Madhur Jaffrey's
FAR EASTERN
COOKERY

ALSO BY MADHUR JAFFREY

MADHUR JAFFREY'S COOKBOOK: EASY EAST/WEST MENUS FOR FAMILY AND FRIENDS
(Harper & Row)

A TASTE OF INDIA
(Atheneum)

MADHUR JAFFREY'S INDIAN COOKERY
(Barrons)

MADHUR JAFFREY'S WORLD-OF-THE-EAST VEGETARIAN COOKING
(Alfred A. Knopf)

AN INVITATION TO INDIAN COOKING
(Alfred A. Knopf)

SEASONS OF SPLENDOR
(Atheneum)

(children's book)

Madhur Jaffrey's
FAR EASTERN
COOKERY

PERENNIAL LIBRARY

HARPER & ROW, PUBLISHERS, NEW YORK

GRAND RAPIDS, PHILADELPHIA, ST. LOUIS, SAN FRANCISCO
LONDON, SINGAPORE, SYDNEY, TOKYO, TORONTO

Frontispiece:
*Produce at a
Market, Korea*

Dedication:
*Madhur Jaffrey
with mushrooms,
ginko nuts, and
dates, Korea*

This book was originally published in 1989 by BBC
Books, a division of BBC Enterprises Limited. It is
here reprinted through arrangement with BBC
Books.

FIRST U.S. EDITION

DESIGNED BY JOEL AVIROM

Library of Congress Cataloging-in-Publication Data
Jaffrey, Madhur.
   [Far Eastern cookery]
   Madhur Jaffrey's Far Eastern cookery.—1st perennial
     library ed.
       p.   cm.
   Reprint. Originally published: BBC Books, 1989.
   Includes index.
     ISBN 0-06-096398-0 (pbk.)   ISBN 0-06-055173-9
     1. Cookery, Oriental.   I. Title.
TK724.5.A1J32   1989
641.595—dc19   89-45096

89 90 91 92 93 DT/RAI 10 9 8 7 6 5 4 3 2 1
89 90 91 92 93 DT/RAI 10 9 8 7 6 5 4 3 2 1 (pbk.)

TO SANFORD WITH ALL MY LOVE

CONTENTS

ACKNOWLEDGMENTS

*T*here were, literally, hundreds of people who helped me through this enormous project. I would like to express my gratitude to all of them, especially to:

Malaysia

Zainal Arshad, Puan Rashidah, Lim Suan Har, Hasna Abu Bakar, Ahminahbi, Mrs. Zaidah Ahmed, Lim Bian Yam, William Chan and the Nyonya Heritage Museum, Zainal Aziz, Penang Development Corporation, Tourist Development Corporation of Malaysia, Boon Cheong

Thailand

Pieng Chom Darbanand, Chompunute and Akorn Hoontrakul, Duangmarn Mekswat, Chalie Amatyakul, Chai and Daeng Jongmu, Kruamas Woodtikarn, Mrs. Ubol, Mrs. Boonyoun, Tourism Authority of Thailand

Indonesia

Sri Owen, Mrs. Sanuar, Amri Yahya, Jonqui and Sian Januar, Martini Jufri, Usman and Rosalina Beka, Risnawati Agus, Lastri Krisnarto, Department of Tourism, Cri Murthi Adi, Muriel Peters

Korea

Mrs. Han Chung Kyu, Mrs. Choi Sang In, Sang Kyung Lee, Dr. Park Hun-Seop, Chilwon Village, Korea National Tourist Corporation, Mrs. Han Chung Hea

Philippines

Mila Rodriguez, Sandra Cahill, Reynaldo Alejandro, Sandy Daza, Glenda Barretto, Ruby and Buddy Roa, Doreen and Willy Fernandez, Ruska Gamboa, Ramon Hofilena, Dr. Fe Elseyer, Tina Lapres, Philippines Department of Tourism

Vietnam

Biche Lombatière, Indrajit Ghosh, Ram and Shangri-La Gopal, Richard G. Tallboys, Thuy Pellissier, Lîu Thanh Nhàn, Mrs. Vường, Ngùyêñ Văn Y, Ministry of Information

Hong Kong

Willy and Mimi Mark, Grace and Kendall Oei, Mrs. Audrey Fung, Priscilla Chen, Margaret Leeming, Hong Kong Tourist Association, Irene Ho, Professor K. C. Chang at Harvard University, Cambridge, Massachusetts

Japan

Professor Shizuo Tsuji and the staff of the École Technique Hôtelière Tauji, Keiko Okamoto, Tawaraya Inn, John J. McGovern, Tsuruya Ryotei, and Japan National Tourist Organization.

INTRODUCTION

*T*he young women stood poised on the craggy black rocks that edge Korea's southernmost island, Cheju, their trim bodies silhouetted against the blue of the sky and the sea. Then, one by one, they dived off and disappeared into the cold waters. Several minutes later they surfaced with a bounty of abalone, oysters and sea urchins. These briny creatures were not destined to go far! They were prized open, right there on the rocks, dabbed with a heady sauce made of fermented soybeans, chilies and garlic and sold by the women to waiting customers (including this one) who did not seem to know when to stop eating.

I started traveling to the Far East almost twenty-five years ago, marveling on each trip at how *well* people ate, at the freshness of their ingredients and at their combinations of cooking techniques and seasonings that produced highly nutritious and delicious foods with such ease. In a market in Indonesia I once bought *gadangan* from a woman with a basket. This was a medley of blanched vegetables tossed lightly with a "dressing" of grated coconut, red chilies, lime juice, sugar and salt. It was so simple and so utterly glorious. On another occasion I was sitting in a dusty, unpromising office in Vietnam. Some staff members were about to prepare lunch on the premises. Files were cleared off tables and a kerosene stove lit. Soon an amazing salad emerged. It consisted of plain raw kohlrabi mixed with *very* freshly roasted and lightly crushed peanuts, mint, fresh coriander, vinegar, sugar and ground red pepper. It could not have been improved upon. In Japan I have had grilled mushroom caps stuffed with ground chicken and dressed with soy sauce and vinegar; in Thailand I have eaten a superb dish of stir-fried ground chicken blanketed with crisply fried basil leaves; and in the Philippines I have enjoyed an exquisitely delicate first course of mackerel strips "cooked" in lime juice.

There is so much good food in this region. You might have sampled some Thai, Japanese or Vietnamese dishes in local restaurants and been afraid to try cooking them at home. You should not be put off by the "foreignness" of some of the ingredients. Just remember that, for all of Europe, at one time potatoes, tomatoes and corn were "foreign" (they came from the New World) and so were mangoes, black pepper and cinnamon (they came from Asia). Ingredients, indeed whole dishes, once traveled through the world at the cumbersome pace of the mortals who transported them—on foot, by boat or on horseback. Today a chef can eat a dish in Hong Kong on one day, and recreate it in his kitchen in New York the following week; a recipe for a curry from Malaysia can be faxed to London on the same day and the ingredients for it, what with air transportation and refrigeration, found in many supermarkets.

For this book I have decided to concentrate on eight countries of East Asia—Korea, Japan, Hong Kong, the Philippines, Vietnam, Thailand, Malaysia and Indonesia. The climates of these countries vary from temperate to tropical—Indonesia is actually on the equator—and their cuisines are quite distinct from each other. There are, however, some common elements. What binds all these countries together is their healthy emphasis on grains. Unlike in the West, where the focal point of a meal is meat or eggs, the place of honor in East Asia is given either to wheat, in the form of noodles, pancakes or steamed buns, or it is given to rice.

It is not certain where rice originated, though the latest research seems to point to Thailand. At any rate, rice quickly spread through much of Southeast Asia and eventually inched its way north to China and Japan as farming techniques improved. In the entire Far Eastern region, with a few exceptions, rice is synonymous with the meal itself, and an invitation to dine very often translates as "Come and have rice with me." In a Chinese dialect, to have a job is to "have grains to chew," and to have lost it is to "have broken the rice bowl." Chinese children are warned that if they leave a single grain of rice in their bowl they will end up with a pockmarked spouse!

While almost all East Asians eat rice, they do not all prefer the same kind. The Chinese generally like a long-grain variety while the Japanese and Koreans frown on anything but their somewhat more glutinous short-grain varieties. In Bali in Indonesia I have had the fluffiest, lightest rice; in Malaysia I have eaten a pudding made with black rice; in the Philippines, a cake made with purple rice; and in northern Thailand, following the local custom, I have made small balls out of glutinous rice and eaten them with my pork curry.

The soybean is another ingredient that gives Far Eastern foods their special character and nutritional value. Pound for pound, it is richer in protein than red meat, richer in digestible calcium than equal amounts of milk, and contains more iron than ox liver. And it has no saturated fat. But it is hard to digest in its normal state and so needs to be processed in some way. This has led to the availability of a host of soybean products such as bean curd and soy sauce. Made from the beans in combination with wheat, barley or rice, briny fermented soy sauce adds protein, flavor and saltiness to thousands of dishes from Korea to Indonesia.

Soy sauce is not the only flavoring-cum-salting sauce in the region. Fish sauce performs a very similar function in Vietnam, Thailand and the Philippines. Even though this is made from fermented fish, it is neither malodorous nor overpowering and it *is* very rich in protein, calcium and phosphorus! When used properly, as in a Vietnamese dipping sauce that calls for the addition of water, lime juice, sugar and chilies, it is so good as to be almost drinkable.

Then there is that felicitous Chinese creation, the noodle. Originating probably before the start of the Christian era—in fact, as soon as the Chinese were able to grind grains into a fine flour—the noodle quickly made its way into the hearts—

and mouths—of the entire Far East. Today there are rice noodles, wheat noodles and buckwheat noodles. These Chinese symbols of longevity may be immersed in soups, stir-fried with meats and put into cold salads. They are as perfect for eating and easy entertaining as Italian pasta.

The one seasoning that is used throughout the Far East is ginger. You probably know it well from Chinese and Indian cookery. Fifth-century Chinese sailors used to carry it on their ships, embedded in earth to make it last. They knew it prevented scurvy (it is rich in vitamin C). They also knew that it had "heating" properties, and to this day, ginger tea is served after a meal of "cooling" crabs.

The Chinese have, for centuries, felt that the human body functions best when "cooling" and "heating" (*yin* and *yang* respectively) forces are properly balanced. In 1368 Chia Ming, a medieval foodie, catalogued every edible substance, marking its degree of "hotness" and "coolness." He ate carefully himself and lived to be 106! The Chinese, wherever they are—and as well as populating Hong Kong they have spread widely in the Philippines, Thailand, Malaysia and Indonesia—are very aware of this as they cook and eat. I was offered not only ginger tea after a heady meal of many, many roe-filled crabs but also chrysanthemum tea (it is cooling) after we had gorged ourselves on barbecued beef and chicken (they are heating) at a bayside Hong Kong picnic.

An ancient Chinese poem, attempting to entice the soul back to earth, offers it a meal where dishes of "all flavors" are present, "bitter, salt, sour, pungent and sweet." These are still the five flavors the Chinese try to balance at every meal. The Koreans took cognizance of a flavor the Chinese seemingly missed—the "nutty" flavor found in sesame seeds. There is, however, a taste that the Chinese and the Koreans were not to know till the sixteenth century—the fire of the red-hot chili.

Chilies came marching into Asia with the Portuguese (who found them in the Americas) and conquered the Old World forever, transforming the cuisines of Indonesia, Malaysia, Thailand, Vietnam, Korea and some provinces of China such as Szechuan and Hunan. It is hard to say what it is about chilies that causes an addiction. Perhaps it is the exquisite pain they bring that heightens the pleasure of eating, but once you have enjoyed them, there is no turning back: you are hooked forever.

The culinary art of the Far East lies in the magical mingling and balancing of flavors and textures. Western taboos just do not hold: fish and pork strips are thrown together in a fiery stew in Korea; a paste made of minced pork and crab meat is slathered onto triangles of bread before they are fried in Vietnam. The soft, the smooth, the crunchy and the slithery as well as the sweet, salty, hot and sour are all present in a kaleidoscope of inventive permutations.

The source of meat for much of this region (excepting Japan) has traditionally been the pig. This prolific animal could be raised on scraps while precious grains from the fields could be wisely saved for the growing numbers of humans. Cattle could be saved for plowing the fields that raised the grains. Changes came from Indonesia, Malaysia and the southern Philippines with the spread of Islam. Pigs, of religious necessity, were out. Goats and, when people could afford it, cattle were slaughtered instead. As farming methods improved, more and more cows were raised for slaughter. Today, Korea has a few cattle farms that rival those in Texas.

What much of this region thrives on, however, is fresh fish. People demand the freshest of fish and get it. The price of fish drops dramatically if it is a day old. Eels, carp, crabs and octopus, all live, wriggle around in tanks and tubs. Even before dawn, hundreds of shrimps are lined up on scrubbed counters like repeating commas. By midday the shrimps will have been stir-fried with asparagus in Hong Kong, dipped in batter and fried in Tokyo, and stirred into a coconut-enriched sauce in Malaysia.

The demand for freshness extends to vegetables as well. It is said that in China only 60 percent of the credit for a good meal goes to the person who cooks: 40 percent goes to the person who shops. Straw mushrooms, it is clear, should be free of spots, and who would buy green beans if they did not snap when they were broken? Vietnam was the poorest country we visited, yet its markets had a fresh herb section that was as verdant as a summer garden.

In Japan the need for freshness is carried a step further. First you buy a very fresh vegetable. Then you make it look even fresher than nature can make it. For example, a cucumber was to be sliced into rounds. It had just been picked; it was perfect. It was, nonetheless, dropped into boiling water for a second and then rinsed in cold water before cutting. The taste remained unchanged but its skin turned a lusher green. Now the cucumber was *more* perfect than perfect!

In spite of their many common ingredients and cooking techniques, the cuisines of each of the eight countries chosen for this book are quite distinctive. Let me tell you a little about each of them.

Malaysia

Malaysian cuisine combines the delicacy of Chinese food with the exuberance of Indian spices and the aromas of Southeast Asian herbs. This cuisine has developed interestingly. The original Malay diet consisted mostly of rice and fish. The two could be moistened with coconut and flavored with a host of local seasonings such as shrimp paste *(blachan)*, black pepper, ginger, turmeric, shallots, lemongrass and tamarind. But then things began to change.

A look at a map will reveal that peninsular Malaysia, sticking out like a finger into the sea, seems to be a natural meeting point between East and West Asia. It was actually more than that. From the earliest times favorable northeast and southwest monsoon winds literally blew in the ships of Indian, Arab and Chinese traders. By the early fifteenth century Malacca, a southern port, had become a hotbed of commerce, with trade flourishing in silk, jewels and spices. Each group not only traded but also left behind some of its members who settled and intermarried with local women. Starting with its sultan, a slow conversion to Islam also began. The following century brought the Portuguese, bearing chilies from the West, then the Dutch and English, all of whom stayed on to rule. In the nineteenth century rubber plantations and tin mines needed labor, so Hindu and Muslim Tamil Indians and Hokkien-speaking Chinese were imported by the British. The Europeans eventually left but the Asians stayed.

As peoples of all three major races—the Malays, Chinese and Indians—commingled and merged, so did their cuisines. Malaysia is one of the world's few true melting pots. The sharp edges of racism have been softened by the constant rubbing of multicolored shoulders, and the sharp differences in the cuisines have been blurred by the constant exchange of techniques and ingredients. Today one finds that, while some foods have kept their original form, most have been modified subtly or drastically, making it hard to fit many dishes into a clear niche or to pinpoint their exact origin.

I remember once attending a gathering of the Penang Women's Institute, where a dozen women had collected in the home of one of them to prepare a Malay-style meal. Shoes had been left at the front door, as is the custom, and the Muslim

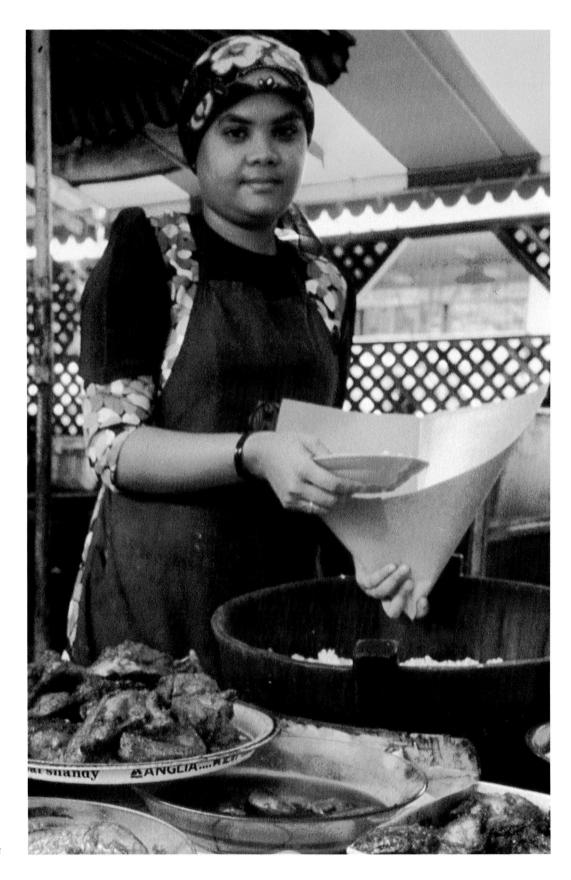

Take-away food stall, Kuala Lumpur, Malaysia

MADHUR JAFFREY'S FAR EASTERN COOKERY

Malay ladies, in their long-sleeved, ankle-length dresses and headscarves, were padding around happily, pounding chilies, slicing shallots and squeezing out coconut milk. Hasna Abu Baker was to make a shrimp and bottle gourd curry. She boiled the ground spices—cumin, coriander, fennel, pepper and chilies—in water, then added the shrimps, the gourd and coconut milk. When they were cooked, she heated a little oil, browned shallots, garlic and whole fennel seeds in it, and then threw the oil and seasonings into the curry as a final flavoring. I had never seen this last step done anywhere except in India. The dish was a miraculously good hybrid.

On the other hand, the Indian Muslim community offered me one of their scrumptious marvels, *nasi kandar,* a meal of rice, beef curry, fish curry and hard-boiled eggs, that I had never seen in India. The name of the dish comes from two cultures: *nasi* is the Malay word for cooked rice and *kandar* may come from an Indian word for shoulder. To get this meal you would, some years ago, have to stop a vendor who carried a pole on his shoulder from which were suspended two baskets carrying all the dishes. You would be spooned a little of everything, with the sauce from the meat going over the eggs. Today the itinerant vendors have virtually disappeared, but specialized restaurants and caterers keep up the tradition. In Kuala Lumpur I watched one caterer, Puan Rashidah, prepare the curries. Most of the seasonings were Indian, but not all. For what went into the pots included the very Chinese star anise, the very Malay lemongrass—and soy sauce!

Throughout the nation Muslim Malays, while avoiding pork, have taken to Indian spice mixtures with a passion; Indian Hindus, while continuing to cook their traditional rice and split pea pancakes *(dosas)* and to avoid beef, now routinely add lemongrass and galangal to their coconut-enriched curries; the Chinese, while not giving up their Teo Chew–style duck braised in wine, enjoy eating Hokkien-style noodles with a fiery chutney *(sambal)* made with shrimp paste and red chilies. Today rice noodles can be found floating in a spicy coconut curry sauce *(curry mee).* Western-style cakes and breads are often flavored with the aromatic pandanus leaves of the region.

The intermarriage between the Malay men and Chinese women in the Straits settlements of Penang and Malacca (as well as Singapore) has led to a new mixed culture—that of the "Straits Chinese"—and to a style of cooking now gaining much favor in restaurants. Named after the women in the community, this cuisine is known as the food of the Nonyas. The Straits Chinese gave up the use of chopsticks and took to their fingers. They began to perfume and enliven their pork, shrimps and chicken with coconut milk, candlenuts and tamarind. They still enjoyed mild, gentle dishes such as Chicken with Bamboo Shoots in Black Bean Sauce and their airy stuffed pancakes *(Po piah)* but ate many fiery ones as well. Cooking skills were passed on from mother to daughter, a young girl's eligibility often depending on her ability to chop, cut and pound!

Nowadays the young Straits Chinese spend much less time in the kitchen as the entire nation seems to have become aware of the pleasures of eating out. Malaysia sits just above the equator and the climate is tropical. There are restaurants, of course, to go to, but food can be enjoyed even more as one takes the breeze if bought from obliging hawkers. From breakfast until dinner, hawkers sell an infinite variety of some of the world's most scrumptious snacks. On the way to the office, many workers stop to pick up *nasi lemak,* a banana leaf packet containing, at its simplest, some rice cooked with coconut milk, fried whitebait, a couple of tamarind-flavored shrimps, a few cucumber or pineapple slices and a dollop of fiery chili sauce made with roasted shrimp paste and pounded red chilies. For lunch you can go to the open-air hawkers' center on a high-rise rooftop such as the one I visited in Penang. Food here is served on green or orange plates. This is an Islamic nation and green signifies that the food is *halal*—that is, approved for Muslim consumption; orange plates may well have pork on them. This way friends of different faiths can sit together and know instantly what foods they must not touch and which are safe to eat. You might wish to end the day on Penang's seafront, Gurney Drive. Here, calmed by the soft lapping of the waves and the cooling breeze, you can take a last bite from one of those gorgeous sweet pancakes, *ban chan kuay*, spongily light and stuffed with sesame seeds and peanuts.

RECIPES FROM MALAYSIA IN THIS BOOK INCLUDE

STIR-FRIED SHRIMPS WITH TAMARIND AND CHILIES
SAMBAL UDANG
SQUID IN CHILI AND GARLIC SAUCE
SOTONG DAN CHILI DAN BAWANG PUTIH

BEEF CURRY WITH THICK ONION SAUCE
DAGING NASI KANDAR

CHICKEN WITH BAMBOO SHOOTS AND MUSHROOMS IN BLACK BEAN SAUCE
AYAM PONGTAY
HEARTY CHICKEN CURRY WITH POTATOES
LAUK AYAM
DUCK BRAISED IN WINE
TEO CHEW–STYLE DUCK
EGG CURRY
GULAI TELOR

SQUID IN BLACK SAUCE
SOTONG MASAK KICAP
SPICY SHRIMP AND CUCUMBER CURRY
GULAI LABU

EGGPLANT IN A THICK, HOT, SWEET AND SOUR CHILI SAUCE
PACHERI TERONG
BEAN SPROUTS WITH A SPICY COCONUT DRESSING
KERABU TAWGEH
SPICY YELLOW SPLIT PEAS
PARPU

PERFUMED RICE WITH VEGETABLES NONYA-STYLE
NASI ULAM
TOMATO RICE
NASI TOMAT
RICE NOODLES IN A COCONUT CURRY SOUP
CURRY MEE

FLUFFY PANCAKES WITH SWEET SESAME-PEANUT FILLING
BAN CHAN KUAY, MARTABAK

Thailand

$\mathcal{T}$hai food virtually bursts with contrasting hot, sweet, sour and salt flavors. The Thais have taken some of the best ideas from the cooking of the Malays, Chinese and Indians, thrown in their own zesty spirit and their love of the raw, crunchy, aromatic and colorful and have come up with a cuisine that is unmatched in its combination of lightness and seductive earthiness.

Take the Chicken, Shrimp and Fruit Salad (*Yam Polamai*, page 65). Who, first of all, would think of putting such disparate ingredients together—shredded chicken, shrimps, grapes, oranges, fried garlic, fried shallots and roasted peanuts —and then of dressing them with lime juice, sugar, salt and green chilies? Only the Thais. Yet this salad is so inspired and so good that, when I serve it, my guests cannot stop marveling—or stop eating. Thailand has a bountiful repertoire of such salads—chicken combined with cucumber and chilies, shrimps with oyster mushrooms, ground beef with mint and shallots—each more glorious than the next.

A Thai meal for a fairly well-off family in the Bangkok area is built around rice. Thailand exports its fine rices around the world and yet produces enough to allow each inhabitant to eat about 1 lb a day at a very reasonable price. The rice is accompanied by a soup or a soupy stew, a stir-fried dish and a saladlike dish, all served at the same time and eaten either with the fingers or with a fork and a spoon, the fork being used only to shove the food into the latter implement. Many Thai restaurants catering to foreigners serve soups as a first course. All soups, including the stunning Hot and Sour Shrimp Soup (*Tom Yam Kung*) with its hot and sour, lemongrass-flavored broth and its floating shrimps and straw mushrooms, are best enjoyed with spoonfuls of plain rice. The neutrality of the soft grain serves to absorb the heat of the soup and accentuate its flavors. Meals here tend to end with fruit: papayas carved like roses, mangoes carved like leaves, pineapples carved like pears and watermelon pieces carved as pineapples. It is quite an art, requiring lethal knives and great patience.

Thai foods can be hot—really hot. Generally, hot dishes are balanced with mild ones. There are always side dishes of raw vegetables and fruit to nibble upon— forests of mint, lettuce leaves, long beans and bean sprouts. These often look like

Khlong Toey market, Bangkok **(Lindie Lapin)**

garnishes but they are meant to be eaten, offering both a change of texture and taste.

Aromatic herbs grow abundantly in this tropical country and are used generously. They include enormous families of mints and basils, coriander (the leaf and the root), kaffir lime leaves, the highly scented pandanus leaves and lemongrass. "Indian" spices, such as cumin, coriander, turmeric, cinnamon, cardamom and cloves, *are* used but only for curries and in such small quantities as to leave more of an herby flavor than a spicy one. Gingers are used, particularly galangal, as well as various limes and tamarind for souring. Fish sauce *(nam pla)* and shrimp paste provide saltiness and added flavoring.

Thai curries are exquisite and vary throughout the country. The north, where pork reigns supreme, serves a dark and hearty Indo-Burmese–style curry, filled with large chunks of meat, which is eaten with little balls of hard glutinous rice. The south softens its curries with coconut milk, uses many more fresh herbs and cuts its meats (or shrimps or chicken) into small pieces.

Vegetables are often cooked with small amounts of meat, generally pork. In one northern village I was treated to cauliflower stir-fried with minced pork. In Bangkok I often took myself for a cheap meal of green beans, stir-fried with minced pork and chilies, served behind my ritzy hotel; and I remember buying a quite scrumptious dish of *gai lan*, a green leafy vegetable, stir-fried with smoked pork. Pork lubricates the vegetable and gives it an added dimension.

Noodles are eaten in enormous quantities, especially at lunchtime. My favorite was the noodle soup made in two minutes flat by hawkers who sell nothing else. The noodles of your choice are lowered into boiling water and then dropped into your bowl. Green beans, bits of chicken and bean sprouts are lowered into stock until blanched and then draped over your noodles. A ladle of broth goes over everything. You then take this steaming bowl to your streetside table and season it with fish sauce, sugar, crushed chilies and roasted peanuts.

Sometimes a cuisine can best be gauged by its treatment of seafood. Many restaurants in and around Bangkok have large tanks of fresh fish. So first you go and pick it: "I want *those* shrimps, *that* crab, etc." Then you seat yourself in some airy pavilion and wait. Soon the dishes begin to arrive: small shrimps in a delicate broth wherein float little creamy pieces of young coconut; large shrimps that have been grilled over wet straw (the smoke penetrates the meat) and which you eat with fish sauce, vinegar and a chili dipping sauce; juicy crabs that have been stir-fried with green chilies, mint and lemongrass. There is a phrase in Thailand which says, "There is rice in the fields and fish in the water." It means that all is well. Certainly in the culinary sense all seems to be very well in this marvelous country.

Watermelons, Or Tor Kor Market, Bangkok, Thailand

Right: *Ready-made curry paste, Bangkok* **(Lindie Lapin)**

Durian, Bangkok **(Lindie Lapin)**

Right: *Garlic and fiery red chilies, Chiang Mai, Thailand*

RECIPES FROM THAILAND IN THIS BOOK INCLUDE

HOT AND SOUR SHRIMP SOUP
TOM YAM KUNG

CHICKEN, SHRIMP AND FRUIT SALAD
YAM POLAMAI

THAI PORK CURRY IN THE BURMESE STYLE
KAENG HUNGLAY

SPICY BEEF SALAD
LAAB

EASY BEEF CURRY
KAENG PHET NUA

RED CHICKEN CURRY
KAENG PET KAI

GROUND CHICKEN STIR-FRIED WITH BASIL
KAI PAD BAI KAPROW

CHICKEN WITH GARLIC AND BLACK PEPPER
KAI TOD KRATIUM PRIKTAI

SQUID SALAD
YAM PLA MUK

FISH POACHED IN AROMATIC TAMARIND BROTH
KAENG SOM

FISH STEAMED WITH LEMONGRASS
TOM SOM PLA

STIR-FRIED GREEN BEANS WITH PORK AND CHILIES
MOO PAD PRIK SAI TUA FAK YAO

GREENS WITH GARLIC AND OYSTER SAUCE, OR "FLYING" GREENS
PAK BUNG LOY FA

SPINACH WITH GARLIC AND FISH SAUCE
PAD PAK BUNG

COCONUT MILK CUSTARD
SANKHAYA

Indonesia

rs. Zainar's simple country cottage is built on a high hill overlooking the sea. She waits for us on a bench set under a star fruit tree. We have come to see her kitchen garden. Unlike gardens in the West, this garden in Padang, West Sumatra, has no cabbages or cauliflowers. This is a tropical garden—the equator goes right through the island of Sumatra—and Mrs. Zainar grows turmeric, galangal, ginger, chilies, lemongrass, tamarind, nutmeg, basils, mints and cloves. She also has coconuts and eggplants. She is pretty self-sufficient—at least, in spices.

It is to Indonesia that traders—Indians, Arabs and eventually the Dutch—came for spices. They grow easily here and quite abundantly as well. To see these spices being used in everyday cooking, let us watch a fish curry (*gulai ikan*) being made farther up the island by Mrs. Sanuar. The fish was alive a short while ago, swimming in the family tank. It has been mercifully dispatched and cut into steaks. A daughter is grinding the spices on a stone slab set in the counter: red chilies, shallots, ginger, galangal, fresh turmeric and candlenuts (so called because they can actually be lit). The spice mixture (or *bumbu*) is combined with the fish, coconut milk and herbs such as the leaves of turmeric and mint, and then left to cook. It will be a spectacular curry. I know; I have eaten it before.

The first time I came here was during the Muslim holy days that follow Idul Fitri, when all homes keep glass jars filled with pineapple pastries, little curry puffs and small Dutch-style cakes for visitors who drop by. Mrs. Sanuar had treats of her own, including some wonderful peanuts that she had fried with garlic, shallots and Chinese celery. She invited us to stay for lunch. A cloth was spread out on the living room floor (I had seen this Muslim custom in India) and all foods placed, in traditional style, in the middle. Food was to be enjoyed communally. The fish curry was set down. So was some rice (the staple), cabbage greens cooked with a red chili, shallot and garlic paste, some crisp wafers (*krupuk*) and the most renowned dish of the region, beef *rendang*.

Rendang is cooked for weddings and feasts. It is also called "traveler's food" because it keeps well. Made with lots of coconut milk and flavored with lemongrass and chilies, it cooks and cooks until most of the liquid is gone. It is a quite

North Sumatra fishing village, Indonesia (Peter Ramsden)

outstanding dish and the best example of West Sumatra's spicy style of food. Strangely enough, Padang, a small town in West Sumatra, has exported its cuisine all over Indonesia through the proliferation of what are now known as Padang restaurants. You can find them in any city. The food is hot, lots of dishes are brought to your table dramatically layered on the arms of the waiters and you pay only for what you eat. It's a good deal!

As it happens, there are more than 13,000 islands in the nation and each has a different culinary slant. Bali, for example, never turned to Islam as the rest of the nation did, so its inhabitants eat pork and turtle with great enthusiasm. The Balinese also specialize in cooking a whole duck or chicken by smothering it with a spice paste of chilies, shallots and turmeric, wrapping up the bird in banana leaves and baking it slowly over charcoal. It is moist, spicy and good. For some reason the Balinese do not like to eat fish; the rest of the islands do, however. From north Sulawesi comes *ikan rica rica,* a marvelous fish dish: fish marinated with lime juice and salt is grilled and then smothered with a fried paste of coarsely crushed ginger, shallots and chilies. The Arabs brought skewered kebabs to Java. The East Javanese have now claimed them as their very own, transforming them with their sweet soy sauce *(kecap manis)* into delectable sweet and salty morsels called *satays. Satays* are sold nationally, with the spicing changing dramatically from region to region.

Among my own favorites in Indonesia are the salads, such as *gado-gado.* Blanched and boiled vegetables—bean sprouts, cabbage, green beans and potatoes—are all arranged on a plate and then doused with a heavenly hot, sweet, sour and nutty sauce made with peanuts.

Indonesia has no grand cuisine. The food tends to be egalitarian: everyone in a region tends to eat the same dishes. You eat with the right hand and pass food with the left. Food, with the exception of soup, is served at room temperature and is meant to be shared. Sweet teas and ginger coffees are drunk. Muslims generally do not drink alcohol, but the Hindu Balinese have a roaring time with a rice liquor, *brem*. Fruits here are superb and end a meal most satisfactorily. Those with a sweet tooth can take themselves off to the market to buy a sweet *martabak*, a thick light pancake spread with butter and then dusted with sugar, crushed peanuts and tiny chocolate vermicelli. It drips all over the place when eaten but is irresistible.

RECIPES FROM INDONESIA IN THIS BOOK INCLUDE

SHRIMP WAFERS
KRUPUK UDANG
SPICY CHICKEN SOUP WITH MANY FLAVORS
SOTO AYAM

BEEF CHUNKS COOKED IN COCONUT MILK
KALIYO OR RENDANG DAGING

STUFFED WHOLE CHICKEN IN A PARCEL
BETUTU AYAM
SPICY CHICKEN KEBABS WITH A PEANUT SAUCE
SATAY AYAM
WHOLE GRILLED FISH, SOUR AND SPICY
IKAN PANGGANG
WEST SUMATRAN FISH CURRY WITH COCONUT MILK
GULAI IKAN

SALAD OF ASSORTED VEGETABLES WITH A DELICIOUS PEANUT DRESSING
GADO-GADO
CAULIFLOWER AND CARROTS WITH A COCONUT DRESSING
GADANGAN
SPICED MUSHROOMS IN A PACKET
PEPES JAMUR
CABBAGE STIR-FRIED WITH RED PEPPER PASTE
SALA LOBAK
GREEN BEANS AND CARROTS WITH GINGER AND CHILIES
TUMIS BUNCHIS

SPECIAL FRIED RICE WITH BEEF AND SHRIMPS
NASI GORENG ISTIMEWA

FLUFFY PANCAKES WITH SWEET SESAME-PEANUT FILLING
BAN CHAN KUAY, MARTABAK
GINGER COFFEE
KOPI JAHE

Korea

*L*et me, for a moment, pretend that I am a camera and zoom in—at dinner time, of course—on a middle-class Korean family. All members are seated on the floor around a low rectangular table. Each person has a metal bowl filled with rice. The short-grain rice, of a slightly sticky variety, is being picked up dexterously with strangely thin, knitting needlelike chopsticks. These chopsticks, as well as long-handled metal spoons, now reach out helter-skelter toward the center of the table where there is a dish of blanched spinach, very lightly seasoned with sprinklings of sesame oil, roasted sesame seeds and soy sauce. In a heavy earthenware casserole can be seen a fiery-looking stew of fish, beef slices and bean curd cubes, still steamy from the retained heat. Near it sits a spicy stir-fried dish of pork and red peppers and, next to that, a bowl of cabbage pickle. Each person has a glass of hot barley tea. The mother of the family, who has cooked dinner, has trendily coiffured hair and pinkish-bronze rouge on her wide cheekbones. She works in a shop that sells jeans and other sportswear. The father's haircut is much more conservative. He works for a company exporting cars to the United States. There are two small children and their grandmother, who cares for them during the day. The flat is modern and small, a ninth-floor refuge in a suburban development, a long bus ride out of Seoul. Inside the flat it is warm and cozy. Outside it is snowing.

This scene serves to tell much of my story. South Koreans are a rough-tough people of Mongol ancestry who have pushed their country from a developing third world nation into a hive of modern industry. China, which looms further to the north and across the waters to the east, has invaded many times and left a firm imprint. The Japanese were more recent—and much-hated—occupiers. They are rarely mentioned, though their silent mark may occasionally be felt. Today Confucian ideals and modern mammon are equally revered in a fine balancing act while the Koreans hold on to their unique identity.

As in much of Asia, rice is essential to most meals, having supplanted the millet of ancient times. It is the same sort of rice that is eaten in Japan. Sometimes this rice is cooked together with barley or millet, making it richer nutritionally and nuttier in flavor. Noodles, especially those made of buckwheat and mung beans, are highly popular. On my very first trip to Korea, almost a decade ago, I remember succumbing to the cool flavors of a summer noodle soup, *naeng myon*. Cold buckwheat noodles had been topped with thin slices of cucumber, cold beef and crisp pear-apples. Then the entire lot had been dressed in a cold and utterly delicious meat broth. If this sounds tempting enough, just wait. The soup was meant to be seasoned further at the table with mustard, a sauce of soy and vinegar and some liquid from a pickle. It was heavenly!

At everyday Korean meals, soupy dishes or stews are almost always present. They are served side by side with grilled and stir-fried foods. Some dishes are very hot, others gentle and mild, the latter serving to calm the effects of the former. The seasonings in general use are soy sauce, vinegar, sesame oil, roasted sesame seeds, sugar, ginger, garlic, red chilies and a family of pastes (the *changs*) made of fermented soybeans.

More needs to be said about the last three—and about Korean pickles. First, the garlic.

It is said that the birth of Korea was the direct result of a union between the son of the divine creator, a bear and twenty cloves of garlic. The bear wanted to become human so the god gave it the garlic to eat and suggested that it retire for 100 days. It emerged as a woman and had a son by the god. This child, Tan'gun, then went on to found Korea. The Koreans may or may not have divinity in their blood. They certainly have a lot of garlic in it. They eat it morning, noon and night, sometimes raw, sometimes grilled, sometimes pickled, and almost always as a seasoning for their marinated and grilled meats and stews. I find it rather amusing

 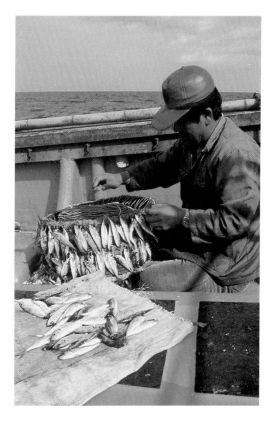

Fish seller, Songsan Port, Cheju Island, Korea

Right: *A fisherman's bait, Korea* (Julian Charrington)

that Western nutritionists are now beginninng to tell us what Asian folk wisdom has known for centuries—that garlic cleanses the blood and keeps it flowing freely.

I cannot say for sure which country in this world eats the hottest foods, but South Korea must rank easily in the top three. Fiery chili pods ripen to a rich red color in the autumn here, at which time they are either cut into hair-thin slices before drying (old women are generally assigned this tedious task) or dried first and then pounded into some of the world's best ground red pepper. Its bright carmine color can be seen smothering squid rings, oysters and all manner of vegetables.

A visit to any Korean home reveals tall ceramic jars standing like silent sentinels on balconies, roofs and yards. These hold the pastes and pickles that give Korean meats their special character. The pastes, such as *toen chang* and *kochu chang,* are made of fermented soybeans and grains. The former, like Japanese *miso,* is mild; the latter, filled with chilies, a virtual firebird. Both may be added to stews to thicken and flavor them, and to boost their nutritional content.

Korean pickles *(kimchee)* are a world in themselves and *no* meal, from breakfast to dinner, is complete without them. There is a *kimchee* museum in Seoul that lists 160 varieties made of vegetables ranging from ordinary pumpkins to the precious ginseng root. The staple, however, remains the *kimchee* made of large Chinese or Napa cabbages (rather like Chinese celery cabbage). The vegetables are brined, then stuffed with a mixture containing, among other things, scallions, ginger, garlic, radishes and red chilies. They are then packed into vats and left to seethe and bubble until they have turned sufficiently sour, by which time they are rich in minerals and vitamin C and are addictively wonderful.

The Korean peninsula is surrounded by the sea on three sides and creatures from these waters are consumed daily, sometimes by themselves, sometimes in the most imaginative combinations with meat. A fish stew may have slices of beef in it and a dozen cockles may be set loose in a sea of pork broth.

Rice, fish and pickles are taken for granted in Korea. It is beef, a relatively new item as far as common consumption goes, that is prized—in particular the mari-

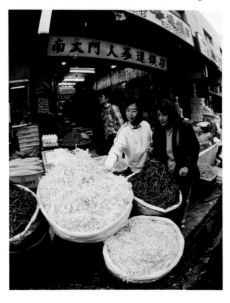

A market featuring bean sprouts, bracken, and Chinese bellflowers, Korea

MADHUR JAFFREY'S FAR EASTERN COOKERY

*Dried fish stall,
East Gate Market,
Seoul, Korea*

nated and grilled-at-the-table beef strips called *bulgogi*. Tasting of the ginger and garlic, soy sauce, scallions and sesame seeds that are in their marinade, they hiss and sizzle in front of the diners, teasing them with their heavenly aroma. After a recent poll of children on their likes, the *Korean Times* discovered that mother came first, beef was second and father was third. I feel sorry for father, but here's a hurray for beef—especially *bulgogi*!

RECIPES FROM SOUTH KOREA IN THIS BOOK INCLUDE

BEAN SPROUT AND RADISH SOUP
KONGNAMUL KUK

MEATBALL SOUP
WANJA KUK
STIR-FRIED PORK WITH RED BELL PEPPER
TWAEJI BOKKUM
MARINATED AND GRILLED BEEF STRIPS
BULGOGI

CHICKEN PATTIES WITH GINGER AND SESAME SEEDS
TAK KOGI SOPSANJOK
SPICY CHICKEN STEW WITH CARROTS AND POTATOES
TAK TORI TANG
SAVORY EGG CUSTARD WITH SHRIMPS AND MUSHROOMS
KERAN CHIM
FISH, SHELLFISH AND BEAN CURD STEW
SAENGSUN CHIGAE

STIR-FRIED ZUCCHINI WITH SESAME SEEDS
HOBAK NAMUL
SEASONED SPINACH
SIGUMCHI NAMUL

CELLOPHANE NOODLES WITH BEEF AND VEGETABLES
CHAPCHAE
POTATO PANCAKES
GANJA BUCHIN

HOT FERMENTED BEAN PASTE
KOCHU CHANG
CABBAGE PICKLE
KIMCHEE

CANDIED WALNUT HALVES
HOTOO TWIKIM

The Philippines

*I*t is fiesta time in the small Negros village. Long tables have been set under shady trees and covered over with banana leaves. A whole pig *(lechon),* roasted to a turn on a spit, its skin crackling-crisp, is stretched across the center like an edible epergne. It has been stuffed in the old traditional manner with sour tamarind leaves. It has been basted, in the new traditional manner, with bottled American-style ginger ale.

On either side of the pig are whole steamed and roasted chickens *(rellenong manok).* They have been boned, marinated overnight in soy sauce and the juice of the small *kalamansi* lime, then stuffed with, among other things, ground meats such as pork, veal, Chinese ham and Spanish sausage, as well as olives, pimentos, several American-style pickles, golden raisins and Parmesan cheese. There are also generous platters of rice *paella,* chock-full of shrimps, chicken pieces and sausage.

Ginger ale, Spanish sausage, olives, *paella?*

Like most Southeast Asian countries, the Philippines has seen waves of Chinese traders and settlers who brought noodles, bean curd, soy sauce, pancakes and spring rolls in their wake. They intermarried with the local Malays to such an extent that much of the country is of Chinese-Malay extraction. Muslims came too, Arabs and Indians, bearing Islam, cumin and coriander. But the people who had the most influence on the country—its religion, customs and food—were the ones who followed, the Spaniards and the Americans.

The Spanish came in 1521 and ruled until 1898, when the Americans took over, staying through World War II until 1946. The Spanish occupation not only gave the Philippines its name (after Philip II of Spain) and its major religion, Catholicism, but introduced a Mediterranean style of eating. Spanish food was mostly cooked in olive oil, with seasonings limited to garlic, onions, tomatoes, sweet peppers and vinegar. The Filipinos were not about to give up their own Chinese-Malay dishes, but they did begin to add Spanish ingredients to their own recipes and to cook the newcomers' fancy food as well. They thought it rather grand, however, to call most dishes by Spanish names, especially on menus.

With the Americans came a large military presence and vast stocks of exotic

Opposite:
Coconut plantation, Philippines

Fish drying, Guinilaharan Village, Negros Island, Philippines

goodies such as canned evaporated and condensed milk, canned fruit, bottled mayonnaise, hot dogs, sweet bottled pickles and canned tomato sauce. It was considered a decided improvement to make the Spanish dessert *flan* (caramel custard) with evaporated milk instead of water buffalo milk and quite trendy to eat steaks.

Rice, fish and pork have remained the national staples. Rice is eaten from breakfast to dinner and made into thousands of different cakes, noodles and pancakes. This is a nation of 7,000 islands, and fish—fresh or dried—is eaten daily, especially in the villages. It is also made into fish sauce *(patis)*, which is used here almost as much as soy sauce in China. A village meal might well consist of vegetables cooked with cockles, fried dried fish and rice.

Pork is a much-loved meat and is eaten often by those who can afford it. The national dish is probably *adobo*. Even though chicken and squid *adobos* are very popular, pork is the universal favorite. This dish, originally of Spanish extraction, now involves marinating pork pieces in soy sauce and vinegar with garlic, bay leaves and peppercorns, and then cooking them until they brown in their own juices. It is uncommonly good—and lasts well because of the vinegar. (In my house, however, it does not last at all. It gets eaten the minute it is made!)

A common breakfast is rice stir-fried with garlic, and cured meat, the two washed down with glasses of ginger tea. Breakfast for the rich, though, could turn into a three-hour meal with thick, frothy chocolate in demitasse cups; fluffy, sugared, coiled buns *(ensaimada);* "sardined" fish cooked with onions and peppers; an

A tranquil scene in the Philippines (Bein S. Bautista)

array of smoked fish; salted duck eggs; fried eggs; Chinese ham; Spanish sausages and glutinous rice lozenges to be eaten with ripe mangoes.

Lunch could bring a stew of mung beans and shrimps *(mongo)*, often eaten with a few drops of olive oil and lime juice, a goat and potato stew *(caldereta)* and an eggplant salad *(ensaladang balasenas)*, all to be eaten with rice.

Filipinos seem to eat all the time and, perhaps finding the gap between lunch and dinner too long, have come up with a whole meal of snacks known as *merienda*. Almost anything can be made to fit here: noodles decked with plump oysters, mango and guapple pies (a guapple being a large, hard, applelike guava), little ground rice cupcakes *(puto)*, stuffed pancakes *(lumpia)* and tiny pastry envelopes filled with mango and banana jam *(panyo-panyo)*. To drink there is the refreshing *kalamansi* lime juice and hot chocolate.

The Filipinos are not done. They happily go on to dinner. They might visit a simple *turo-turo* (literally "point-point") cafeteria to enjoy a hearty pork and chick pea stew *(menudo)*, or they might take themselves to a dressier restaurant and start with coconut-enriched seafood soup filled with clams, mussels and shrimps and flavored lightly with ginger, then go on to a deep-fried pork knuckle, beautifully crisp outside and showered with bits of fried garlic and chilies. And for the dessert? Well, how about a large wedge of American-style lemon meringue pie?

RECIPES FROM THE PHILIPPINES IN THIS BOOK INCLUDE

MUNG BEAN SOUP
MONGO GUISADO

GLORIOUS SEAFOOD SOUP
AMA TITO REY SOUP

MACKEREL "COOKED" IN LIME JUICE
KILAWING TANGUIGUE

PORK COOKED IN A PICKLING STYLE
ADOBONG BABOY

LAMB OR GOAT STEW WITH POTATOES, PEPPERS AND OLIVES
CALDERETA

KNOCKOUT KNUCKLE
PATANG BAWANG

PORK WITH CALF'S LIVER AND CHICK PEAS
MENUDO

PIQUANT SHRIMPS
GAMBAS PICANTES

SQUID WITH TOMATOES
ADOBONG PUSIT

SNOW PEAS STIR-FRIED WITH SHRIMPS
SITSARO GUISADO

RICE WITH SEAFOOD, CHICKEN AND SAUSAGES
PAELLA

CARAMEL CUSTARD FILIPINO-STYLE
LECHE FLAN

GINGER TEA
SALABAT

APPLE (OR GUAPPLE) PIE

Vietnam

*I*t was late afternoon in December and uncomfortably chilly. A phalanx of bicycles rushed down a wide Hanoi boulevard. One cyclist, wearing a heavy navy blue jacket, stopped at the entrance to the market and then wheeled his bicycle inside. He bought a huge bunch of swamp cabbage, a green vegetable rich in minerals and vitamins, and strapped it to the back of his bicycle. He intended to cook the vegetables with fish sauce (called *nuoc mam* here) and red chilies, and eat it with fresh noodles. He then walked past the writhing eels and the woman roasting large rice flour wafers encrusted with sesame seeds, stopping once again in front of a woman who squatted before a basket of flowers—pink asters, bright yellow chrysanthemums and an array of the most desirable old-fashioned roses. He put down his money and took the roses. Then, holding them jauntily aloft in one hand and steering with the other, he rejoined the moving river of cyclists and headed home.

Vietnam is indeed a devastated land. Fields are still dotted with bomb craters. But the people have not lost their flair or their style. The country is changing fast. Northern cities, once unable to obtain the more abundant foodstuffs of the south, are doing better as the road system improves. There is much more money in the south, particularly in Hồ Chí Minh City, much of it coming in hard currency from relatives abroad. In the warm evenings there, the young zoom round and round the town center on motorcycles, stopping at one of the many restaurants to listen to Linda Ronstadt or Abba on tape, drink Saigon Beer and eat the world's best spring rolls made with tissue-thin edible rice paper, or spicily cooked chicken pieces flavored with lemongrass, or whole smoked eggplants smothered with a lime sauce.

The Vietnamese people are of mixed Malay and Chinese stock and have a history of foreign influences. The upper part of the country was either occupied or dominated by China for a thousand years, well into the middle of the tenth century. Indians came—somewhat more peacefully—to the south, where they traded their spices. Western powers, looking first for trade and then colonies, followed, starting around the sixteenth century. France had virtually taken over the country by the late sixteenth century. The Americans came last. Each left their mark.

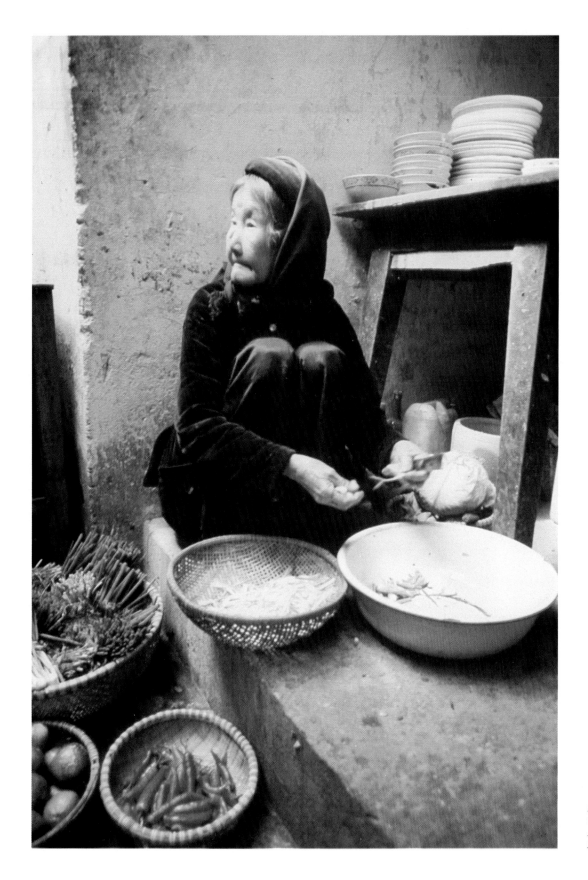

Scallion slicing,
Chà Cá
Restaurant,
Hanoi, Vietnam

The Chinese influence is quite pervasive. It can be seen in the use of chopsticks, in the small and delicate spring rolls, in the use of bean curd, fermented soybeans, star anise and Chinese medicinal herbs. It can be seen in the mixture of pork and crab for soups and fillings. It can also be seen in the Vietnamese love of noodles, especially of *phở*. This is a noodle soup, a glorious breakfast soup, though it can be eaten at any time.

The Vietnamese day starts early. Offices open at 7:30 A.M. in summer, 8:00 A.M. in winter. Before that there are exercises to be done and breakfast to be had in one of the many state-run or private restaurants. Most people opt for *phở*. The stock for this, a meat broth flavored with roasted ginger and star anise, bubbles in a cauldron. As an order comes in, rice noodles are heated in water and put in a bowl. Cooked beef slices go on top and then slices of raw beef. This is topped with green coriander, mint and scallions. Boiling stock is ladled over the top. The stock magically releases the fragrances of the herbs and turns the raw beef into rare beef. (In these days of hardship the beef is more often replaced by chicken, which is cheaper.) The soup is seasoned further at the table with a red chili sauce that adds heat and color, fish sauce that adds saltiness and rounds off the flavor of the stock, and a generous squeeze of lime. *Phở* is eaten with chopsticks and a Chinese-style spoon.

The Indian influence can be seen in the use of curry powders in the south, and in the ground rice pancakes. Perhaps the best example of the latter is *banh cuon*,

Above:
*Marketplace,
Vietnam* (Julian
Charrington)

*Banana seller,
1912 Market,
Hanoi, Vietnam*

an exquisitely delicate creation. Thin batter is poured onto a piece of muslin to steam briefly. Then the soft pancake is almost scraped off and used to enfold a very Chinese stuffing of minced pork and black fungus. It is served posthaste with crisply fried shallots on the top and a dipping sauce of pork stock seasoned with fish sauce, vinegar, sugar and chilies. If you are lucky, a few drops of jasminelike essence that comes from a special beetle are put into it as well. It is glorious!

You can tell that the French were here by the dashing berets the men wear. French bread is sold in every city. Quick lunches can be made by splitting a loaf in half, slathering it with butter from the Soviet Union and then stuffing it with slices of pâté or sausage or the Spamlike *chả lua*. Coffee, once very popular among the Westernized Vietnamese, is hard to find, but tea is drunk all the time. Every office has thermos flasks of hot water and a slightly bitter tea is made up quickly in small teapots and served in tiny, Chinese-style handleless cups.

What really distinguishes Vietnam's food from its neighbors' is its use of fresh herbs. Mounds are used for each meal. Every mouthful becomes a little perfumed package. If, say, a piece of fish cooked in coconut milk is to be eaten, a portion is put onto a piece of lettuce. This is topped with fresh coriander, mints, basils, scallions, and peanuts. It is wrapped up, dipped in a sauce and *then* eaten. The same happens to a piece of meat that has been marinated with garlic, shallots and lemongrass, and to small, bite-size spring rolls. Aromatic herbs keep exploding in the mouth, each fresher than the last.

Dill is commonly used, especially in conjunction with fish. One of Hanoi's specialties is *chả cá*. A restaurant and a street are named after it. Chunks of firm river fish are marinated in a mixture of turmeric, galangal, shrimp paste, lime juice and tamarind, then grilled over charcoal and brought to the table where a frying pan set over a portable stove awaits. The fish is reheated in a small amount of lard and fish sauce and then smothered with a blanket of fresh dill and scallions. As soon as the herbs wilt, the fish can be devoured with the assistance of fresh rice noodles, chopped peanuts and deliciously sour dipping sauces.

It is not just the herbs that give Vietnamese food its special character. It is the mixture of the herbs; the flavors of lemongrass, galangal and fried shallots; the taste of crushed, freshly roasted peanuts; and the use of salty, hot and sour dipping sauces that make Vietnamese food so wonderfully unique.

RECIPES FROM VIETNAM IN THIS BOOK INCLUDE

SAVORY PORK AND CRAB TOASTS
BÁNH MÌ CHIÊN
PORK AND CRAB SOUP
CANH THỊT NẤU CUA
SMALL SPRING ROLLS
NEM RÁN

AROMATIC AND SPICY BEEF STEW
THỊT BÒ KHO
NAPOLEON BEEF ON A SKEWER
THỊT BÒ LỤI
EASY BEEF KEBABS
BÒ NƯỚNG CHẢ

SPICY STIR-FRIED CHICKEN WITH LEMONGRASS
GÀ XÀO XẢ ỚT
ROAST CHICKEN WITH FIVE-SPICE POWDER
GÀ XỐI MỠ

STEAMED FISH WITH GINGER AND COCONUT MILK
CÁ LÓC HẤP
FISH BRAISED IN TEA
CÁ KHO
MONKFISH WITH DILL
CHẢ CÁ

KOHLRABI OR BROCCOLI STEM SALAD
NỘM SU HÀO
SMOKY EGGPLANTS IN A LIME SAUCE
CÀ TÍM NƯỚNG
ZUCCHINI WITH PORK AND SHRIMPS
BÀU XÀO

RICE NOODLES IN SOUP WITH BEEF
PHỞ

Hong Kong

*T*he crabs, of leafy green hue, squirm in mild protest. Their fierce claws have been tied to their bodies with matching grass and they have been laid out in baskets with regimental neatness. Each worthy crab is destined for the pot. It is October in Hong Kong and the two-month season for Shanghai's hairy crabs has just started. Trains from the northeast have been rumbling in with their valuable catch. Each small crab is more expensive than a lobster is in the West. Yet three or four per person will be eaten at each meal! The Chinese here know that in October they should eat the females as they just ooze with the much-prized roe; November is the time to tackle the males. They also know that each crab should be steamed alive and that it should be kept tied as it cooks to keep the meat sweet and to prevent the crab from releasing its juices—and its roe—as it struggles. Traditions have also armed them with the knowledge that crabs are very *yin*, or cooling. So they will eat them with shreds of young ginger, which is *yang*, or heating, and, for good measure, drink ginger tea afterward.

Hong Kong—big, brash and bustling—is a modern city with an ancient culture. Its 6,500,000 people, who use ferries, buses, underground trains and hydrofoils to zigzag across its many islands at frenzied speed, know how to make money and how to eat. With the sea on one side and fertile subtropical country on the others, they have constant access to a rich supply of the fruits of earth and sea. Spoiled by nature's abundance and fine-tuned by an ancient culinary tradition that is easily one of the world's finest, they demand the best ingredients and are not satisfied unless they get them. They know that a bearded kitchen god watches each hearth, ready to report all errors to his superior above.

Hong Kong, ceded to the British in the nineteenth century, is almost completely encircled by the 3,696,100 square miles that are China. Its cuisine is very much a mirror of the varying cultural traditions of the mother country. Indeed, half of Hong Kong's food and water is brought from there.

Most moderately equipped kitchens here contain certain staples: rice; soy sauces, light and dark; vinegars of varying hues; oil for cooking (peanut) and flavoring (sesame); as well as preserved and pickled foods. The spice rack may hold red chilies, Szechuan peppercorns, star anise, cassia bark and sesame seeds.

Other ingredients must be bought fresh. I have watched shrimps being rejected because they were kicking their legs too lazily, lobsters dropped back into tanks because their tails did not curl smartly and crabs failing to find a buyer because their bellies were squishy. Live cockles you buy may be cooked with black bean sauce; shrimps may be steamed with garlic oil and scallions; a whole fish steamed with ginger, pork shreds and sour pickle; and crab may be combined with chicken and winter melon for a soup. Over 30,000 fishermen supply the Hong Kong area with almost 100,000 tons of fish a year.

Daily shoppers are just as choosy about a vast selection of vegetable produce. There are, first of all, herbs and seasonings such as fresh coriander, chives and ginger; bland foods that will serve to absorb flavors and add textures, including bean curd and bamboo shoots; fungi that will add taste as well as protein and vitamin C; squashes to be stir-fried; and cabbages and radishes that can be put into soups and stews.

The day starts early with a choice of breakfasts. Is it to be a bowl of rice porridge *(congee)*, a deep-fried Chinese long doughnut *(you tiao)* or a steamed bun *(baozi)*? There would, of course, be tea, the national drink.

For midmorning tea there is the tea house. Just as there are pubs in England that turn into clubs for the local clientele, so it is with tea houses in Hong Kong. Some are used by wheelers and dealers of the financial world, others by bird fanciers who bring in their pet birds for a bit of appreciation—and perhaps a fight. The business of tea drinking *(yam cha)* is a serious one. First you pick your tea leaves from the many green, half-fermented and fermented teas. Then you go through the motion of "washing" your cup in a bowl of hot water at the table, then you brew the tea. Regular patrons leave their teas in marked caddies at the

Happy Valley Market, Hong Kong

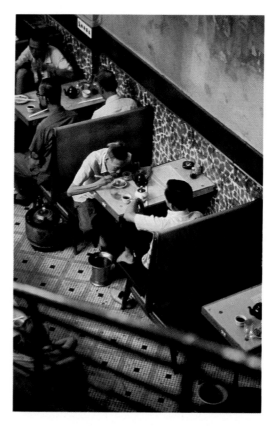

tea house. To accompany the tea there is a wide choice of *dim sum,* little snacks whose name means "order what you fancy": steamed shrimp dumplings with their translucent gossamerlike covering; bits of roast pork baked in savory pastry; or even a masterfully engineered dumpling filled with soup!

Lunch or dinner could take the form of noodles bought from a neighborhood stall or it could mean a visit to a restaurant embedded in one of the newer plazas where the meal might be preceded by ice skating, bowling or buying a Gucci handbag! The choice in styles of food available reflects in microcosm what may be found throughout all of China. Lovers of the fiery cuisines of the western regions of Sichuan and Hunan might wish to dine on Cold Chicken with Sesame and Chili Sauce or the crispy, sweet and hot Fried Shredded Beef with Carrots and Chilies or Pork in Hot and Sour Soup. A Beijing-style restaurant might supply the northern delicacies Lamb with Scallions, Scallion Bread or Peking Duck. The north eats more wheat than rice, using it to make fried and steamed breads as well as noodles. If you have membership and feel like the mellow, slightly sweet food of the eastern region, you might take yourself to the Shanghai Club and order their Fried Chicken with Scallion Sauce. It is marvelously crisp on the outside and smothered with a sauce of minced fresh herbs.

You could pick Cantonese food, the local cuisine. Mild and gently seasoned, it is designed, as the Cantonese say, "to let the ingredients shine through." The freshest of fish fillets are stir-fried with black bean sauce, and young shrimps combined with jade-green asparagus.

A few words about etiquette. The Chinese invented chopsticks and use the "nimble brothers" with masterful ease. Chopsticks should never be left in a crossed position (except after eating *dim sum,* to indicate that you have finished). Soup spoons are used not only for soup but also for the liquid in stews. All foods, except the individual bowls of rice, are communal and placed in the center of the table. Rice bowls should be brought near the mouth when you eat from them, not left on the table. When eating a whole cooked fish, you should never turn it over to get at the flesh on the other side (if you do, a fishing boat will tip over!). And yes, you may slurp your soup!

Vegetables, Happy Valley Market, Hong Kong

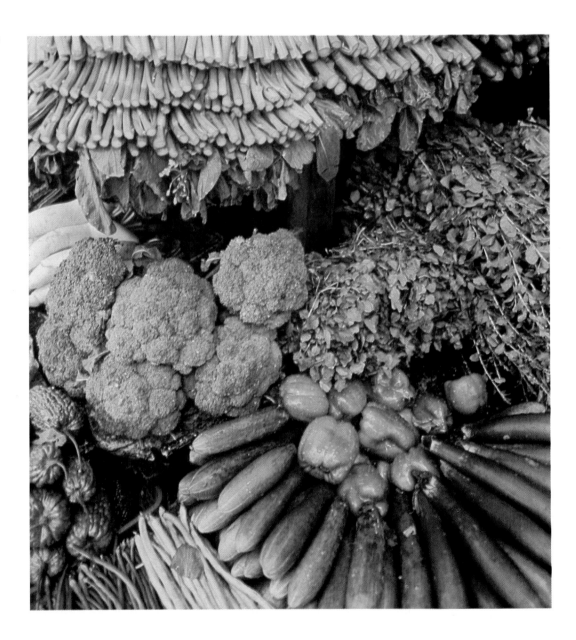

RECIPES FROM HONG KONG IN THIS BOOK INCLUDE

SUMMER SOUP WITH PORK AND CUCUMBER
WEI LING QINGGUA ROU JIN JIANG

LAMB WITH SCALLIONS
CONG BAO YANG ROLL
GLAZED GINGERY SPARERIBS
HONG SHAO LEIGU
PORK WITH LONG BEANS AND CHIVES
SIJIDOU CHAO ZHULIU
SICHUAN-STYLE FRIED SHREDDED BEEF WITH CARROTS AND CHILIES
GONGBAO NIULIU

COLD CHICKEN WITH SESAME AND CHILI SAUCE
MALAJI
CHICKEN STIR-FRIED WITH CELERY
JIANCAI JIDING
FRIED CHICKEN WITH SCALLION SAUCE
YOUPI ZIJI

SHRIMPS WITH ASPARAGUS
XIAN LUSUN CHAD XIAQIU
FISH FILLETS WITH BLACK BEAN SAUCE
DOUSHI YI

BRAISED LIMA BEANS
SHENGBIAN CANDOU
BEAN CURD WITH OYSTER SAUCE
HAOYOU DOUFU
SALAD OF CARROTS, CELERY, CUCUMBER AND HAM
LIANG BAN YANGCAI

COLD SESAME NOODLES WITH CHICKEN AND VEGETABLES
BON BON JIHAN BANMIAN
NOODLES WITH PORK IN HOT AND SOUR SOUP
SUANLA ZHA JIANGMIAN

SWEET WALNUT SOUP
WAIYOU HETAO TANG

Japan

*M*any years ago my husband and I were taken to one of the better eating establishments on one of the uglier outskirts of Kyoto city. The day was hot and miserable, the city congested and the traffic a nightmare. But the minute we entered the restaurant, our world changed. Our private room was cool and serene. We were seated facing the one large window. All we could see from it was a hill, a stream and an exquisitely proportioned tree. The window frame had been ingeniously placed to crop out all vulgarity and disarray.

Japanese food is meant to serve the same purpose—to create order out of chaos, to bring a sense of simplicity and perfection to a confused and entangled world. The principles belong to Zen Buddhism and apply to most aspects of Japanese culture. Foods are prepared so that their natural flavors remain unmasked and they are served in small, almost austere portions. The arrangement of food on the plate is always three-dimensional—it may be in little hillocks, or one food may lean against another—and, especially in the classy restaurants, it is made to resemble "nature" as much as possible. Tiny long-stemmed mushrooms float in a soup like fresh-fallen flowers in a stream. Bits of skewered and broiled chicken are set on a plate with leaves and look like small buds in a tree. It is said that a good Japanese restaurant is rated on three things: a third of the marks go to the cooking, a third to the presentation and the remaining third to the general ambience.

Not everyone can rise to the heights of the great Japanese chefs, but the principles hold true even for everyday meals. A very simple Japanese breakfast might consist of rice, a soup of fermented bean paste (*miso*) with perhaps a few cubes of bean curd floating in it, some pickles and tea. The only eating implement would be chopsticks, the liquid part of the soup being drunk by bringing the soup bowl to the mouth. *Miso* is made of fermented soybeans and grains. There is a world of such pastes in Japan. They range in color from white to almost black and in texture from smooth to very grainy. With judicious mixing, the flavor of your morning soup can be varied daily.

I find it interesting that many of these breakfast habits are changing. People now walk into coffee shops and order "morning," which brings them coffee, toast

A yakitori bar, Japan

and an egg, if they like! The Japanese have even invented a bread-making machine where all you have to do is put in the right measure of flour and the machine kneads, rests and bakes a loaf!

Newfangled inventions notwithstanding, rice is the staple grain. Japan has very little arable land and rice is made to grow on every available patch, however small it may be. The Japanese pay a lot for their short-grain, somewhat glutinous rice. They could import it; it would be far cheaper that way. But the Japanese are fiercely independent and do not wish to rely on others for a basic foodstuff. Besides, they like the flavor of their own grain.

As in the entire Far East, noodles are very popular. There are restaurants, both humble and expensive, that specialize in them. In the heat of the summer I have sat by a stream and had cold noodles float by me in a moat built into the counter. Once I had fished out the noodles, I had only to dip them in a citron-flavored dip before devouring them. In the cold autumn I have been served a steaming noodle casserole filled with mushrooms just picked from fallen logs and topped with a poached egg. It is best, my hosts explained, to suck the hot noodles in. The slurping allows an intake of air which cools them off.

The Japanese like to stress the seasons in their meals. In summer a moss-eating fish might be served to you on a bed of cool-looking pebbles; in autumn you might get chrysanthemum petals in your salad; winter might bring steaming savory custards and bean curd casseroles (bean curd retains its heat for a long time); and spring might produce fiddlehead ferns and young bamboo shoots.

Until the nineteenth century the only flesh consumed by the Japanese came from fish and birds. It then began to be felt that the Japanese race might grow taller and stronger if it ate red meat. So recipes for pork and beef were developed,

Grilled fish in
Nishiki Street,
Kyoto, Japan

MADHUR JAFFREY'S FAR EASTERN COOKERY

Construction worker in Kyoto, Japan, enjoying a bento box lunch

such as breaded pork cutlets or *tonkatsu; sukiyaki,* in which thick slices of beef and vegetables are braised together at the table; and *shabu shabu,* a kind of fondue in which meats and vegetables are dipped at the table into a bowl of simmering kelp stock and to cook them and then into a choice of sauces to season them. All these dishes made for delicious meals and tempted many Japanese to eat red meat.

Fish still predominates in the Japanese diet, however. The basic Japanese stock *(dashi)* used in everything from soups to sauces is made from shavings of dried bonito (a large mackerel-like fish) and dried kelp. The nation delights in raw fish, which can come in the form of *sashimi,* thin fish slices eaten with a dip of horse-radish-flavored soy sauce, or in the form of *sushi,* where sliced raw fish of all sorts is put together with small portions of lightly seasoned rice and eaten as canapés might be. Fish may be grilled simply with just a sprinkling of salt or basted as it grills with a thicker sauce of soy and sweet rice wine *(mirin).* It may be tossed with rice wine *(sake),* steamed and then served with a sauce of lemon and soy. It may also be dipped in batter and fried, making the glorious *tempura.* There are just as many ways of cooking chicken. Perhaps the most-loved chicken dish, though, is *yakitori,* a kind of chicken kebab dipped into a sweetish soy sauce mixture during the grilling.

It may by now be apparent that Japanese seasonings and sauces are made of careful permutations of the same few ingredients: soy sauce, rice wine *(sake),* sweet rice wine *(mirin),* sugar, fish and kelp stock *(dashi),* the juice of various sour citrus fruits and occasionally an aromatic Japanese pepper *(sansho).* The national drink is *sake;* these days, however, whisky or beer may be drunk right through a meal, and French wines, too, are encroaching.

For an informal meal, a family might serve grilled fish, a saladlike dish of spinach or beans dressed with sesame seeds, and perhaps carrots braised in stock. There would also be soup, rice, pickles and tea to round off the meal.

Rice, pickles and tea complete the most formal of dinners as well. I have known Japanese men to eat for three hours at official banquets but refrain from devouring that final triumvirate. "My wife will be waiting up," they say. "I will have my rice with her." Rice symbolizes the meal, and the man who has his rice at home is eating his meal with his wife. Symbols mean a lot in Japan.

RECIPES FROM JAPAN IN THIS BOOK INCLUDE

STUFFED MUSHROOMS
SHIITAKE NIKOZUME
FERMENTED BEAN PASTE SOUP WITH BEAN CURD
MISO SHIRU
CUCUMBER AND SHRIMP SALAD
EBI TO KYURI NO SUNOMONO

BREADED PORK CUTLETS
TONKATSU
BREADED PORK CUTLETS OVER RICE
KATSUDON

CHICKEN BITS ON A SKEWER
YAKITORI
CHICKEN WITH A SWEET SAKE GLAZE
TORINIKU NO TERIYAKI

GRILLED MACKEREL WITH SWEET SOY SAUCE
SAKE NO TERIYAKI
SHRIMP AND VEGETABLE FRITTERS
TEMPURA

GREEN BEANS WITH SESAME DRESSING
SANDO MAME NO GOMA AYE
MUSHROOMS IN A SCALLION DRESSING
KINOKO NO AEMONO
NOODLES IN BROTH WITH POACHED EGG AND VEGETABLES
SANSAI UDON
MIXED RICE
KAYAKU GOHAN
GINGER SHREDS IN SWEET VINEGAR
HARI SHOGA

SAKE

TECHNIQUES

*T*he general techniques used in Far Eastern cookery are not all that different from those used in the West. A few pointers may, however, be of some help.

CUTTING MEATS AND VEGETABLES

Meats and vegetables are frequently cut into strips or dice before they are cooked, so that the pieces cook evenly. This is particularly important for quick stir-frying and for the general look of the food. Aesthetics play a very special role in this region, reaching a pinnacle in Japan, where restaurants are judged on the look of their food as much as on its taste.

To debone a chicken leg (see below)
The chicken recipes in this book often call for boneless dark leg meat, as it stays much more moist than white meat and has a better flavor. Deboning a chicken leg is actually quite easy. (a) Using a sharp knife, make a deep slit along the length of the bone and drumstick. (b) Free the meat at both ends, cutting at right angles to the bones. (c) Now cut—almost scrape—the meat off the thigh bone and drumstick, freeing the meat from the middle joint as you do so. (d) The chicken meat may now be cut into pieces of the desired size.

a

b

c

To cut vegetables into julienne strips and dice (see above)

Each vegetable demands its own cutting technique. Generally speaking, you should first cut the vegetable into slices of the required width. Then cut them lengthwise into strips. These strips can be cut crosswise if small dice are required.

To cut a carrot into julienne strips 2 inches long, cut off the top and tip and then cut the carrot crosswise into 2-inch chunks. (a) Cut each chunk lengthwise into slices of the desired thickness. (b) Cut each slice lengthwise again, to make the strips. (c) Cut each strip into dice, if required.

To slice meat into thin slices and strips

It frequently helps (though it is not essential) to partially freeze, say, a beef steak, before you cut it against the grain into thin slices. If strips are called for, stack a few slices together at a time to make the cutting quicker.

TO PEEL AND DEVEIN A SHRIMP
(a) First pull off the tail. Then peel off the shell and, with it, the tiny legs. (b) Make a shallow cut down the back of the shrimp. (c) Remove the fine digestive cord which runs the length of it.

TO CLEAN SQUID
Twist off the head (with the tentacles). The inner body sac will probably come away with it. Discard the sac and the hard eye area, which you may have to cut off with a knife. Retain the tentacles. If possible, pull off some of the brown skin on the tentacles. (You may safely leave this, if you wish.) Peel the brownish skin from the tube-like body. Discard this skin and pull out the smooth inner cartilage (or pen). The squid can now be washed and used as your recipe requires.

MARINATING

Meats are often cut up and put into marinades before they are cooked. A marinade tenderizes meat and injects it with all the flavors and aromas of its myriad ingredients. The meat can then be grilled or quickly stir-fried while retaining the tastes of all its seasonings.

BASTING SAUCES

As meat, fish or poultry is grilling, it is often basted. Sometimes, as in Japan, the basting sauce has sugar in it so it not only provides flavor but a final glaze as well. In Malaysia basting sauces may contain coconut milk, which provides the lubrication needed to keep the meat, poultry or fish from drying out. In Indonesia a most practical (and aromatic) brush is made from a stick of lemongrass that is lightly pounded at the end!

SPICE PASTES

Most curry-style dishes require that a spice paste be prepared first. To this end, fresh and dried spices are pounded in a mortar and then fried in oil to get rid of their raw taste. Freshly pounded spice pastes of good quality are sold in most Thai and Malaysian markets. We in the West have to prepare our own, but we have blenders, food processors and coffee grinders to make our lives easier.

Fresh hot red chilies, pounded to a paste, are a major ingredient in Thai, Indonesian and Malaysian dishes. While many people pound their own chilies at home in a mortar, others are content to buy them, already pounded, in small plastic bags. When I cannot get fresh hot red chilies, I blend together sweet red bell peppers and ground red pepper (cayenne); this mixture gives just the right color to the dishes where it is needed.

COOKING COCONUT MILK

When cooking coconut milk, care must be taken that it does not curdle. Stir it constantly as it cooks. I often add it only toward the end of the cooking period and just bring it to a simmer and leave it at that. Coconut milk may be simmered for a long period, but only if it is stirred most of the time.

GARNISHES AS FLAVORINGS

A garnish in the West often means a radish or a tomato cut into a flower. This sits on the edge of the plate, to be admired and perhaps even nibbled upon. It frequently has no real connection with the food it enhances. In the East what might look like a garnish is often an integral part of the dish. For example, crisply fried shallots and crushed roasted peanuts may be sprinkled over a dish at the last minute. They are there because without their flavor and texture the dish would be incomplete.

BROILING

Broiling is very popular throughout the Far East. Tiny pieces of meat skewered on bamboo sticks (*satays*) and freshly grilled on charcoal are sold in the bazaars of Indonesia, Malaysia and Thailand, as everyone loves to eat out. The Koreans cut their meat into strips, marinate it and grill it on their dining tables. Each home is equipped with special portable burners and grills just for this purpose. The Japanese pierce a fillet of fish with several skewers, then grill it with frequent bastings of sweetish sauces. The skewers are very helpful when it comes to turning the fillets over. As they are inserted against the grain, the fish does not fall apart. Bamboo skewers should be soaked in water for 30 minutes before use so that they do not burn.

Although most of the grilled dishes in this book can be cooked under an oven broiler, the taste will be more authentic if you are able to use a charcoal or gas grill instead. When grilling on charcoal, it is important to get the coals white-hot before you start.

STEAMING

Steaming is used for cooking anything from plain rice to complete dishes such as Fish Steamed with Lemongrass and Savory Egg Custard with Shrimps and Mushrooms. Just as every home in the West has a roasting pan, so every home in the Far East tends to have a steamer. Steaming cooks gently and preserves flavor.

One of the most satisfactory utensils for steaming is a wok because its width easily accommodates a whole fish, a casserole or a large plate of food. Use a wok with a flat base or set a round-based wok on a wire stand. Put a metal or wooden rack into the wok.

Now pour in some water. Bring it to a gentle boil and lower in the food. The water should stay about ¾ inch below the level of the food that is being steamed. Extra boiling water should be kept at hand just in case it is needed.

Cover the whole wok, including the food, with a wok lid or a large sheet of aluminum foil.

STIR-FRYING

This is fast cooking over high heat in a small amount of oil. A wok is essential for this. The oil is heated and often flavorings such as garlic and ginger are tossed around in it before cut meats and vegetables are added. These, too, are tossed around quickly until they are cooked.

DEEP-FRYING

You need several inches of oil in a wok or frying pan and a good deal more in a deep-fat fryer in order to deep-fry. The oil must be heated to the required temperature before you drop in a single morsel of food. Properly deep-fried foods are not at all greasy; the outside is beautifully crisp while the inside is completely cooked.

Oil that has been used for deep-frying may be reused. Let it cool completely and then strain it. Store it in a bottle. When you cook again, use half old oil and half fresh oil. Oil that has been used for frying fish should be reused only for fish.

Place a wire rack inside the wok upon which the food is put for steaming.

DRY-ROASTING

Spices are often dry-roasted before use. It is best to do this in a heavy cast-iron frying pan that has first been heated. No oil is used: the spices are just stirred around until they brown lightly. Roasted spices develop a heightened, nutty aroma. They can be stored for at least several months in an airtight jar.

BLANCHING AND REFRESHING

In order to keep vegetables crisp and their color bright, they may, after preparation, be plunged very briefly into a large pan of water at a rolling boil—that is, boiling furiously. The reason for using a lot of boiling water is that you do not want the temperature of the water to drop when the vegetables are put into it: this would slow their cooking time and therefore affect both their color and crispness. The vegetables should be cooked in the water until barely tender (but still crisp), drained quickly and then either plunged into a large quantity of iced water or rinsed under cold running water. This helps to set their color and stop the cooking process.

POACHING

Many recipes require that chicken breasts be poached in water to just cover. Breast meat is fairly dry and it toughens easily. To poach properly, it is important that the water be barely simmering. If it boils too rapidly, it will toughen the meat.

BRAISING

This also involves cooking foods slowly in liquid but over a long period. Whole birds and fish can be cooked in this way. The liquid is always flavored. It may be stock or water flavored with wine, herbs and spices; or, as in one recipe in this book, the braising liquid could be tea.

EQUISPMENT

his book does not require unusual equipment. However, it does help to have the following:

A WOK

This is an all-purpose utensil that may be used for steaming, simmering, stir-frying or deep-frying.

A wok is traditionally a round-bottomed pan. Because of its shape, flames can encircle it and allow it to heat quickly and efficiently. It is most economical for deep-frying as it will hold a good depth of oil without needing the quantity a straight-sided pan would require. It is ideal for stir-frying as foods can be vigorously tossed around in it. As they hit nothing but well-heated surfaces, they cook fast and retain their moisture at the same time.

Choosing a wok
What kind of wok should you buy? Advances are being made all the time and every year seems to bring new woks into the marketplace. Traditional woks of good quality are made either of thin tempered iron or carbon steel. The ideal wok is 14 inches in diameter and fairly deep. (Saucer-shaped shallow woks are quite useless.) A round-bottomed wok works well on a gas stove. A new, somewhat flat-bottomed wok has been invented for people who have electric stoves. I cannot say I love it. Instead I opted for a yet newer invention in my country house, which has an all-electric kitchen. This is an electric wok

—but a very special one. The brand name is Maxim. It is the only electric wok I know that heats very quickly, becomes *very* hot and allows food to be both stir-fried and simmered.

Seasoning a wok
The iron and carbon steel woks leave the factory coated with oil. This needs to be scrubbed off with dish detergent. Then a wok needs to be seasoned. Rinse it in water and set it over low heat. Now brush it all over with about 2 tablespoons vegetable oil. Let it heat for 10–15 minutes. Wipe the oil off with a piece of paper toweling. Brush the wok with more oil and repeat the process 3–4 times. The wok is now seasoned. Do not scrub it again; just wash it with hot water and then wipe it dry. It will *not* have a scrubbed look. It will, however, become more and more "nonstick" as it is used.

Wok accessories
For use on a gas stove, a wok needs a stand that not only stabilizes it but allows air to circulate underneath. The perfect stand is made of wire. The collar variety with punched holes seems to kill free circulation of air and heat and should not be used on gas stoves.

When you buy a wok, it is also a good idea to invest in a curved spatula, a steaming rack and a lid.

CAST-IRON FRYING PANS

I find a 5-inch cast-iron frying pan ideal for roasting spices and a large one perfect for pan-broiling thin slices of meat. All cast-iron frying pans can be heated without any liquid and they retain an even temperature. Once properly seasoned, they should never be scrubbed with abrasive cleansers.

BLENDER, FOOD PROCESSOR AND COFFEE GRINDER

In the Far East mortars, pestles and grinding stones of varying shapes, sizes and materials are used to pulverize everything from sesame seeds to fresh hot red chilies. I find it much easier to use an electric blender or food processor for wet ingredients and a clean electric coffee grinder for dry ones. Mouli has come up with small "wet-dry" grinders that may be used to grind small quantities of both dry seasonings and wet pastes.

GRATER

The Japanese make a special grater for ginger and horseradish. It has tiny hairlike spikes that are perfect for their purpose. If you ever find one, do buy it. Otherwise use the finest part of an ordinary grater for grating fresh ginger.

DOUBLE BOILER

This is simply one pan balanced over another. The lower pan holds boiling water and allows the ingredients in the other pan to cook very gently.

Double boilers are available from good kitchenware shops but can be easily improvised.

ELECTRIC RICE COOKER

Many households in the Far East seem to have one of these gadgets. Its main use is to free all burners on the stove for other purposes and make the cooking of rice an easy, almost mindless task. I do have one and use it only for plain rice.

DEEP-FAT FRYER

For those who are afraid of deep-frying, this is a godsend. Because it has a lid that closes over all splattering foods, this piece of equipment also helps to make deep-frying a painless, safe and clean task.

RACKS FOR BROILING FISH

In Indonesia hinged double racks are used for broiling fish over charcoal. The fish lies sandwiched between the two racks and can be easily turned and basted. Many types of fish racks are available in the West, some even shaped like a fish. I find them exceedingly useful.

FOOD SCALE

A food scale that measures ounces can be extremely useful, especially for weighing fresh herbs and vegetables. Inexpensive scales can be found at some supermarkets, department stores and cookware and gourmet shops.

First Courses

CHICKEN, SHRIMP AND FRUIT SALAD

Thailand

From Chalie Amatyakul at Bangkok's Oriental Hotel Cooking School

YAM POLAMAI

There is such exuberance about Thai salads. Not only are meat, fish and fruit all put together, but they also are seasoned quite brilliantly with hot, sweet, sour and salty flavors as well as with crisply fried slivers of shallots and garlic. This salad does have several parts to it but each takes very little time to prepare. You will, I promise, be more than compensated when your family and friends cry out with delight at the very first mouthful—this is a superb dish.

In Thailand the fruit in the salad can include such exotic fare as pomelos, water chestnuts, mangoes, rose apples, mangosteens and litchis, all of which should be diced. Do use these fruits if you can find them. The amount of sugar, salt, lime juice and chilies will vary not just according to your taste but also according to the natural flavors of the fruit. Taste as you mix the salad and make your own adjustments. If you do not want tiny explosions of "heat" as you eat, leave out the green chilies and use ground red (cayenne) pepper instead. You may use cooked instead of uncooked shrimps, in which case you will not need to poach them.

All the ingredients and separate parts of the salad may be prepared several hours ahead of time. The salad should, however, be mixed only at the last minute so that the texture is crisp.   *Serves 6 as a first course or 4 as a main course*

Salt

1 large, firm, sour dessert apple (such as a Granny Smith)

1 cup medium to large red grapes, preferably seedless

1 cup medium to large green grapes, preferably seedless

1 medium orange

5 garlic cloves

7 medium shallots (or 1 medium onion)

Oil for deep-frying

1/4 lb chicken breast, boned and skinned

8 medium or 16 small shrimps

4 tablespoons Roasted Peanuts (see page 247)

1 teaspoon sugar

3 tablespoons fresh lime or lemon juice

2–3 fresh hot green chilies

2 tablespoons fresh coriander leaves

Combine 1 teaspoon salt with 2½ cups water in a small bowl. Peel and core the apple and cut it into ¼–⅓-inch dice. As you cut and dice, put the apple pieces into the salted water. Set aside.

Halve the grapes lengthwise and remove the seeds where necessary. Put the grapes into a bowl. Peel the or-

Bottom: *Chicken, Shrimp, and Fruit Salad (this page);* **top right:** *Stir-Fried Shrimps with Tamarind and Chilies (page 67);* **top left:** *Savory Pork and Crab Toasts (page 68)* ange, separate the segments and skin them as best you can. Cut each segment crosswise at ⅓-inch intervals. Lay the orange pieces over the grapes. Cover and set aside.

Peel the garlic, cut into thin slices and cut the slices into fine slivers. Peel the shallots, halve them lengthwise and thinly slice them.

Pour the oil to a depth of 1 inch into a medium-sized frying pan or wok. Place over a medium-low heat. While you are waiting for the oil to get hot, set a sieve over a bowl and place it on a work surface near the pan. Spread some paper toweling over a large plate. When the oil is hot, put in the garlic slivers and stir and fry until they turn golden. Empty the oil and garlic into the sieve; then, when the garlic has drained, spread it out over one half of the paper toweling.

Put the oil in the bowl back into the frying pan and set it over a medium heat. Replace the sieve over the bowl. When the oil has reheated, put in the shallots and stir and fry until they are golden brown and crisp. Empty the contents of the pan into the sieve. When the shallots have drained, spread them out over the remaining paper toweling. (Save the flavored oil for cooking other foods.)

Cut the chicken into long thin strips and put these into a clean medium-sized frying pan. Add water to cover and ¼ teaspoon salt, and bring to a simmer. Simmer gently for about 5 minutes or until the chicken is just done. Remove the chicken from the water and tear it into shreds 1 inch long or cut it into ¼–⅓-inch dice. Save the water in which it was cooked.

Peel and devein the shrimps. Bring the chicken poaching water to a simmer and add the shrimps. Turn the heat to medium-low. Stir and poach the shrimps for 2–3 minutes or until they are just cooked through. Drain. Cut the shrimps into ¼–⅓-inch dice. Combine the chicken and shrimps, cover and set aside.

Crush the peanuts lightly—an easy way is to put them into a plastic bag and hit them gently with a hammer. Set them aside.

Combine 1 teaspoon salt, the sugar and the lime juice in a small bowl and mix. Set aside. Cut the chilies into very fine rounds. Wash and dry the coriander. Cover and set aside.

Immediately before you are ready to serve, drain the apples and pat them dry. Set aside a little of the fried shallots and Chinese parsley for garnishing, then toss all the other ingredients together in a large bowl. Check the seasoning. Bring the salad to the table on individual plates, garnished with the reserved shallots and coriander.

STIR-FRIED SHRIMPS WITH TAMARIND AND CHILIES

SAMBAL UDANG

*H*ot, sour and simple to prepare, this is a delicious way to cook shrimps.
Serves 4

2–10 *whole dried hot red chilies (2 will make a very mild dish, 10 a hot one)*

6 *candlenuts or 8 cashew nuts*

7 *medium shallots (or 1 medium onion)*

1 *teaspoon shrimp or anchovy paste*

1 *lb medium shrimps*

8 *tablespoons vegetable oil*

2 *tablespoons tamarind paste (see page 303) or 4 teaspoons lime or lemon juice*

½ *teaspoon salt*

2 *teaspoons sugar*

Crumble the chilies into a cup. Add the nuts and 5 tablespoons water. Set aside for 1 hour. Peel the shallots and chop them coarsely. When the chilies and nuts have finished soaking, put them and their soaking liquid into a blender. Add the chopped shallots and shrimp paste. Blend to a smooth paste, adding up to 3 tablespoons water if needed. Peel and devein the shrimps; wash them and pat dry.

Place the oil in a wok or large frying pan over a high heat. When it is hot, put in the paste from the blender. Stir-fry for 1 minute. Turn the heat down to medium, and continue to stir-fry for 2–3 minutes. Turn the heat up again and add the shrimps. Stir-fry for 1 minute. Lower the heat to medium and add the tamarind (or lime or lemon juice), salt and sugar. Stir-fry for 3–5 minutes or until the shrimps are cooked. Check the seasoning.

SAVORY PORK AND CRAB TOASTS

BÁNH MÌ CHIÊN

You may serve these as a savory at the end of a meal or as a first course. When I invite people over for drinks I find that these toasts are just the perfect nibble to pass around. Rather like the triangles of shrimp toast that you might have eaten in Chinese restaurants, they are triangles of ground pork and shredded crab meat. They are simple to prepare. All that they require is that you fry them just before you serve them—usually for less than 2 minutes per batch.

If you are using frozen crab meat make sure that you defrost it completely and squeeze out all the moisture from it beforehand. If you are grinding the pork yourself, put the garlic and shallots into the food processor along with the meat.

Makes about 32 triangles of toast

2 large garlic cloves
1 medium shallot (or ½ small onion)
3 oz cooked crab meat, finely shredded
¼ lb lean pork, very finely ground
1 large egg
Freshly ground black pepper
1½ teaspoons sugar
1½ teaspoons fish sauce or salt to taste
About 8 slices white bread, about ¼–⅓ inch thick
Vegetable oil for frying

Peel the garlic and shallot and mince them finely. Combine the garlic, shallot, crab meat and ground pork in a bowl. Beat the egg in a separate bowl. Add 2 tablespoons of the beaten egg to the pork-crab mixture. Add also a generous amount of black pepper, the sugar and the fish sauce. Mix well to form a paste. This mixture may be made ahead of time, covered and stored in the refrigerator.

Stacking a few slices of bread together at a time, cut off the crusts. Now cut the slices in half diagonally, making large triangles, then cut these triangles in half again to make small triangles. Using a knife, spread the prepared paste over one side of each triangle to a thickness of ⅛ inch.

Pour the oil into a large frying pan to a depth of just under ½ inch and set it over a medium-low heat. When it is hot (a cube of bread dropped in should begin to sizzle immediately if the temperature is right), put in as many triangles of bread as will fit in a single layer, meat side down, and cook for 1½ minutes or until the meat is golden brown. Turn the bread triangles over and cook on the second side for 30–60 seconds or until golden. Remove them with a slotted spoon and drain on paper towels. Fry all the triangles in this way. Serve hot.

CUCUMBER AND SHRIMP SALAD

EBI TO KYURI NO SUNOMONO

*I*n Japan a *sunomono* is a "vinegared thing," a salad which is usually served in small portions at the start of a meal. I have used Japanese rice vinegar here; it is milder and slightly sweeter than distilled white vinegar. To make an approximation of it yourself for this recipe, combine 3 teaspoons distilled white vinegar with 1 teaspoon water and a pinch of sugar.

It is best to use small shrimps for this dish. You may buy cooked ones, if that is more convenient, or else you could buy fresh ones and then drop them into simmering water for a minute or two, after which they will need to be peeled and deveined. Larger shrimps should be cut into ½-inch pieces.   *Serves 4*

2 Kirby cucumbers or 1 regular 6-inch
   cucumber

Salt

4 teaspoons Japanese rice vinegar

2 teaspoons Japanese soy sauce (shoyu)

½ teaspoon sugar

2 teaspoons Japanese Soup Stock (see page
   78) or unsalted chicken stock,
   homemade (see page 77) or canned

½ teaspoon sesame oil

¼ lb small cooked peeled shrimps

Peel the cucumbers only if the skin is very thick and cut crosswise into very thin rounds. Put the slices in a bowl. Add a very scant ½ teaspoon salt and toss. Set aside for 30–45 minutes. Squeeze as much liquid as possible out of the cucumber slices and pat them dry with paper towels.

Mix the vinegar, soy sauce, sugar, Japanese Soup Stock and sesame oil in a small bowl.

Just before serving, drain the cucumber slices again, pat them dry and put them in a bowl. Add the shrimps and the vinegar dressing. Toss to mix. Put the salad into the center of each of four small individual plates or bowls, heaping it up to form little hillocks.

MACKEREL "COOKED" IN LIME JUICE

KILAWING TANGUIGUE

*I*n this startlingly good and refreshing first course, particularly suitable for the summer, the mackerel is actually not cooked at all, making the dish a very easy one to prepare. The fish does not, however, taste in the slightest bit raw. That is because it is marinated in lime juice, which firms the flesh and turns it opaque—in essence doing to the fish what cooking would do to it, only with less effort on your part. If you have never eaten raw fish, you simply must try this. It is sour and gingery and best served as a first course over a bed of salad greens. *Kilawing tanguigue* is not all that different from the Latin American *ceviche* and was probably brought to the Philippines by the Spaniards, who most likely picked it up in Central or South America. It is now very popular in the northern province of Ilocos Norte, where it is sometimes made with a very special local vinegar.

You may make this mackerel dish a day in advance. Keep it well covered and refrigerated.   *Serves 4*

---

9 oz mackerel fillets, skinned
4–5 tablespoons lime juice
1-inch cube fresh ginger
½ medium carrot
½ small onion
½ teaspoon salt
Freshly ground black pepper

Mackerel fillets that are supposedly boned invariably have a few bones left in them. Feel for them with your hands and pull them out either with your fingers or with a pair of tweezers. Cut the fillets into ½-inch cubes and put these into a stainless-steel or non-metallic bowl. Cover with lime juice. Toss well and set aside for 1 hour.

Meanwhile, peel the ginger and cut it into very thin slices. Stacking a few slices together at a time, cut the slices first into very thin strips and then halve the strips. Peel the carrot and cut first into thin slices and then into minute dice. Peel the onion and mince it. Drain the fish carefully and add to it the ginger, carrot and onion. Add also the salt and some black pepper. Toss well. Cover and refrigerate for at least 2 hours. Serve cold.

Squid in Chili and Garlic Sauce

SOTONG DAN CHILI DAN BAWANG PUTIH

*I*n Malaysia the sauce for this dish is made with fresh red chilies. Since they are hard to find here, I use a mixture of dried chilies and paprika. The dish still tastes very good.   *Serves 4*

4–9 whole dried hot red chilies (4 will make a mild dish, 9 a hot one)

½ teaspoon paprika

½ teaspoon shrimp or anchovy paste

1 lb squid, cleaned (see page 57)

3 garlic cloves

1 large onion

5 tablespoons vegetable oil

½ teaspoon salt

½ teaspoon sugar

1 teaspoon lime or lemon juice

Crumble the chilies into a cup. Add 4 tablespoons warm water and set aside for about 30 minutes. Put the chilies and their soaking liquid into an electric blender and blend until smooth. Return the mixture to the cup and add the paprika and shrimp paste. Stir to mix.

Wash the squid and pat it dry. Cut the tubular body of the squid cross-wise into ¾-inch rings. The tentacles may be left clumped together or separated into 2–3 clumps. Peel the garlic and chop finely. Finely slice the onion.

Place 3 tablespoons of the oil in a frying pan over a high heat. When it is hot, put in the garlic. Stir and fry for about 30 seconds or until the garlic is golden. Add the squid. Stir and cook for 3–4 minutes or until the squid has turned opaque all the way through. Empty the contents of the frying pan into a bowl and set aside.

Wipe the frying pan clean with paper towels. Put in the remaining 2 tablespoons oil and set the pan over a medium-high heat. When the oil is hot, put in the onion. Stir and fry for about 3 minutes or until the onion is soft. Add the paste from the cup, the salt, sugar and lime juice. Stir and cook for 1 minute. Add the squid and all the juices in the bowl. Mix, heat thoroughly and serve.

SMALL SPRING ROLLS

NEM RÁN

Called *nem* in North Vietnam and *chả giò* in South Vietnam, these delicious bite-sized crab-and-pork-filled spring rolls are usually wrapped in soft lettuce leaves and dipped into a sauce before being eaten. Fresh herbs such as mint and basil are put into these lettuce bundles as well.

A word about the Vietnamese spring roll wrappers: unlike the Chinese spring roll skins, which are made of plain wheat flour, these are made from rice flour. When bought, they look like round translucent sheets of paper with the markings of the cross-woven mats on which they dried firmly imprinted on them. The ideal size is about 4 inches in diameter, but this size is hard to find in the West. Mrs. Vường, the chef at whose elbow I learned this recipe in Hanoi, used two very thin wrappers, one placed more or less on top of the other, to make each spring roll. Since the wrappers were stiff, she softened them by smearing the outside wrapper with a little caramel-flavored water. I find that the wrappers I have managed to obtain at ethnic grocers' in the West are often much larger and coarser in texture, and either need repeated brushings with caramel water or a quick dip in a sinkful of warm water to soften them. They may also need to be halved or quartered. As they crumble easily, it is best to wet them first, then cut them with a sharp knife. After they have been stuffed, you will need a little flour paste to stick the last end of the wrapper down firmly in place.

Vietnamese spring roll wrappers are sold by Chinese and Far Eastern grocers, where they are usually labeled ''rice paper.'' If you cannot get authentic rice paper wrappers, the best substitute is filo pastry, which is sold in many supermarkets and delicatessens. To use the pastry, just spread one large sheet on a slightly dampened cloth. Brush it with warm vegetable oil and cover it with another sheet. Brush that with oil as well. Cut the sheets, in place, into 4-inch squares. As you work with one square, keep the rest covered with a damp cloth. You will not need the caramel water or flour paste. Instead of frying the pastry rolls, you can arrange them, one next to the other, on a baking tray, brush them all with oil and then bake them in the oven at 400°F for 20–30 minutes, turning them over halfway through the cooking time.

One of the ingredients called for here is a fungus known variously as wood-ears, cloud-ears, *moer*-mushrooms or just black fungus. Used routinely in Chinese cookery, these ''mushrooms'' look like miniature elephant's ears and have a mild earthy taste and a crunchy texture. They are also meant to be very good for the heart! The Vietnamese often use them in their fresh form. In the West, we can obtain them only in their dried form at Chinese grocers'. (Consult page 286 for more details on this interesting ingredient and what variety to look for.) If you cannot obtain dried black fungus, increase the number of dried Chinese mushrooms from 8 to 14.   *Makes about 50 bite-sized rolls*

2 tablespoons dried black fungus
  (cloud-ears)
8 dried Chinese mushrooms
½ oz cellophane noodles
½ scallion
½ medium onion
¼ lb lean pork, finely ground
¼ lb cooked white crab meat, shredded
¼ teaspoon salt
Freshly ground black pepper
1 large egg
1 large head soft lettuce
1 bunch fresh mint sprigs
4 tablespoons Caramel Water (see page
  242) or warm water may be used as a
  substitute
2 tablespoons unbleached, white flour
Vietnamese rice papers
Oil for deep-frying
Fish Sauce Seasoned with Lime Juice
  (see page 239)

Soak the black fungus in 1¼ cups hot water for 30 minutes. Lift the fungus out of the water and rinse it under cold running water. Feel for the hard "eyes" and cut them off. Chop the fungus very finely. You should have about 4 tablespoons.

Soak the dried mushrooms in a separate 1¼ cups hot water for 30 minutes or until they are soft. Lift them out of the liquid and cut off the hard stems. Chop the caps finely.

Soak the cellophane noodles in a large bowl of hot water for 15–30 minutes or until they are soft. Drain and cut them into ½-inch lengths.

Finely chop the scallion. Peel the onion and chop it finely. In a bowl combine the pork, crab meat (make sure that it has no bits of shell left in it), black fungus, mushrooms, cellophane noodles, scallion, onion, salt, black pepper and egg. Mix well.

Wash the lettuce, separating all the leaves, and drain it. Wash the mint, break it into very small sprigs, and drain it. Make the Caramel Water. Combine the flour with 3–3½ tablespoons water to make a paste.

Add 2½ cups hot water to the Caramel Water, which should now be warm. Brush a piece of rice paper on both sides with the diluted Caramel Water. If it turns soft and pliable, proceed with the next step; otherwise brush it again with the Caramel Water. If you have the 4-inch rice papers, leave them as they are. If you have the 9-inch papers, cut them into quarters. Work with one quarter at a time.

Put a heaped teaspoon of the pork-crab mixture roughly in the center, but closer to the edge nearest you (see diagram). Spread the mixture into a sausage shape about 1¾ inches long. Fold the side nearest the filling over it. Then fold the two adjacent sides over to the center. Now roll the parcel away from you and seal the edge with a little flour paste. Make all the spring rolls in this way and set them aside on a plate. (If you find that the rice paper is too thin and unmanageable, use 2 papers, one on top of the other.)

Heat the oil in a wok or deep-fat fryer over a medium heat. When the oil is hot, put in as many spring rolls as will fit easily in one layer. Fry them until they are golden. Remove them with a slotted spoon and drain them on paper toweling. Continue until you have fried all the spring rolls in this way.

Arrange the spring rolls on a plate. Arrange the lettuce leaves and mint sprigs on another plate. Put a small bowl of Fish Sauce Seasoned with Lime Juice near each diner, or place a bowl between 2 diners for them to share. To eat, take a lettuce leaf, or part of one, and put a spring roll and a few mint leaves on it; roll it up and dip it into the sauce.

PREPARING A SPRING ROLL

a   Brush the piece of rice paper with diluted Caramel Water on both sides.

b   When the rice paper is soft and pliable, put a heaped teaspoon of pork-crab mixture near the center, but closer to one side. The mixture should be in a sausage shape, about 1¾ inches long.

c   Fold the side nearest the filling right over it.

d   Now fold an adjacent side over toward the center.

e   Then fold the opposite side over.

f   Finally, roll the parcel away from you to use up the remaining rice paper until you are left with a neat parcel.

STUFFED MUSHROOMS

SHIITAKE NIKOZUME

A yakitori bar in Japan produces not just tantalizing tidbits of broiled chicken on skewers (see page 126), but also a whole range of snacks that may be served with drinks or as a first course at a somewhat formal dinner. These mushrooms, for which I must confess a passion, are one such example. They are simple enough to make. Mushroom caps are stuffed with ginger-flavored ground chicken and then cooked on a hot, lightly oiled surface. What gives them a heady lift is the final dousing they get in a tart sauce of soy and vinegar. A little mustard is served on the side to add further piquancy. A serving in the *yakitori* bars I frequented consisted of three mushrooms—four is considered an unlucky number. You may, of course, serve as many as you please.   *Serves 6*

1-inch cube fresh ginger

1 medium egg

10 oz chicken, skinned and ground (use dark or light meat, or a mixture)

Freshly ground black pepper

2–3 blades fresh chives or 1 scallion (optional)

18 large well-formed mushrooms

1 tablespoon vegetable oil

6 tablespoons Japanese soy sauce (shoyu)

2 tablespoons distilled white vinegar or 3 tablespoons Japanese rice vinegar

Prepared English or any other mustard to serve on the side

Peel the ginger and grate it finely. Collect it all on your finger tips. Hold it over a bowl and squeeze as much juice from it as you can. Discard the grated ginger, keeping the juice. Break the egg into the same bowl and beat it lightly. Add the ground chicken and

black pepper to taste. Finely chop about 2 teaspoons chives or scallion and add to the stuffing. Mix gently.

Gently break off the mushroom stems. Wipe the mushroom caps with damp paper toweling. Stuff each mushroom cavity with a heaped teaspoon of the chicken mixture, flattening off the top.

Put the oil into a large nonstick frying pan and set it over a medium-high heat. When it is hot, put in the mushroom caps, stuffed side down. Cook for 4–5 minutes or until lightly browned. Turn the caps over, turn the heat down to medium, cover and cook for 3–4 minutes. Meanwhile, mix the soy sauce and vinegar in a bowl.

Put three caps on each of six individual salad plates, stuffed side up. Spoon an equal amount of sauce over each plate of mushrooms. Serve hot with the mustard on the side.

SHRIMP WAFERS

KRUPUK UDANG

*K*rupuk, sold by Southeast Asian and some Chinese grocers (see Ingredients, page 275), are wafers which, rather like the Indian poppadums, add a pleasing crunch to a meal. They may be found sitting neatly at the edge of a plate of *Gado-Gado* (Salad of Assorted Vegetables with a Delicious Peanut Dressing, page 207), their crispness balancing nicely with the blanched vegetables, or on a plate of *Nasi Goreng Istimewa* (Special Fried Rice with Beef and Shrimps, page 214). They nearly always appear at festive banquets, are amazingly good with drinks—try them with a dip of *Sambal Terasi* (Red Pepper Sauce with Shrimp Paste, page 243)—and may be eaten on their own as a snack. There are many, many varieties of *krupuk*. They may be flavored with shrimps, cassava or nuts. One of my favorites, found only in the hills of Western Sumatra, is made of cassava and comes thinly smeared with a sweet and hot red chili jam.

Krupuk udang, made of shrimps and starch, come in many sizes and colors, some rather startling. I have seen bright blue, pink, green and yellow *krupuk* gracing many a table. Krupuk need to be fried quickly—passed through hot oil, you might say—before they are served. To ensure crispness, the wafers must be bone dry before they hit the oil. Indonesian housewives routinely put *krupuk* in the sun for a brief period first. You could place them in a warm oven for 10 minutes. Once they are in the hot oil, they expand quite a bit and assume a lighter, airier texture. Ideally they should be cooked shortly before they are eaten. If you cannot manage that, store them in an airtight container after they have cooked. Uncooked *krupuk* should also be stored in very tightly lidded jars.

Here is the general method for preparing these wafers. Put enough oil in a wok to have at least 1½ inches in the center. When it is very hot—about 365°F—drop in 2 or 3 small *krupuk* (fewer if they are large). They will sink, rise almost immediately and greatly expand in size. Spoon oil over them during the few seconds that they take to cook. Do not let them brown. Adjust the heat if necessary. Remove the wafers with a slotted spoon and transfer them to a plate lined with paper toweling. Cook as many *krupuk* as you need in this way.

CHICKEN STOCK

Good chicken stock is needed for many recipes in this book, so it is useful to keep a supply handy in your refrigerator or freezer. Here are a few tips:

1. Whenever you poach a chicken breast, strain the liquid and save it. Use it when small amounts are called for.

2. Save all chicken bones and carcasses and store in the freezer; they can be added to the pot when making stock.

3. When cooking stock, maintain it at a low simmer or it will turn cloudy. It should bubble only very slightly. Skim the stock frequently as it cooks, especially in the first 30 minutes.

4. Sometimes just a little salt can be added to the stock at the end of the cooking time to bring out its flavor. You should leave the salt out when making stock for use in Japanese cooking.

5. Before freezing stock you can boil it down to half its original quantity so that it occupies less space. It can easily be reconstituted later.

6. Pour cooled, degreased stock into ice-cube trays and freeze. When frozen, the cubes can be transferred to freezer bags. You will then be able to use small quantities of stock as you need them and will be spared the mess of defrosting large amounts unnecessarily.

7. Frozen stock can be defrosted very quickly in a microwave oven.

Makes about 3 quarts

---

3 lb chicken necks, wings, backs and bones
2 lb chicken pieces (such as legs)
2 thin slices fresh ginger
2 scallions
Salt (optional)

Wash the chicken pieces and put them into a large pan. Add 3¾ quarts water and bring it to a simmer. Maintain the simmer and do not let the stock boil. Over the next 30 minutes, keep removing the scum that rises to the top. Now put in the ginger slices. Trim the scallions, discarding the green section, and add the white part to the stock. Cook partially covered, maintaining the heat at a bare simmer for 3–4 hours. Strain into a bowl through a triple layer of dampened muslin, cheesecloth or a large clean handkerchief and add a little salt if required. Stand the bowl in a large basin or sink of cold water to cool it off quickly. Pour the stock into containers, cover and refrigerate. Remove the fat when it has solidified. You can now freeze the stock.

JAPANESE SOUP STOCK

DASHI

Unlike much of the world, the Japanese make their basic stock out of fish and sea kelp. The most common fish used for stock is bonito, a member of the mackerel family. It is sold in Japan in a dried, filleted form that looks rather like a piece of smooth, hard, petrified wood, and in fact needs to be shaved with a plane. The delicate, curled shavings are at their best when they are freshly done and when they are a pale pinkish brown color. The finest of Japanese food establishments would consider using no other, just as the best French restaurant would always make its stock from scratch. The discriminating Japanese housewife does not shave her own bonito, but she can go into any good market and get it shaved for her on the spot. The average Japanese, on the other hand, either buys packaged bonito shavings, which come in plastic bags or in cornflakelike boxes, or uses instant soup stock *(dashi-no-moto)*, which is available in granular form.

The other ingredients used in good *dashi*—and for vegetarians it is often the only ingredient—is *konbu*, a special kelp sold in the form of large, dried leaves. Only sections of it are used at a time. The kelp needs to be of good quality. Its flavor is said to reside on its surface, so it is never washed, just wiped lightly with a damp cloth. This kelp should never be boiled vigorously; it is either soaked overnight or allowed to simmer very gently.

Whether you will be able to get shaved bonito *(hana-katsuo)* and the right kelp *(dashi-konbu)* is another matter. You should make an effort, as their flavors are the purest. If you cannot, use instant *dashi-no-moto*, though it is very often salted. As a last resort, you may use very light, unsalted chicken stock.

The correct way to make authentic *dashi* was demonstrated to me by Mr. Saito at the École Technique Hôtelière Tsuji, the largest school training professional chefs in Japan. First, a hunk of woodlike bonito was quickly rinsed and dried. Odd bits of dried skin and dried blood were scraped off. Just before the stock was made, the bonito was shaved with a plane that was affixed to a box. The shavings fell neatly and conveniently into a drawer! *Makes 1 quart*

1-oz piece kelp (konbu)
1 oz dried bonito shavings (hana-katsuo)

Wipe the kelp lightly with a damp cloth and put it into a medium-sized pan. Pour in 1 quart water and very slowly bring it to a simmer over a medium-low heat. If you are using the stock to make clear soup, remove the kelp just before the water comes to a boil. If you are using the stock for anything else—such as Fermented Bean Paste Soup with Bean Curd (page 85), noodles, sauces or for cooking vegetables—let the kelp simmer gently for 10 minutes without ever let-ting the water come to the boil. Re-move the kelp and then add the bonito shavings. Immediately take the pan off the heat. Do not stir. Within the next minute or so, the shavings will sink to the bottom. Strain the soup through a piece of dampened cloth.

While stock for clear soups is best when freshly made, all other Japanese Soup Stock may be made ahead of time and refrigerated. It should keep thus for 3 days and may be reheated by being brought to a bare simmer. Japanese Soup Stock is generally sea-soned with a little salt and/or soy sauce when it is used for clear soups.

BEEF STOCK

NƯỚC PHỞ

Good beef stock requires both beef bones and meat. While bones provide the body, the depth of flavor can come only from meat. Ideally you should use equal quantities of bones and meat, though you can save a little money by using more bones. I like to save odd bones from roasts, freezing them until I decide to make stock.

If you are starting from scratch, ask the butcher for soup bones (marrow bones are best) and have him saw them into smaller pieces. As far as the meat is concerned, you may use brisket, removing it when it is tender; it takes about 2½ hours to cook. You can also use stewing beef and just leave it to cook for the entire period. Some people like to use shanks, cut up of course, as they provide both meat and bones. You may take the meat off the bone after 2½ hours and let just the bones cook on.

Although it is usually best to salt stock when the cooking is completed, in this recipe I add a small quantity of salt earlier just to give the meat a little flavor. The brisket may be cut into thin slices for use in salads and soups, such as Rice Noodles in Soup with Beef (page 226) and Bean Sprout and Radish Soup (page 84).

This stock recipe is from Vietnam, but if you make it with salt to taste instead of the fish sauce and leave out the star anise and cinnamon, it may be used for all recipes in this book that require beef stock.

Makes about 2½ quarts

1 large onion

3-inch piece fresh ginger

4 lb beef marrow bones, sawed into smaller pieces

3 lb beef brisket or stewing beef

2-inch cinnamon stick

2 whole star anise

1 teaspoon salt

2 tablespoons fish sauce or extra salt to taste

Preheat the oven to 450°F.

Peel the onion. It is not necessary to peel the ginger. Put the onions and ginger in the oven and let them roast for 30 minutes. They should brown a little. Remove them and set aside.

Put the marrow bones and brisket into a very large pan. Add 5½ quarts water and slowly bring it to a simmer. Over the next 15 minutes, keep removing the scum that rises to the top. Then put in the onion, ginger, cinnamon stick, star anise and salt. Cover partially and cook very gently for about 2½ hours or until the brisket is tender. Remove the brisket and set it aside. Once it has cooled, it can be wrapped and stored in the refrigerator for use in other dishes. Continue to cook the stock gently, with the pan still partially covered, for another 2–2½ hours. Add the fish sauce a little at a time, tasting the stock until it is of the desired saltiness. It should be slightly undersalted.

Strain the stock into a large bowl through a double thickness of dampened muslin, cheesecloth or a large clean handkerchief. Cool it quickly by standing the bowl in a large basin or sink of cold water. Pour the stock into containers, cover and refrigerate. When the stock is cold, remove the fat—if you are in a hurry, you will have to do this with a spoon before the fat has solidified. The stock may now be frozen—see Chicken Stock, points 5–7 (page 77), for instructions.

HOT AND SOUR SHRIMP SOUP

Thailand

*From Pieng
Chom Darbanand
at the Imperial
Hotel, Bangkok*

TOM YAM KUNG

I would definitely classify this as one of the world's greatest soups. I have enjoyed it for some twenty years and have never had quite the same version twice. Traditionally the stock is made only with shrimps. Whole shrimps that still have their flavorful heads attached to their bodies are boiled in water seasoned with aromatic lemongrass and lime leaves. They are then removed, peeled, and their heads and shells thrown back into the stock pot for added flavor. Since most of us cannot find fresh shrimps with heads, it is best to use a rich chicken stock instead and add the shrimp shells to intensify its taste.

This soup can be made as fiery hot as you can handle. The amount of both the chili paste and the hot green chilies can easily be increased. My recipe is for a soup of medium heat, though the fresh green chilies, when bitten into, do carry their own explosive power with them. If you cannot find the Thai chili paste known as *nam prik pow*, use ¼ teaspoon ground red (cayenne) pepper combined with ¼ teaspoon sugar and ½ teaspoon vegetable oil.

Although Thai hotels and plush Westernized restaurants tend to serve this soup as a first course, in homes it is usually one of several main dishes served with plain rice.   *Serves 6 as a soup or 4 as a main course*

continued

1 lb medium shrimps

2 sticks fresh or 2 tablespoons dried sliced lemongrass

4 fresh or dried kaffir lime leaves or 1 tablespoon finely grated lemon rind

1½ quarts Chicken Stock, homemade (see page 77) or canned

1 tablespoon fish sauce or salt to taste

3 tablespoons fresh lime juice or to taste

1 teaspoon chili paste (nam prik pow; see page 278)

15 oz can straw mushrooms or 12 medium fresh mushrooms

3 fresh hot green chilies

3 tablespoons fresh coriander leaves

Wash the shrimps well. Peel and devein them, saving the shells. Wash the shrimps again, drain and pat them dry. Cover and refrigerate.

If you are using fresh lemongrass, cut each stick into 3 × 2-inch pieces, starting from the rounded bottom end. Discard the strawlike top. Lightly crush the 6 pieces with a heavy pestle, a hammer or the blade of a knife.

Combine the lemongrass (fresh or dried), the kaffir lime leaves (or lemon rind), the stock and shrimp shells in a pan. Bring to a boil. Lower the heat and simmer very gently for 20 minutes. Strain this stock and to it add the fish sauce, the lime juice and the chili paste. Mix and taste again, adding more fish sauce or lime juice if you need it. Drain the straw mushrooms and add them to the seasoned stock. (If you are using fresh mushrooms, quarter them and drop them in lightly salted boiling water. Boil for 1 minute. Drain and add to the seasoned stock.)

This much of the soup may be prepared several hours ahead of time and stored in the refrigerator if necessary.

Prepare the garnishes shortly before you are ready to serve the soup. Cut the green chilies into very fine rounds and wash and dry the fresh coriander leaves. Just before serving, heat the stock with the mushrooms in it. When it begins to bubble, drop in the peeled shrimps. Cook on a medium heat for about 2 minutes or just until the shrimps turn opaque. Put the soup into a large serving bowl or into individual serving bowls. Garnish with the green chilies and whole fresh coriander leaves and serve hot.

MUNG BEAN SOUP

Philippines

*From Glenda
Barretto at the
Via Mare
Restaurant*

MONGO GUISADO

*H*ere is an easy-to-prepare, delicious and very nourishing soup. Generally it is quite thick and is eaten with rice, but many restaruants now serve it in a somewhat simplified version. Fish sauce, olive oil and lime wedges are usually passed around at the table for those who wish to add a little more seasoning. A common garnish for the soup is pork cracklings (fried pork skins). If you wish to use it, you will need 1 tablespoon crumbled cracklings per serving.   *Serves 4*

1⅔ cups mung beans

3¾ cups rich Chicken Stock (see page 77),
   pork stock or chicken-and-pork stock
   (canned chicken broth may be used)

1 large onion

1 large garlic clove

¼ lb medium shrimps

3 tablespoons olive oil

¾ teaspoon salt or to taste

Freshly ground black pepper

Fresh lime or lemon wedges, fish sauce
   (optional) and extra olive oil (optional)
   to serve on the side

Pick over the beans and wash them in several changes of water. Drain them and put them into a medium-sized pan. Cover with water by about 2 inches and bring to a boil. Lower the heat and simmer for 2 minutes. Turn off the heat and let the pan and its contents sit for 1 hour. Then drain the beans and put them back into the pan.

Add the stock and bring to the boil again. Cover loosely, turn the heat to low and simmer gently for about 1 hour or until the beans are tender. Mash them lightly in the pan.

Peel and thinly slice the onion. Peel the garlic and chop it finely. Peel and devein the shrimps, wash them and pat them dry. Cut the shrimps cross-wise into ½-inch segments.

Put the olive oil in a medium-sized frying pan and set it over a medium-high heat. When the oil is hot, put in the onions and garlic. Stir and fry them until they turn golden and are just beginning to brown. Put in the shrimp pieces and stir and fry for about a minute or until they turn opaque. Empty the contents of the frying pan, including the oil, into the pan containing the beans. Add the salt and black pepper. Stir to mix.

Reheat the soup and serve with lime wedges and, if you like, fish sauce and olive oil.

BEAN SPROUT AND RADISH SOUP

KONGNAMUL KUK

During my very first stay in Korea many years ago I frequently had this soup for breakfast, along with rice, pickles and barley tea. The thin slices of beef in the soup are cut from the brisket used in Beef Stock (page 80). If you are making Beef Stock especially for this soup, leave out the fish sauce, cinnamon and star anise. If you have made a stock using bones but no brisket, you can prepare this soup without including any meat.

Korean white radish is very thick, very long and sweet. The one I used here was 1½ inches in diameter. If the only white radish you can find is very sharp, use the sweeter and more commonly available red radishes instead, cutting them in half lengthwise. They will lose a little of their red color in the soup, but that does not matter. You may also substitute young, sweet turnips.   *Serves 4*

7 oz long white Oriental radish
1½ oz sliced boiled brisket from Beef Stock
5 cups Beef Stock, homemade or canned
¾ lb fresh bean sprouts
3 scallions
Salt

Peel the radish and cut it crosswise into 2-inch sections. Cut each section lengthwise into ¼-inch slabs. If you are using brisket, cut the meat against the grain into very thin slices. Each slice should be about 1½ inches long.

Combine the radish, brisket and stock in a pan and bring to the boil. Cover, lower the heat and simmer gently for 15 minutes. The radish should by now be almost translucent.

Meanwhile, wash the bean sprouts and drain them. Pull off their thread-like ends if you feel up to it (see page 277). Cut the scallions into 2-inch lengths. Cut the white part lengthwise into halves or quarters, depending on thickness. When the soup has cooked for 15 minutes, put in the bean sprouts and scallions. Add salt to taste and simmer for 5 minutes more. Serve hot.

FERMENTED BEAN PASTE SOUP WITH BEAN CURD

MISO SHIRU

My favorite Japanese breakfast consists of nothing more than a tart pre-served plum, so tart that it puckers the mouth and jolts me awake (as well as filling me with vitamin C), a hot bowl of this *miso* soup, rice, pickles and tea. Millions of Japanese drink *miso* soup in the morning; those, of course, who have not suc-cumbed to the more modern, fashionable notion of toast and coffee. *Miso* soup may also be served at the beginning or end of a meal.

Miso is a paste made from fermented soybeans, though it can contain mixtures of other fermented grains as well. It is easy to digest, full of protein and, for vegetarians, a major source of nutrients.

There are many different types of *miso* available in Japan. Whole sections of shops contain row upon row of wooden tubs, each heaped with *miso* of a different color (ranging from white to almost black), a different texture (from coarse grains to a smooth paste) and a different degree of saltiness (from very salty to somewhat sweet—these days there are also low-salt *misos*). Most of these may be used to make soup.

For us in the West, the choice is much more limited. Most of us have access to health food shops, which tend to stock three or four varieties. There are nearly always yellowish, brown and reddish brown *misos*. Start with *aka miso*, the reddish brown one. You may later even decide to mix several *misos* together, once you get to learn the characteristics of each one.   *Serves 4*

1 scallion

¼ lb bean curd

1 quart Japanese Soup Stock (see page 78) or light unsalted Chicken Stock, homemade (see page 77) or canned

4 tablespoons aka miso (*the reddish brown one*)

Cut the entire scallion (including the green section) into very thin rounds. Cut the bean curd into ½-inch cubes. Heat the stock in a medium-sized pan until it is hot, but not boiling. Take it off the heat. Lower a small sieve into it so that only its lower half is sub-merged in the liquid. Put the *miso* into the sieve and push as much of it through as possible. Discard any lumps which may be left in the sieve. Put the soup back on a medium heat and add the bean curd and scallion. Bring the soup to a simmer. When the first bubbles appear, remove it from the heat and serve.

GLORIOUS SEAFOOD SOUP

AMA TITO REY SOUP

Seafood is plentiful in the Philippines and at Tito Rey's Restaurant it is cooked to perfection. This soup combines Spanish techniques with Filipino ingredients in the most delectable way. Needless to say, it should be made only if fresh mussels and clams are available. If you can find only one of these mollusks, use it to replace the other. You can improvise freely here and add seafood that you happen to like. I often put in squid, cut into rings, and cubes of filleted white fish, such as sole. When selecting shellfish, avoid mussels or clams that have broken shells.

Serves 4

8 mussels

4 clams

¼ lb medium shrimps

½-inch cube fresh ginger

½ medium onion

5 cups Chicken Stock, homemade (see page 77) or canned

1 teaspoon whole black peppercorns

Salt

3 tablespoons unsalted butter

3 tablespoons unbleached, all-purpose flour

⅛ lb cooked or uncooked white crab meat

5 tablespoons thick coconut milk (see page 282)

A little fresh parsley

Bottom: *Glorious Seafood Soup (this page);* top: *Small Spring Rolls (page 72);* center left: *Fish Sauce Seasoned with Lime Juice (page 239)*

Scrub the mussels and clams well with a stiff brush under cold running water. Pull the ''beards'' from the mussels. Peel and devein the shrimps, wash them and pat them dry. Cut each shrimp crosswise into 3 segments. Cut the ginger crosswise into 4–5 slices. Peel the onion.

Combine the stock, ginger, whole onion and peppercorns in a pan and bring to a simmer. Cover and simmer for 15 minutes. Strain the stock and put it back into the pan. Add salt to taste —it should be slightly undersalted as shellfish are briny—and keep it hot.

Melt the butter in a wide heavy pan over a medium-low heat. When it is melted and bubbly, put in the flour and turn the heat to low. Stir and cook for 2 minutes, letting the mixture bubble and froth but not brown. Slowly pour in the hot stock, stirring rapidly with a whisk as you go. Bring the stock to a gentle simmer for 3–4 minutes. If you see even a few lumps in the soup, strain it at this stage.

Put the mussels and clams into the soup and bring to a boil. Cover, turn the heat to medium and cook for 5 minutes. Remove the lid. The mussels and clams should have opened up. (If some have not, cook for another minute, then discard any that still have not opened.) Put in the shrimps, crab meat and coconut milk. Cook for another minute over a low heat.

Mince the parsley. Pour the soup into wide soup plates, dividing the shells evenly between them. Garnish with the parsley and serve.

SPICY CHICKEN SOUP WITH MANY FLAVORS

SOTO AYAM

*T*here are probably as many recipes for *soto ayam* as there are families in Indonesia. This soup can be a light and delicate teaser or it can, with the addition of fried potato balls, noodles and hard-boiled eggs, transform itself into a whole meal. I have decided to place my *soto ayam* smack in the middle of its range of possibilities. It is light enough to qualify as a first course and yet it has enough of the titillating additions—bean sprouts, bits of chicken, crisply fried shallot flakes, scallions and red chili sauce—to give it its complex Indonesian flavor.

When this soup is made in Indonesia, a whole chicken is first boiled with a few spices. The liquid becomes the stock and the chicken meat is then pulled off the bone, shredded and put back into the stock. I do not do this for two reasons. I like to cook my stock long and slowly, using necks, backs, wings and odd bones and carcasses I have lying in wait in the freezer. Also, for my taste, good quality chicken meat either gets too tough over such a long cooking period or it is overcooked. I prefer to make my stock separately and then, since we can buy chicken pieces so easily in the West, lightly poach skinned and boned chicken breast to provide the meat content of the soup.

Making the liquid part of the soup, poaching the chicken meat and preparing the bean sprouts, the Red Pepper Sauce, shallots, potatoes and green seasonings can all be done ahead of time. Just before serving, the sprouts can be thrown into boiling water to heat them and the stock can be brought to a simmer.   *Serves 4*

FOR THE GARNISHES, FLAVORINGS AND SAUCE

5 medium shallots (or ½ large onion)
½ medium potato
Vegetable oil for shallow-frying
Salt
1 scallion
1 handful tender celery leaves
½ lime or lemon
½ medium red bell pepper, seeded
1 tablespoon distilled white vinegar
¼ teaspoon sugar
½ teaspoon ground red (cayenne) pepper

FOR THE FLAVORED STOCK

7 medium shallots (or 1 medium onion)
3 garlic cloves
6 candlenuts or 12 cashew nuts
Salt
*1½ quarts Chicken Stock, homemade
   (see page 77) or canned*

YOU ALSO NEED

¼ lb chicken breast, boned and skinned
Salt
¾ lb fresh bean sprouts

First prepare the garnishes, flavorings and sauce. Peel the shallots and cut them lengthwise into fine slivers. Peel the potato and cut it first into ⅛-inch-thick slices and then into ⅛-inch-wide julienne strips.

Place a bowl on the work surface near your stove and balance a sieve over it. Put about ¼ inch oil in a frying pan and set it on a medium heat. When the oil is hot, put in the shallots. Stir and fry until golden-brown and crisp. Empty the contents of the pan into the sieve. Drain the shallots well and then spread them out on a plate lined with paper towels. Put the oil back into the frying pan and heat it again over a medium heat. When it is hot, put in the potato sticks. Stir and dry until they are golden and crisp. Empty the contents of the frying pan again into the sieve set over the bowl. Drain the potatoes well and spread them out on another plate lined with paper toweling. Sprinkle the potatoes very lightly with salt. When the shallots and potatoes have cooled, they can be put into small airtight jars until needed. (Save the oil for the stock.)

Cut the scallion crosswise into very, very fine rounds along its entire length, including the green section. Soak the rounds in cold water (this makes them milder). Coarsely chop the celery leaves. Cover them with plastic wrap and set them aside. Cut the lime (or lemon) into 4 wedges. Cover and set aside.

Combine the red pepper, vinegar, ½ teaspoon salt, sugar and ground red pepper in an electric blender. Blend until smooth. Empty into a small attractive serving bowl. Cover and set aside.

Make the flavored stock. Peel the shallots and chop them coarsely. Peel the garlic and chop it coarsely. Coarsely chop the nuts. Blend the shallots, garlic, nuts and 4 tablespoons water in a blender until smooth.

Put 4 tablespoons of the reserved oil in a medium-sized pan (preferably nonstick) and set it on a medium-high heat. When the oil is hot, add the paste from the blender. Stir and fry for 4–5 minutes or until the paste is lightly browned. Add the stock and bring it to a boil. Turn the heat to low and simmer gently for 15 minutes. Add salt to taste, stir in well, then set aside.

Cut the chicken lengthwise into ¾-inch-wide strips. Put these into a pan and cover with about ½ inch water. Add ¼ teaspoon salt and bring slowly to a simmer. Simmer gently for 2–3 minutes or until the chicken turns white all the way through. Lift the chicken out of the liquid and let it cool slightly. Using both hands, pull the meat into long—not too thin—shreds. Cover with plastic wrap. (The poaching liquid can be strained and reserved for use in another dish.)

Trim away the long threadlike ends of the bean sprouts if you feel up to it and drop them into a pan of boiling water for 30 seconds. Drain and immediately rinse under cold water. Drain well, cover and set aside.

All the elements of the soup are now assembled. To serve, uncover the sauce and put it on the table. Drain the scallion and pat dry. Arrange the fried shallots, fried potatoes, scallion, celery leaves and lime wedges on a platter. Heat the flavored stock. Drop the bean sprouts into boiling water for 10 seconds to heat them through. Drain them and divide between 4 soup bowls or plates. Top with the chicken, which should also be divided up equally. Ladle the hot stock over the top and take the soup to the table. Diners should add to the soup: sauce, lime wedges, shallots, potatoes, scallion and celery, roughly in that order.

PORK AND CRAB SOUP

CANH THỊT NẤU CUA

Here is another pork and crab combination that the Vietnamese do so well. This time it is in a soup which is quite Chinese in its origins. In Vietnam the soup is served with a generous squeeze of fresh lime juice and some Red Pepper Sauce (see page 242) for those who want it.

If you cannot find black fungus, increase the number of dried Chinese mushrooms to 12, and if you cannot get those either, use 12 good-sized, fresh cultivated mushrooms in the place of both fungi, cutting them into thin slices and putting the slices into the soup at the same time as you would add the dried fungi. The fresh mushrooms will, of course, need no soaking.   *Serves 4–5*

8 dried Chinese mushrooms

*1 tablespoon small dried black fungus
(cloud-ears)*

*4–5 oz lean boneless loin of pork or pork
loin chops*

2 teaspoons plus 2 tablespoons cornstarch

2 teaspoons sesame oil

1 teaspoon fish sauce or ¼ teaspoon salt

1 egg

1 scallion

*5 cups Chicken Stock, homemade (see page
77) or canned*

Salt

*¼ lb cooked white crab meat, finely
shredded*

Lime wedges (optional)

*Red Pepper Sauce (optional) to serve on
the side*

Soak the dried mushrooms in about 1 cup hot water for 30 minutes or until they are soft. Soak the black fungus in 1 cup hot water for 30 minutes or until it is soft.

Cut the pork against the grain into ⅛-inch slices. Stacking a few slices at a time together, cut the meat, again against the grain, into long shreds about ⅛ inch wide. Put the pork in a bowl. Add the 2 teaspoons cornstarch, sesame oil and fish sauce. Mix. Cover and set aside for 20 minutes or longer, refrigerating if necessary.

Lift the mushrooms out of their soaking liquid. Strain the soaking liquid through a cloth and set it aside. Cut off the hard mushroom stems and discard them. Cut the caps into ⅛-inch strips. Lift the black fungus out of its soaking liquid and discard the liquid. Feel the fungus for hard "eyes." Cut off any you find and discard them. Chop the fungus coarsely.

Put the remaining 2 tablespoons cornstarch into a small cup. Add 3 tablespoons of the reserved mushroom-soaking liquid or water. Mix and set aside. Beat the egg lightly and set it aside. Cut the scallion crosswise into very fine rounds.

Put the stock and any remaining mushroom-soaking liquid into a pan. Add the two kinds of mushrooms and bring the stock to a simmer. Cover and simmer on a low heat for 5 minutes. Then put in the pork. Bring to a boil gently and simmer until the pork is just cooked through, stirring and breaking up any meat lumps as you do so. Taste the soup and add salt if it is needed. Put in the crab meat. Give the cornstarch mixture a stir and pour that in as well. Stir and cook on a lowish heat until the soup is thick and bubbling.

Take the soup off the heat. Immediately pour in the beaten egg in a slow steady stream using a fork to stir the top of the soup in a figure 8 pattern. This procedure makes perfect "egg drop" slivers. Put in the scallion and stir the soup for a few seconds more to allow the scallion to wilt. Serve with lime wedges and Red Pepper Sauce.

Hong Kong
From Willy Mark

SUMMER SOUP WITH PORK AND CUCUMBER

WEI LING QINGGUA ROU JIN JIANG

*F*resh ingredients and delicate flavors—that is what Cantonese food is all about, and nothing exemplifies it more than this soup. Even though the soup is ideal for summer, you may serve it successfully in winter as well. The cucumber in it, you might be interested to know, does not stay raw. It cooks, however briefly, to turn into a most interesting vegetable. As far as the pork is concerned, you could buy either ½ lb of pork tenderloin, or 2 pork loin chops weighing in total about 14 oz, and then just cut the meat off the bone.

You can prepare the stock, marinate and parboil the meat, and slice the cucumbers well ahead of time. The soup should be assembled and heated only at the last minute. *Serves 4–5*

continued

*½ lb pork tenderloin or 14 oz loin chops,
  boned*

½ teaspoon cornstarch

2 teaspoons sesame oil

⅔ egg white

Salt

1-inch cube fresh ginger

*1 oz. fresh coriander leaves (with stems
  and roots if possible)*

*5¾ cups Chicken Stock, homemade (see
  page 77) or canned*

*2 Kirby cucumbers or 1 small regular
  cucumber*

Remove any fat from the pork and then cut the lean pork into thin slices about 1½ × 1 × ¹⁄₁₆ inches. Put the meat in a bowl. Add the cornstarch, sesame oil, egg white and ¼ teaspoon salt. Mix well and set aside for 30 minutes or more, refrigerating if necessary.

Peel the ginger and cut it into thin slices. Wash the fresh coriander well and pat it dry. Remove the leaves (reserving the stems and roots), cover them with plastic wrap and set them aside. Combine the chicken stock, ginger slices and coriander stems and roots in a pan. Bring to a boil, turn the heat to low and simmer for 20 minutes. Strain and add salt to taste.

Pour about ¾ inch water into a medium-sized frying pan and bring it to a boil. Put in the pork and then turn the heat to low. Stir the pork about until it turns white all the way through. (It is not necessary for the water to come to the boil again.) Remove the pork with a slotted spoon and set it aside. Peel the cucumber and cut it into very thin rounds.

Just before eating, heat the seasoned stock until it is bubbling. Put in the pork and cucumber and let them just heat through. This should take 30–40 seconds. Remove the pan from the heat and put in the coriander leaves. Serve immediately.

Meat

NAPOLEON BEEF ON A SKEWER

THỊT BÒ LỤI

Many Vietnamese in Hanoi refer to this dish either as *boeuf brochette* or *boeuf Napoleon*. (I suppose it is the sort of thing an army on the move might cook!) Thin slices of meat are marinated in a mixture of fried spices, skewered and then grilled over charcoal or wood. The meat is then taken off the skewer and put on a plate. It is eaten, as many other Vietnamese dishes are, in little packages. You take a soft lettuce leaf and put a few pieces of meat on it. On top of the meat you put a few fresh mint leaves, a few small sprigs of fresh coriander, a few fresh bean sprouts, some sliced scallion, some cucumber slices, some Crisply Fried Shallot Flakes (page 250) and some crushed Roasted Peanuts (page 247). Next you wrap the lettuce leaf round all this to form a bundle, dip the bundle into Fish Sauce Seasoned with Lime Juice (page 239)—and eat it.

If you do not feel like making packages, there is another way of serving the meat, a method that I use quite frequently. I put only ½ teaspoon of salt in the marinade. When the meat is cooked, I take it off the skewers and put it on a plate. I dribble Fish Sauce Seasoned with Lime Juice over it generously, then scatter crushed Roasted Peanuts and some Crisply Fried Shallot Flakes on the top. With this I serve a side salad of lettuce, cucumbers, ripe tomatoes, fresh mint and fresh coriander leaves.

All the cooking in north Vietnam seems to be done in lard. I have used vegetable oil here, but you may use lard if you wish.   *Serves 4*

1 stick fresh or 2 tablespoons dried sliced
   lemongrass
1 large onion
½ large red bell pepper
1 teaspoon salt
Freshly ground black pepper
¼ teaspoon ground red (cayenne) pepper
   or to taste
4 tablespoons vegetable oil
1 lb lean steak or flank steak, about 1 inch
   thick

If you are using fresh lemongrass, slice it crosswise as thinly as possible, starting at the bulbous end and going up about 6 inches. Discard the strawlike top. If you are using dried sliced lemongrass, soak it in 4 tablespoons hot water for 1 hour.

Peel the onion and chop it coarsely. Remove the seeds from the red pepper and chop it coarsely. Combine the lemongrass, its soaking liquid (if you are using the dried variety), the onion, red pepper, salt, black pepper and ground red pepper in an electric blender. Blend to a smooth paste, adding a few tablespoons of water if necessary.

Put the oil in a medium-sized, preferably nonstick, frying pan and set it over a medium-high heat. When the oil is hot, add the paste from the blender. Stir and fry for 6–8 minutes or until the paste has darkened in color. (You may need to turn the heat down toward the end of this cooking time.) Leave the paste to cool.

Assuming that you are right-handed, hold a large knife at a 135-degree angle to your work surface (45-degree for left-handers) and cut the slab of meat against the grain into very thin slices (in other words, you are cutting at a slight diagonal just as you would for London broil). Cut these slices into 1-inch pieces and put the pieces into a bowl. Add the paste and oil from the frying pan and mix well. Cover and set aside, refrigerating if necessary, for 1–24 hours. (You may put the meat on its skewers before you set it aside, if that is more convenient.)

Preheat an oven broiler or an outdoor charcoal grill.

Thread the meat fairly tightly onto 2–4 skewers—the number of skewers required will depend upon their length. Grill or broil the meat about 5 inches from the source of heat for about 5 minutes on one side and for 3–4 minutes on the opposite side. Serve as suggested above.

Korea

From Mrs. Han Chung Kyu

MARINATED AND BROILED BEEF STRIPS

BULGOGI

Koreans have a great fondness for beef, especially *bulgogi*. Now, with prosperity high and the price of beef reasonable, many a housewife lovingly cooks it for her husband's dinner. If it is not available at home, there are restaurants aplenty, scattered across the length and breadth of the land, that specialize in it and, like magnets, draw thousands of eager customers to their smoke-filled rooms.

Bulgogi is a broiled or grilled meat. This grilling is done over charcoal or gas and may take place at the table or outdoors. The grill itself is usually portable and varies from a ridged, heavy, metal plate that is raised in the center to a more conventional cross-hatched surface. Since I do not have a Korean *bulgogi* grill, I use a large, well-heated, cast-iron frying pan. I happen to have a trusted 14-inch pan that is perfect for the job but a smaller cast-iron frying pan will do. You could also cook the meat, spread out, under a very hot broiler.

In Korea thin slices of meat, marinated in a mixture of soy sauce, sugar, scallions, ginger and garlic, are flung over the fire. Diners cook the meat themselves, turning it over with their chopsticks until it is cooked as they like it. Other ingredients can be added to the marinade as well, such as roasted sesame seeds and—very uncommon for us in the West—pear. This pear is the hard, round and very crisp "pear-apple" that is found in Korea and China. It has a mellowing, softening effect on a mixture of somewhat sharper flavors. I use any hard pear that is available and find that it works well as a substitute.

This beef is generally eaten with rice, Cabbage Pickle (page 248) and vegetables such as Seasoned Spinach (page 204) or Stir-Fried Zucchini with Sesame Seeds (page 206). Sometimes leaves of soft lettuce are served on the side for diners to make small packages of the meat, rice and vegetables. A package is usually dipped in soy sauce before it is eaten.   *Serves 4*

1¼ lb lean tender beef steak

½ medium hard pear

4–5 garlic cloves

2-inch cube fresh ginger

4 tablespoons Japanese soy sauce (shoyu)

5 medium mushrooms

2 small onions

3 scallions

1 medium carrot

2 tablespoons sesame oil

1 tablespoon roasted sesame seeds
  (see page 299)

2½ tablespoons sugar

Cut the meat against the grain into 3 × 2-inch rectangles that are about ⅛ inch thick.

Peel and core the pear half and then chop it coarsely. Peel the garlic and ginger and chop them coarsely. Put the pear, garlic, ginger and soy sauce into an electric blender and blend until smooth.

Cut the mushrooms into ⅛-inch slices. Peel and thickly slice the onions. Cut the scallions into 2½-inch lengths. Peel the carrot and cut it into 2½-inch chunks. Then cut each chunk lengthwise into ⅛-inch slices.

Put the meat in a bowl. Add the paste from the blender, the mushrooms, onions, scallions, carrot, sesame oil, sesame seeds and sugar. Mix well. Cover and marinate for 1–24 hours.

Set a large cast-iron frying pan on a high heat. Let it get almost white-hot. Put in as many of the meat slices as will fit in one layer. Cook, turning the meat pieces over as soon as they brown a little. You may leave the meat rare if you like. Remove the meat as soon as it is ready. Cook all the meat in this way. Then put in the vegetables and the marinade. Cook on a high heat for a minute or so. Then spoon the mixture over or beside the meat. Serve immediately.

SPICY BEEF SALAD

LAAB

As steak tartare, that piquant mixture of raw ground beef and seasonings, is named after the nomadic Asians who thought it up, it should come as no surprise that the Far East has a host of fairly similar dishes. Take *laab,* an exquisite Thai salad. It comes from the northeast part of the country, an area that borders Laos. The ground beef in this case is sometimes left raw or it may be quickly stirred in a very hot wok so that it qualifies as rare. It is then magically seasoned with sliced shallots, lime juice and mint. There is a secret ingredient that binds the salad and gives it a nutty aroma. It is rice—rice that has been roasted and ground!

A plate of *laab* usually has the seasoned meat on one side and a whole forest of fresh herbs and raw vegetables on the other. The two are then eaten together, the spicy meat nicely balanced by the crisp vegetables. Incidentally, you may also make this salad with leftover roast beef. Cut it into very thin slices and then cut the slices into 1 × 2-inch strips. You do not, of course, need to cook them.

Serves 4

FOR THE VEGETABLES ON THE SIDE

About 12 crisp inner leaves of iceberg, or other lettuce

4–8 sprigs fresh mint

½ lb fresh bean sprouts

12 tender green beans or about 8 long beans

7 fresh hot red chilies or 1 red bell pepper

FOR THE SPICED BEEF

3 tablespoons long-grain rice

6 medium shallots or 1 small onion (preferably red)

2 garlic cloves

2 tablespoons vegetable oil

1 lb tender beef (such as a good-quality steak), ground

4 tablespoons lime or lemon juice

4 tablespoons fish sauce or salt to taste

1 tablespoon sugar

A generous handful fresh mint leaves

1 fresh hot red or green chili

¼ teaspoon ground red (cayenne) pepper

First prepare the vegetables. Wash the lettuce and pat it dry. Put it in a plastic bag and refrigerate. Remove the large coarse stems from the mint, if any; otherwise leave it in sprigs. Wash these and pat them dry. Put them in a plastic bag and refrigerate. Top and tail the bean sprouts (see page 277) if you are up to it. Wash them and leave them floating in a bowl of cold water. You may refrigerate them. Drain them well before using them. Wash and trim the beans. Long beans should be cut into thirds. Cover and refrigerate. The red chilies may be cut into flowers (see page 279) or into long strips. If you are using a red pepper, seed it and cut it into strips. Cover and refrigerate.

Set a small cast-iron frying pan over a medium-high heat. When it is hot, put in the rice and stir it for 2–3 minutes or until the grains turn golden. Some might even pop. Remove the rice from the pan, cool it slightly and then put it into a clean coffee grinder, food processor or mortar and pulverize it.

Peel the shallots and cut them into very fine, long slivers. (If you are using onions, peel, cut in half lengthwise and then crosswise into fine half-rings.) Peel and mince the garlic.

Just before eating, put a wok on a high heat. When it is hot, swirl in the oil. Let the oil heat. When it is very hot, put in the ground meat and stir-fry for 15–30 seconds. The meat should remain rare. Lift the beef out with a slotted spoon and put it into a bowl. Add the rice, shallots, garlic, lime juice, fish sauce and sugar to the meat. Chop the mint leaves coarsely and finely slice the red or green chili. Add them and the ground red pepper to the mixture. Mix well and check the seasoning.

Put the beef on one side of a large serving plate. Arrange the prepared vegetables prettily on the other side of the plate.

Vietnam

EASY BEEF KEBABS

BŌ NỬỚNG CHA^z

All types of grilled kebabs enjoy great popularity in Vietnam. Here is a very simple version. You could serve this dish with a green salad of lettuce, cucumber, fresh coriander and mint leaves. Fresh rice noodles are generally served on the side in Vietnam. You could serve dried rice noodles or rice itself. *Serves 4*

1 lb flank steak

4 garlic cloves

1 small onion

2 tablespoons fish sauce or a little salt to taste

1½ teaspoons Chinese light soy sauce

4 tablespoons crushed Roasted Peanuts (see page 247)

Fish Sauce with Vinegar and Lime Juice (see page 238)

Assuming that you are right-handed, hold a large knife at a 135-degree angle to your work surface (45-degree for the left-handers) and cut the slab of meat against the grain into very thin slices (in other words, you are cutting at a slight diagonal as you would London broil). Cut these slices into 1-inch-long pieces and put them in a bowl. Peel the garlic and onion and chop them very finely. Add these to the meat to-gether with the fish sauce and soy sauce. (If you are substituting salt for the fish sauce, be sure to add only a little as the dish is served with a well-seasoned sauce.) Mix well and set aside for 1–2 hours.

Preheat an oven broiler or an out-door charcoal grill. Thread the meat fairly tightly onto 2–4 skewers de-pending on their length. Broil or grill about 5 inches from the source of heat for about 5 minutes on one side and 3–4 minutes on the other side.

The meat may be served on or off the skewers, sprinkled with some crushed Roasted Peanuts. Fish Sauce with Vinegar and Lime Juice is poured over the top by each diner.

Hong Kong
From the American Restaurant in Wanchai

SZECHUAN-STYLE FRIED SHREDDED BEEF WITH CARROTS AND CHILIES

GONGBAO NIULIU

*I*n this spicy, slightly sweet, slightly sour dish, beef and carrot shreds are fried until they turn a bit crisp. They are then stir-fried with hot chilies and scallions and doused with a light mixture of vinegar, soy sauce and sugar. The result is quite spectacular. *Serves 3–4*

FOR THE BEEF MARINADE

¾ lb lean beef steak or flank steak
2½ teaspoons Chinese light soy sauce
1 small egg white
1 teaspoon cornstarch
1½ teaspoons sesame oil

YOU ALSO NEED

4 medium carrots
2 garlic cloves

3–4 fresh hot red or green chilies
4 scallions
2½ teaspoons Chinese rice wine or dry sherry
1½ teaspoons distilled white vinegar
2½ teaspoons sugar
1 teaspoon Chinese light soy sauce
2 teaspoons Chinese dark soy sauce
Vegetable oil for deep-frying
1 teaspoon cornstarch

Cut the beef against the grain into very thin slices about 1/16 inch in width. Then stack a few slices at a time together and cut the meat into thin strips about 2½–3 inches long. Put the meat in a bowl. Add all the other marinade ingredients and mix well, ensuring that you break up the egg white. Cover and refrigerate if necessary.

Peel the carrots and cut them into julienne strips, the same size as the beef. Peel the garlic and chop it finely. Cut the chilies lengthwise into fine strips. Cut the scallions crosswise into 3-inch lengths and then cut them lengthwise with the tip of a sharp knife into long fine strips.

Combine the rice wine, vinegar, sugar, light soy sauce and dark soy sauce in a cup. Mix and set aside.

Put about 1½ inches oil in a wok or large frying pan and set it over a medium heat. When it is hot, put in the carrots. Stir and fry for about 5 minutes or until the carrots are slightly crisp. Remove them with a slotted spoon. Now put all the beef in and turn off the heat. Stir the beef around until all the strands have separated and just turned white. You may have to turn the heat back on low to achieve this. Remove the meat with a slotted spoon and put it into a bowl. Sprinkle the meat with 1 teaspoon cornstarch and toss well. Turn the heat under the oil to high. When it is hot, drop the meat in again for 30 seconds and then empty the contents of the wok into a strainer set over a bowl. Drain the meat well.

Put 2 tablespoons of the previously used oil into a clean wok or large frying pan and set it on a high heat. When it is hot, put in the garlic. Stir and fry for 30 seconds or until it is lightly browned. Put in the chilies. Stir once and then add the scallions. Stir rapidly once and add the meat and carrots. Stir for 30 seconds and add the rice wine sauce. Stir rapidly for about 30 seconds and serve.

MEATBALL SOUP

WANJA KUK

A soupy dish in Korea is not always a soup, as we understand it. This meatball soup, for example, is fairly substantial and is usually served as one of the main dishes at a meal that might also include grilled and stir-fried foods. The meatballs here are quite delicate and light. The reason is bean curd—lots of it— which is mashed and combined with ground beef. This results in soft meatballs, the softest you will probably ever encounter.

When I want a light meal, I serve this mild and gentle soup all by itself, with just a green salad on the side for added balance—and crunch.   *Serves 4–5*

5–6 oz bean curd

2 garlic cloves

4 scallions

½ lb ground lean beef

1 tablespoon Japanese soy sauce (shoyu)

2 teaspoons sesame oil

2 teaspoons roasted sesame seeds
  (see page 299)

5 cups chicken, beef or pork stock,
  homemade (see page 77 or 80) or canned

½-inch cube fresh ginger

Salt

½ cup unbleached, all-purpose flour

1 egg

Put the bean curd in the center of a clean cloth, such as a soft dish towel or handkerchief. Gather the ends together and squeeze as much moisture from it as you can. Then mash the bean curd with a fork or push it through a sieve.

Peel the garlic and chop it very finely. Cut 2 of the scallions crosswise into very fine rounds.

In a bowl combine the bean curd, garlic, sliced scallions, ground beef, soy sauce, sesame oil and sesame seeds. Mix well and then make about 20 meatballs. You might find it helpful to wet your hands as you form the meatballs.

Put the stock in a large pan. Cut the remaining scallions into 2-inch lengths. Peel the ginger and cut it into thin slices. Put the scallions and ginger into the stock and bring it to a boil. Lower the heat and simmer gently for 8–10 minutes. Salt the stock to your taste and leave it simmering very gently.

Put the flour on a plate. Break the egg into a saucer and beat it lightly. Roll each meatball first in the flour and then in the egg, and finally drop it into the simmering soup. After the meatballs are in, continue to simmer for another 5 minutes. You may remove the ginger slices before serving.

BEEF CHUNKS COOKED IN COCONUT MILK

Indonesia

From Martini Jufri and the Household of Risnawati Agus

KALIYO *OR* RENDANG DAGING

Perhaps the most loved dish in Muslim West Sumatra, indeed in all of Indonesia, is beef *rendang,* in which large chunks of beef (sometimes water buffalo) are cooked and cooked in a mixture of coconut milk and spices until all the liquid disappears and the meat takes on a very inviting, dark, dry look. Prepared in this way, the beef lasts for days without refrigeration if kept in airtight jars, and it is the preferred food taken by Sumatran travelers on long journeys. No wedding or festive occasion is ever without a *rendang.* Indeed, every time I was fêted it appeared on the menu, much to my delight. Once it was even cooked over wood, which gave it a deliciously complex flavor.

Almost a sister to *rendang* is *kaliyo.* It is exactly the same dish, only in a slightly earlier stage of preparation when the meat still has a nicely thickened sauce clinging to it. I love *rendang,* but I have a passion for *kaliyo.* Its sauce goes so well with the accompanying rice. It also takes less time to cook! This recipe is for both *kaliyo* and *rendang.*   *Serves 4*

3-inch cube fresh or 10–12 slices dried
    galangal

2 sticks fresh or 2 tablespoons dried sliced
    lemongrass

4–6 whole dried hot red chilies

2-inch cinnamon stick

12–14 cloves

1 medium red bell pepper

7–8 medium shallots (or 1 large onion)

1-inch cube fresh ginger

7–8 garlic cloves

12 fresh or dried curry leaves or 4 dried
    bay leaves

8 fresh or dried kaffir lime leaves or
    3 × ¼-inch strip lemon rind

1¾ quarts coconut milk (see page 282)

2 lb stew beef, cut into 1½–2 inch cubes

1¼ teaspoons salt

If you are using fresh galangal, peel and coarsely chop it and set it aside. If you are using dried galangal, combine it in a cup with 4 tablespoons water. If you are using fresh lemongrass, cut off the strawlike top, leaving about 6 inches of the bottom. Lightly crush the very bottom with a hammer or other heavy object and set it aside. If you are using dried lemongrass, put it into the water with the galangal.

Crumble or break the dried red chilies and cinnamon into enough water to cover or add them to the dried galangal and dried lemongrass if you are using them. Also put in the cloves. Soak the spices for 30 minutes. Cut the red bell pepper coarsely into dice, discarding all the seeds. Peel and coarsely chop the shallots, ginger and garlic.

continued

In an electric blender, combine the soaked spices and their liquid, the fresh galangal (if you are using it), the chopped red pepper, shallots, ginger and garlic. Blend until smooth.

Into a wide, preferably nonstick pan put the paste from the blender, the fresh lemongrass (if you are using it), the curry leaves and kaffir lime leaves (or lemon rind). Stir the coconut milk well until smooth and pour that in as well. Bring to a boil, stirring occasionally. Turn the heat to medium and cook the sauce for 15 minutes, stirring now and then to prevent curdling. Put in the meat and salt and bring to a boil again. Reduce the heat to medium. Cook, uncovered, for 1 hour, stirring from time to time. Turn the heat up to medium-high and continue to cook, stirring now and then, for 30 minutes or until the sauce is very thick and brown and the meat tender. (If the sauce begins to splatter too much at any stage, cover the pot very loosely for that period.) This is *kaliyo*. To make *rendang*, continue to stir and cook until all the sauce has disappeared.

Vietnam

From Biche Lombatière

AROMATIC AND SPICY BEEF STEW

THỊT BÕ KHO

Although the West may not associate hearty stews with East Asia, they are, of course, cooked and eaten there. This stew is, perhaps, Vietnam's *boeuf bourguignon*. Some of the seasonings, such as cinnamon (technically cassia bark, a member of the cinnamon family that is used in China and Vietnam) and black pepper, will be quite familiar. Others, such as lemongrass, star anise and yellow bean sauce, may not be, but it is these that give this stew its Eastern aroma and taste. The yellow bean sauce used here is the one with whole or halved beans in it, usually sold as whole or crushed yellow bean sauce.

In Vietnam, this stew is eaten either with rice or with hunks of crusty French bread that is sold in all markets.   *Serves 6*

2 medium onions

5 garlic cloves

10–12 medium shallots or pickling onions

1 stick fresh lemongrass or 3 × 1-inch strip lemon rind

7 tablespoons vegetable oil

3 lb stew beef, cut into 1-inch cubes

6 tablespoons yellow bean sauce

½–1 teaspoon ground red (cayenne) pepper

4 whole star anise

1-inch cinnamon stick

½ teaspoon whole black peppercorns

2 tablespoons sugar

Peel and finely chop the onions and garlic. Peel the shallots and leave them whole. Cut the lemongrass into 2-inch sections, starting from the bottom and going up about 6 inches. Discard the strawlike top. Crush each section lightly with a hammer or other heavy object. (If you are using lemon rind, leave it in one piece.)

Put 3 tablespoons of the oil in a non-stick frying pan and set it on medium-high heat. When it is hot, put in the onions, garlic and shallots. Stir and fry for 2 minutes. Add the lemongrass (but not the lemon rind if you are using it as a substitute). Continue to stir and fry until the onions have browned lightly. Turn off the heat. Pick the shallots out of the pan and set them aside.

Put the remaining 4 tablespoons oil in a large, wide, preferably nonstick pan and set it over a high heat. When it is hot, put in as many meat cubes as the pan will hold in a single layer and brown them, turning them over when necessary. Remove the cubes with a slotted spoon. Brown all the meat in this way.

Return all the browned meat to the large pan. Add 1 quart water as well as the onion-garlic-lemongrass mixture. Coarsely chop the beans in the yellow bean sauce (if they are not already crushed) and add them as well. Also put in the ground red pepper, star anise, cinnamon, peppercorns and sugar. Bring to a boil, then cover, lower the heat and simmer gently for 1¼ hours. Add the reserved shallots (and the lemon rind, if you are using it). Cover again and simmer for another 15 minutes. Remove the lid, raise the heat to medium and cook for a further 15–20 minutes or until sauce has thickened a little and the meat is tender. Spoon the fat off the top before serving.

EASY BEEF CURRY

KAENG PHET NUA

I use skirt steak for this curry. It is such a tender cut of beef and requires hardly any cooking at all. I stand at the stove for about 12 minutes only, 8 of which are spent frying the spices, and the other 4 cooking the beef. This is a perfect dish to serve at a small dinner party. If you cannot get kaffir lime leaves, use a 3 × ½-inch strip of lemon rind that is cut into fine julienne strips. Put it into the curry at the same time as the mint and basil leaves.   *Serves 4*

1 lb skirt steak

1 large red bell pepper

1 large onion

4 large garlic cloves

1 teaspoon shrimp or anchovy paste

½ teaspoon ground red (cayenne) pepper

8 tablespoons vegetable oil

2 tablespoons fish sauce or 1 tablespoon soy sauce mixed with 1 tablespoon water and ¼ teaspoon sugar

1 cup coconut milk (see page 282)

½ teaspoon salt

4 fresh or dried kaffir lime leaves or lemon rind (see above)

10–15 fresh basil leaves

10–15 fresh mint leaves

Cut the beef against the grain into pieces 2–3 inches long, 1 inch wide and ¹⁄₁₆–⅛ inch thick. If you have bought the meat in a long, thin, continuous piece, cut it into 3-inch segments first and then cut each segment against the grain, holding the knife at a 135-degree (45-degree for left-handers) angle to your work surface.

This will give you the required width.

Core the red pepper, remove the seeds and chop it coarsely. Peel the onion and garlic and chop them coarsely. Combine the red bell pepper, onions, garlic, shrimp paste and ground red pepper in an electric blender. Blend until smooth, adding a tablespoon or so of water only if you need to.

Put the oil in a wide shallow saucepan or frying pan and set it over a medium-high heat. When it is hot, put in the spice paste from the blender. Stir and fry for 7–8 minutes or until the paste turns dark and separates from the oil. Add the meat and the fish sauce (or soy sauce mixed with water and sugar). Stir and cook for 2 minutes. Stir the coconut milk and add that, together with the salt and the dried kaffir lime leaves, if you are using them. If the kaffir lime leaves are fresh, tear them in half and remove the center vein before adding. Coarsely tear the basil and mint leaves, and add as well. Stir once, turn off the heat and serve.

BEEF CURRY WITH THICK ONION SAUCE

Malaysia

From Puan Rashidah in Kuala Lumpur

DAGING NASI KANDAR

*D*aging is beef, *nasi* is rice and as far as *kandar* is concerned—well, herein lies a tale. Early Indian settlers, as many others before them, often turned to hawking as a means of livelihood. The Indians suspended two baskets at each end of a pole and balanced this pole on their shoulders or *kandar*. Among the most popular items sold from these baskets was a particular combination of dishes, a whole meal in fact, that took on the name of *nasi kandar,* or "rice meal on a shoulder." There was rice, of course, and a fish curry; hard-boiled eggs, and this beef curry whose thick sauce could also be ladled over the eggs.

Today many hawkers have moved indoors and *nasi kandar* is rarely sold on the move, but there are several restaurants that serve it as their specialty. One, in Penang, is so famous that government ministers from Kuala Lumpur make a beeline for it when they visit there. Puan Rashidah, who gave me this recipe, makes her own, cooking it when catering for private parties besides selling it at a small stall. This curry, which probably started out being Indian, has by now picked up Malay and Chinese seasonings as well. It is a spectacular dish.   *Serves 4*

2 lb stew beef

6–16 whole dried hot red chilies (6 will make a mild dish, 16 a fairly hot one)

2 sticks fresh lemongrass or two 3 × ½-inch slices lemon rind

8 medium onions

¾ cup vegetable oil

5 tablespoons black bean sauce or 3 tablespoons salted dried black beans, washed and mashed with 2 tablespoons oyster sauce

2-inch cinnamon stick

20 fresh curry leaves (optional)

3 tablespoons tamarind paste (see page 303) or 2 tablespoons lime or lemon juice

1 tablespoon sugar

1 teaspoon salt

Cut the beef into 1½-inch cubes and set aside.

Crumble the chilies into a small bowl. Add 4 tablespoons hot water and set aside for 30 minutes or until the chilies soften. Put the chilies and their soaking liquid into an electric blender and blend until smooth.

Cut the lemongrass sticks into 6-inch lengths, starting from the bottom. Discard the strawlike top. Crush the bulbous bottoms of the lemongrass lightly. (If you are using lemon rind, leave it in one piece.)

Peel and finely slice the onions. Put the oil in a large wide pan over a medium-high heat. When it is hot, put in half the sliced onions. Stir and fry for about 15 minutes or until the onions are reddish brown and crisp. (You will probably need to turn the heat down to medium after about 4–5 minutes.) Remove the onions with a slotted spoon and spread them out on a plate lined with paper toweling. Now put in the remaining uncooked sliced onions. Stir and fry for about 5 minutes or until they are soft. Put the chili paste from the blender into the pan. Stir and fry for 30 seconds. Add the black bean sauce and stir for 30 seconds. Next put in the meat, cinnamon stick, curry leaves, tamarind paste (or lime or lemon juice), sugar, whole lemongrass sticks (or lemon rind) and 1 quart water. Stir and bring to a boil. Cover, lower the heat and simmer gently for 1¼ hours or until the meat is almost done. Remove the lid and taste, adding as much of the salt as you think you need. Stir, turn the heat to high and, over the next 10 minutes or so, reduce the sauce until it is thick. Put in the browned onions and mix. Turn the heat to medium and cook for another 2 minutes.

This dish can be made ahead of time and reheated. Remove the lemongrass (or rind) and cinnamon stick before serving.

LAMB WITH SCALLIONS

CONG BAO YANG ROLL

*B*eijing (Peking) may be best known in the West for its roast duck but Hong Kong's knowledgeable residents often order simpler and equally delicious dishes when they go to northern-style restaurants. Here is a simple dish that is as good to eat as it is easy to make. The only labor required is in slicing the meat and scallions. The cooking itself takes just a few minutes.

I use leg of lamb for this recipe. I buy a whole leg, asking the butcher to bone it and remove most of the fat. I cut off the amount I need and freeze the rest for future use. In order to make this dish successfully, it is important that you do not overcook the scallions. They should barely wilt.   *Serves 4*

FOR THE LAMB MARINADE

¾ lb lean tender lamb

2 teaspoons Chinese light soy sauce

2 teaspoons Chinese rice wine or dry sherry

2 teaspoons sesame oil

½ teaspoon roasted and ground Szechuan peppercorns (see page 302) or coarsely ground black peppercorns

FOR THE SAUCE

1 tablespoon Chinese rice wine or dry sherry

4 teaspoons Chinese dark soy sauce

1 tablespoon sesame oil

1 teaspoon distilled white vinegar

YOU ALSO NEED

2 garlic cloves

7 scallions

2 tablespoons fresh coriander leaves

4 tablespoons vegetable oil

Cut the lamb against the grain into very thin slices. Cut the slices into very thin slivers about 3 inches long. Put them into a bowl and add all the other marinade ingredients. Mix well and set aside for 20 minutes.

Combine all the ingredients for the sauce. Mix and set aside.

Peel the garlic and chop it finely. Cut the scallions, including their green sections, crosswise into 3-inch segments. Then cut each piece lengthwise into very fine strips. Wash the coriander and pat it dry.

Put the oil in a wok or a large frying pan and set it over a high heat. When it is smoking hot, put in the garlic. Stir once or twice and then put in the lamb. Stir-fry for about a minute or until the lamb is no longer pink on the outside. Pour in the sauce and stir briefly. Put in the coriander and scallions. Stir for 20–30 seconds or until the scallions just wilt. Serve immediately.

LAMB OR GOAT STEW WITH POTATOES, PEPPERS AND OLIVES

CALDERETA

Many versions of *caldereta* are cooked throughout the Philippines, but here it is prepared in the slightly spicy style well loved in the Western Visayas region. As with many dishes from this former Spanish colony, the Mediterranean influence is evident in the use of tomato paste, red bell pepper and olives. Incidentally, bay leaves, cinnamon sticks and peppercorns, fairly common seasonings for stews, are sold here in a combined version and are known collectively as *ricado*.

Serves 4–5

2 lb boneless lamb or goat meat

3 tablespoons distilled white vinegar

1¼ teaspoons salt

Freshly ground black pepper

5 garlic cloves

1 large onion

4 tablespoons olive oil

3 whole dried hot red chilies

1 teaspoon whole black peppercorns

2-inch cinnamon stick

2 bay leaves

4 teaspoons tomato paste

2 medium potatoes

½ large red bell pepper

8 whole stuffed green olives or other olives of your choice

Cut the meat into 1½-inch cubes and put it in a bowl. Add the vinegar, salt and ground black pepper. Mix and set aside for 30–40 minutes. Drain the meat (saving the liquid) and pat it dry. Peel the garlic and onion and mince.

In a large heavy pan heat the oil over medium-high heat. When it is hot, add the chilies. Stir for a few seconds or until they swell and darken. Remove them with a slotted spoon and set aside. Put as many cubes of meat into the pan as will fit easily in a single layer. Brown the meat on both sides and then remove it with a slotted spoon. Brown all the meat. Next put the garlic and onion into the oil. Stir and cook for 2 minutes, scraping up any pan juices. Put in the black peppercorns, cinnamon and bay leaves. Stir and cook for another minute. Now put in the meat and its accumulated juices, the chilies, the reserved marinade and the tomato paste. Stir and cook for 1 minute. Add 2 cups water and bring it to a boil. Cover, turn the heat to low and cook for 15 minutes.

Meanwhile, peel the potatoes and cut them into 1½-inch cubes. When the meat has cooked for 15 minutes, add the potatoes. Cover and continue to cook for 45–60 minutes or until the meat is tender. Seed the bell pepper and cut it into ¼-inch wide strips. When the meat is tender, put the pepper strips and olives into the stew. Stir and cook for another 3–5 minutes.

PORK COOKED IN A PICKLING STYLE

Philippines

*From Sandy
Daza*

ADOBONG BABOY

One of the most popular pork dishes in the Philippines is *adobo*. It originated well before the age of refrigeration. Meat needed to be preserved and the tastiest way to do it was to cook it with a mixture of vinegar, soy sauce and garlic, thus pickling it into the bargain. Normally pork belly is used, but thin-cut pork loin chops—about ½ inch thick—make a successful substitute. If you wish to use the more authentic pork belly, cut it crosswise into 1-inch cubes. Pork *adobo* is served with plain rice.   *Serves 4*

12 large garlic cloves
6 tablespoons Chinese dark soy sauce
6 tablespoons distilled white vinegar
3 bay leaves
1 teaspoon whole black peppercorns
2 lb thin-cut pork loin chops
3 tablespoons vegetable oil

Peel the garlic cloves. Chop 4 of them finely and set them aside for the marinade. Chop the remaining 8 finely and set them aside separately. Combine the 4 chopped garlic cloves, soy sauce, vinegar, bay leaves and peppercorns in a large bowl and mix well. Add the pork chops and mix again so that they are well coated with the marinade. Set aside for 1 hour, turning the chops over a few times during this period.

Put the oil in a wide saucepan or large frying pan and set it over a medium-high heat. When the oil is hot, put in the 8 chopped cloves of garlic. Stir and fry until they turn light gold in color. Add the pork chops, their marinade and ½ cup water. Bring to a boil. Cover, turn the heat to low and simmer gently for 30 minutes, turning the chops over a few times during this period. Remove the lid from the pan and turn the heat to medium-high. Cook for another 10–15 minutes or until the sauce is thick and the meat is tender. This dish may be prepared a day ahead of time and refrigerated.

MEAT

1 1 1

STIR-FRIED PORK WITH RED BELL PEPPER

TWAEJI BOKKUM

*E*asy to prepare and spicily delicious, this dish is best served with plain rice.
Serves 4

¾ lb boneless loin of pork

1 scallion

1 large garlic clove

1 × ½-inch piece fresh ginger

2 tablespoons Hot Fermented Bean Paste
(see page 240)

½ large red bell pepper

1 medium onion

3 tablespoons vegetable oil

Cut the pork against the grain into slices about 2 × 1 × ⅛ inch. Cut the scallion crosswise into very fine rounds. Peel the garlic and ginger and chop them finely. Combine the pork, scallion, garlic, ginger and Hot Fermented Bean Paste in a bowl. Mix well. Cover and set aside for 30 minutes or longer, refrigerating if necessary.

Seed and cut the pepper into ½-inch squares. Cut the onion into ½-inch cubes and then separate the layers.

Just before serving, put the oil in a large nonstick frying pan and set it over a high heat. When it is hot, put in the pork together with all its marinade. Stir-fry for 3 minutes or until the pork is white all the way through. Add about 6 tablespoons water and the pepper and onion. Stir and cook for another 2 minutes on a high heat.

Bottom: *Stir-Fried Pork with Red Bell Pepper (this page);* **top:** *Knockout Knuckle (page 120)*

GLAZED GINGERY SPARERIBS

HONG SHAO LEIGU

These Shanghai-style pork ribs are braised. There really could not be a simpler way to prepare them. You could also make this dish with thin-cut pork loin chops. *Serves 4*

2 lb pork spareribs

6 tablespoons Chinese dark soy sauce

6 tablespoons sugar

2 1-inch cubes fresh ginger

3 scallions

3 tablespoons Chinese rice wine or dry sherry

Separate the spareribs individually and then cut them into 3-inch lengths. (Persuade your butcher to do this for you if possible.)

Put the spareribs in a wide, preferably nonstick pan. Add the soy sauce and sugar. Peel and lightly crush the ginger cubes and add them to the pan. Add the scallions also. Pour in the rice wine and 1 quart water. Bring to a boil. Cover, turn the heat to medium-low and simmer fairly vigorously for 45 minutes. Turn the meat around every 10 minutes or so to allow even coloring. Remove the lid from the pan and turn the heat to high. Remove and discard the ginger and scallions. Cook for another 20 minutes or so until liquid is thick and syrupy. It should coat the ribs with an even, dark glaze. You may need to stir the ribs around a few times during this period.

PORK WITH CALF'S LIVER AND CHICK PEAS

MENUDO

*T*his is an easy stew, hearty and nourishing and comforting all at once. It is, quite clearly, of Mediterranean origin. It may be eaten with a salad and rice.

Canned chick peas may be used for this dish: drain them first. If you wish to cook your own from scratch, soak about ½ cup dried chick peas overnight in cold water. The following day, drain them, put them in a pan, cover with 1¼ quarts fresh cold water and bring to a boil. Cover, lower the heat and simmer for 45 minutes. Add ½ teaspoon salt and continue to cook for another 30 minutes–1 hour or until the chick peas are tender. (Older chick peas take longer to cook.) Drain them before using them for this recipe. I use the meat from 3–4 thin pork loin chops for this dish. *Serves 4*

5 oz calf's liver
Salt
Freshly ground black pepper
12 oz lean pork
2 small potatoes
1 cup canned peeled tomatoes
3 garlic cloves
1 medium onion
4 tablespoons vegetable oil
¾–1 cup cooked drained chick peas
1 teaspoon paprika

Cut the liver into ½–¾-inch cubes. Dust it lightly with salt and pepper and toss. Cut the pork into ½–¾-inch cubes, discarding most of the fat. Peel the potatoes and cut them into ½–¾-inch cubes; place them in a bowl of water and set aside. Crush the tomatoes lightly and leave them in their liquid. Peel the garlic and cut into fine slivers. Peel the onion and slice it thin.

Put the oil in a large, preferably nonstick frying pan over a high heat. When the oil is hot, put in the liver. Stir and fry until it has browned on the outside but is still soft and slightly rare inside. Remove the liver with a slotted spoon and set it aside. Put the garlic and onion into the same oil. Stir and fry for 1 minute. Then add the diced pork and stir and fry for 3 minutes. Now put in the tomatoes and their liquid. Keep stirring and cooking on a high heat for 1 minute, then cover, turn the heat to low and simmer for 15 minutes. Drain the potatoes and add them to the pan. Also add the chick peas, 1½ teaspoons salt, some black pepper, the paprika and ¾ cup water. Stir and bring to a simmer. Cover and cook for 15–25 minutes, or until the potatoes and pork are tender. Put in the liver, plus any juices that may have run out of it, and heat it through. This dish may be made in advance and reheated.

PORK WITH LONG BEANS AND CHIVES

SIJIDOU CHAO ZHULIU

You could call Willy Mark one of Hong Kong's moving landmarks. He owns restaurants, writes about food and cooks with great knowledge and passion. As it happens, he never seems to cook the same dish twice in exactly the same way. He made this particular Cantonese-style dish for me once with onions and chives, another time with garlic. Each time it was superb and different, which just goes to show that there is great flexibility in Chinese cooking and you should never be afraid to make changes and adjustments.

A note about the ingredients: in Hong Kong, long beans come in two shades of green, light and dark. Willy uses the darker, crisper variety. Use any type of long beans if you can find them. Most Chinese and Southeast Asian grocers stock them. If you cannot obtain them, use any tender green beans, cooking them carefully so that they retain their crispness. The chives Willy picked from the market were topped with closed buds. If you grow chives, as I do, and they happen to be budding, do use them, young bud and all. If you do not grow them, use either Chinese chives or ordinary chives.   *Serves 2–4*

7 oz pork tenderloin, well-trimmed

Salt

4 teaspoons sesame oil

2½ teaspoons cornstarch

7 oz long or green beans

¾ oz fresh chives (Chinese chives, if available)

1 medium onion

¾-inch cube fresh ginger

1 large garlic clove

1 tablespoon oyster sauce

2 teaspoons Chinese light soy sauce

1 tablespoon Chinese rice wine or dry sherry

5 tablespoons vegetable oil

Cut the pork tenderloin into very thin slices about 2 inches long and ½ inch wide. Put them in a small bowl. Add about ⅛ teaspoon salt, 2 teaspoons of the sesame oil, 1 teaspoon of the cornstarch and 2 teaspoons water. Mix well. Cover and set aside, refrigerating if necessary.

Trim the beans and cut them into 2-inch pieces. Cut the chives into 2-inch lengths as well. Peel the onions and cut in half crosswise, then quarter each half and separate the different layers. Peel the ginger and garlic and chop very finely.

In a small bowl combine the oyster sauce, light soy sauce, the remaining

2 teaspoons sesame oil, the rice wine and 5 tablespoons water. Mix well and set aside.

In a cup, combine the remaining 1½ teaspoons cornstarch with 2 tablespoons water and set aside.

Just before eating, put 1 tablespoon oil in a wok or frying pan and set it over a high heat. When the oil is hot, put in half the finely chopped ginger. Stir once or twice. Then add the onion and stir a few times. Put in the green beans and ¼ teaspoon salt. Stir-fry for a minute. Put in 4 tablespoons water and cover immediately. Lower the heat and cook for 4–6 minutes or until the beans are just tender. Uncover and empty the contents of the wok into a bowl.

Clean and dry the wok. Pour in the remaining 4 tablespoons oil and heat it. When it is very hot, put in the pork.

Turn off the heat. Keep moving the pork pieces about until they just turn white. You may need to turn the heat on again to achieve this, but keep it on low. Remove the pork with a slotted spoon and put it into a clean bowl.

Remove all but 1 tablespoon of the oil. Set the wok over a high heat. When the oil is hot, add the remaining ginger and garlic as well as the chives. Stir for 15–30 seconds. Put in the pork. Stir-fry for 1 minute. Put in the green beans and onion and stir them for 30 seconds. Then add the sauce from the bowl and stir for a minute. Take the wok off the heat. Stir the cornstarch mixture in the cup. Make a well in the center of the wok's contents and pour it in. Put the wok back over a low heat. Stir and cook just until the sauce has thickened.

Japan

**With help from
the École
Technique
Hôtelière Tsuji in
Osaka**

BREADED PORK CUTLETS

TONKATSU

Breaded and deep-fried, these cutlets originally came to Japan from the West but they are now so popular that almost every neighborhood has a thriving *ton-katsu* restaurant. One reason could well be that fine food in Japan tends to be very expensive. Among the few good, cheaper eating places are *tonkatsu* restaurants, noodle shops and *yakitori* (chicken kebab) bars.

In Japan *tonkatsu* cutlets are diced into bite-sized pieces so that they can be picked up with chopsticks. They are then reassembled in their cutlet shape and served on a bed of finely shredded lettuce or cabbage. The official dipping sauce, which is available, bottled, all over Japan, seems to be a combination of tomato ketchup, Worcestershire sauce, mustard, soy sauce and *sake*. A soup, a bowl of rice and some pickles are generally served on the side. A Japanese portion would normally consist of one cutlet; I have allowed two per person.   *Serves 4*

8 boneless pork loin chops or 1¼–1½ lb
   pork tenderloin, cut into 8 pieces, each
   about ½ inch thick
Salt
Freshly ground black pepper
*1½–2 tablespoons unbleached,
   all-purpose flour*
2 eggs
*2–3 cups fresh breadcrumbs, made from
   slightly stale bread*
*¼ small head cabbage or crisp lettuce
   (such as iceberg)*
Oil for deep-frying
*East-West Sauce (see page 236) or
   tomato ketchup*
Lime or lemon wedges

*Bottom: Breaded
Pork Cutlets over
Rice (page 122);
top: Glazed
Gingery Spareribs
(page 114)*

Dust the pork pieces on both sides, first with the salt and pepper and then with the flour. Break the eggs into a shallow bowl and beat them lightly.

Empty the breadcrumbs into another shallow bowl. Dip the pork pieces first in the egg and then in the breadcrumbs. Set aside for 30 minutes.

Cut the cabbage or lettuce into fine long shreds and divide between 4 plates.

Heat the oil in a deep frying pan or deep-fat fryer to a medium temperature of about 350°F. When it is hot, put in as many pork pieces as the pan will hold in a single layer and deep-fry for 5–6 minutes or until the meat is brown outside and just cooked through. Drain it on paper toweling. Cook all the meat in this way. Then cut the cooked meat slices neatly into bite-sized cubes and divide them between 4 plates, reforming them into their original cutlet shape and placing 2 reformed cutlets on each bed of cabbage or lettuce. Serve with East-West Sauce and lime or lemon wedges.

KNOCKOUT KNUCKLE

PATANG BAWANG

During my last few trips to the Philippines, I had some of the best food in Manila at the Ang Hang Restaurant. One of its specialties was this dish. Pork is a much-loved meat in the Philippines, as it is in many Pacific Islands, and what often adds to the status of the meat itself is the crispness of the skin on top of it. In this recipe the meat is juicy and tender and the skin is crackling crisp. This is achieved by an easily mastered technique of slow braising and double-frying.

It is quite simple to make this dish; it is harder to find the right cut of meat! What you need is the 3 lb front leg of a pig that—in the words of the chef—"has not been around." This, when translated, means a 3–4 month-old pig. I had great trouble finding the front leg of a pig, let alone that of a pig that had not been around! You have two choices here: you can either buy what is sold as a pork half-leg knuckle; or you can do what I did. I went to the butcher and put in a special order for a front leg. It came, all 5½ lb of it. I wanted only 3 lb, so I asked the butcher to cut away a portion at the thicker end. He took an educated guess, hacked down and came in at 3½ lb. I took both pieces home, one to cook immediately and the thicker end to store in the freezer for later use.

My children declared that this was the best pork they had ever tasted.
Serves 4

---

*3½ lb pork half-leg knuckle or portion of
  front leg of pork*

1 medium onion

2 carrots

2 celery sticks

1 teaspoon whole black peppercorns

3 bay leaves

1 tablespoon salt

9 garlic cloves

6 fresh hot green chilies

*½ cup vegetable oil, plus extra for
  deep-frying*

Put the pork, skin-side up, into a large pan along with 5 quarts water. Bring to a simmer. Maintain a very gentle simmer over the next few minutes and remove as much scum as you can. Peel the onion and carrots. Put them, as well as the celery, peppercorns, bay leaves and salt, into the pan. Cover partially and simmer gently for about 3 hours or until the meat is tender. Remove the meat and leave it to drain and cool. (The meat broth may be strained, cooled, degreased and saved for use in other dishes.)

Peel the garlic and cut it lengthwise into thin slices. Cut the green chilies crosswise into thin slices. Put the ½ cup oil in a frying pan set over a medium-low heat. Put in the garlic. Stir and fry until it just begins to turn golden. Then add the chilies. Continue to stir and fry until the garlic is golden brown and the chilies have crisped a little. Remove the garlic and chilies with a slotted spoon and spread them over paper toweling to drain. Save the garlicky oil.

Heat the oil for deep-frying in a large deep-fat fryer or a large wok to a medium temperature, about 325°F. When it is hot, put in the pork joint, skin-side down. Cover and cook for 5 minutes. Turn the pork over carefully, cover again and cook the second side for 3 minutes. Transfer the pork to a plate. (This much can be done up to 2 hours ahead of time. Do not refrigerate the meat.)

Just before serving, heat the oil again, this time to a high temperature, around 400°F. When it is hot, put in the meat, skin-side down. Fry, uncovered, for 2–3 minutes or until the skin is crisp and brown. Now turn the meat and fry the opposite side for 1 minute. Turn the meat again and fry the skin side for another minute. Make sure that the skin on the sides of the meat browns properly too.

Lift the meat out carefully and drain it briefly. Put it on a plate and then cut the meat off the bone lengthwise in long strips. Lay the strips back over the bone, forming a kind of tent over it. Pour a little of the reserved garlicky oil over the meat. Scatter the fried garlic and chilies over the top and serve.

BREADED PORK CUTLETS OVER RICE

KATSUDON

Τ he Breaded Pork Cutlets (see page 119) may be served in another way: over a large individual bowl of hot rice (Japanese rice is best), with a sauce of stock, soy, *sake* and onions poured over the top. This dish is then known as *katsudon* and it is a great favorite of mine.   *Serves 4*

FOR THE CUTLETS

8 boneless pork loin chops or 1¼–1½ lb pork tenderloin, cut into 8 pieces, each about ½ inch thick

Salt

Freshly ground black pepper

1½–2 tablespoons unbleached, all-purpose flour

2 eggs

3–4 cups fresh breadcrumbs, made from slightly stale bread

YOU ALSO NEED

1 medium onion

4 scallions

2½ cups Japanese Soup Stock (see page 78) or light unsalted Chicken Stock, homemade (see page 77) or canned

5–6 tablespoons Japanese soy sauce (shoyu)

8 tablespoons sake

2 tablespoons sugar

1 tablespoon vegetable oil

Enough Plain Japanese Rice for 4 people (see page 211)

Make the cutlets in exactly the same way as described in the recipe on page 118. Cut them into cubes and keep them hot.

Peel the onion and cut it in half lengthwise. Cut each half crosswise into ⅛-inch slices. Trim the scallions and cut them in half lengthwise, then cut them crosswise into 2-inch lengths. Combine the stock, soy sauce, *sake* and sugar in a bowl.

Put the oil in a medium-sized pan and set it over a medium heat. When the oil is hot, add the onion and sauté it until it is soft but do not let it brown. Add the stock mixture and the scallions. Bring to a simmer gently and then simmer for 3 minutes.

Assemble the *katsudon* quickly now. Put about 1½ cups hot Plain Japanese Rice into each of 4 bowls. Lay the pork cutlets over the rice. Then spoon the stock-onion mixture over the top, dividing it evenly among the 4 bowls. The liquid will moisten the rice and add great flavor to it. Serve hot.

THAI PORK CURRY IN THE BURMESE STYLE

Thailand

From the Home of Kruamas Woodtikarn in Chiang Mai

KAENG HUNGLAY

*E*ven before I got to Chiang Mai, I had been told by friends in Bangkok of this northern dish. "Try and eat it in someone's home," I had been advised. I need not have worried about how I would manage this: Thais are about the most hospitable people I know. Within a day of arriving in Chiang Mai, I was seated with Kruamas "Ting" Woodtikarn's family, devouring not just curry but a tableload of northern delicacies, including black button mushrooms and freshly plucked litchis.

Much of northwestern Thailand not only borders Burma but has also been ruled by it in previous centuries. The cultural give-and-take can still be seen in the lacquered baskets used for storing cooked glutinous rice (this is the rice eaten for breakfast, lunch and dinner), in the cheroot-smoking women of the villages, and in this curry. Those of you who are familiar with India's hot, sweet and sour *vindaloo* will find that this is almost a sister curry. After all, Burma borders India and the ripple effect of cultural exchanges can be quite far-reaching.

Boneless pork from the loin or shoulder may be used in this recipe. A little fat in the meat will keep it more tender. You could cut the meat off chops, if you like, saving the bones for soup. The curry paste can be made ahead of time and frozen. It will need to be defrosted and brought to room temperature before it is used.

Serves 4–6

FOR THE CURRY PASTE

3–8 whole dried hot red chilies, depending on hotness required

¾-inch cube fresh or 5 slices dried galangal or ¾-inch cube fresh ginger

2 sticks fresh or 2 tablespoons dried sliced lemongrass

7–8 medium shallots (or 1 large onion)

10 large garlic cloves

1 teaspoon shrimp or anchovy paste

1 tablespoon ground coriander seeds

2 teaspoons ground cumin seeds

½ teaspoon ground turmeric

YOU ALSO NEED

1¾ lb boneless pork, cut into 1½-inch cubes

1½ tablespoons Japanese soy sauce (shoyu)

3 1-inch cubes fresh ginger (the younger, the better)

10–12 shallots or small pickling onions

10–15 small garlic cloves

2 or more tablespoons tamarind paste (see page 303) or lemon juice

2 or more tablespoons dark brown sugar

Salt (optional)

continued

First make the curry paste. Put 1 cup water in a small bowl and crumble the dried red chilies into it. If using dried galangal and dried lemongrass, add them to the water as well. Leave the dried ingredients to soak for 30 minutes. If you are using fresh galangal (or ginger), peel and coarsely chop it. If you are using fresh lemongrass, cut it into very fine slices crosswise, starting from the bottom and going up the stalk about 6 inches; discard the straw-like top. Peel the shallots and garlic and chop them coarsely.

When the dry seasonings have finished soaking, put them and their soaking liquid as well as all the other ingredients for the curry paste into an electric blender. If you are using fresh galangal (or fresh ginger) or fresh lemongrass, add them to the blender now. Blend until smooth.

Next combine the pork, curry paste and soy sauce in a bowl and marinate for 30 minutes.

Meanwhile, peel the ginger and cut it into very thin slices. Stack a few slices at a time together and cut them into matchstick strips. Peel the shallots and the garlic, leaving them whole.

Put the pork and its marinade into a wide, heavy, preferably nonstick pan, set it over a medium-low heat and bring it to a simmer. Simmer gently for 15–20 minutes or until the meat starts to release its fat. Turn the heat to medium-high. Stir and fry for about 10 minutes or until the spice mixture begins to dry out and brown. Now add 2 cups water, the ginger strips, the whole shallots and the whole garlic cloves. Bring the mixture to a simmer. Cover and cook for 45 minutes or until the meat is tender. Add the tamarind paste (or lemon juice) and brown sugar. Mix and taste, adding more of each if you need it. Add salt if desired. Cook for another 2–3 minutes to allow the flavors to develop and mingle.

Poultry and Eggs

CHICKEN BITS ON A SKEWER

YAKITORI

A yakitori bar in Japan is really a drinking establishment that offers specialized snacks, generally made of chicken and generally cooked on bamboo skewers over charcoal. As offices close in the evenings, men (and nowadays, I noticed, women as well) head toward these bars to drink and have a snack, and even to stay on for a full meal.

Yakitori at its simplest is a chicken shish kebab with a very Japanese flavor. Pieces of dark meat are served either by themselves, neatly speared onto the ends of three small bamboo skewers (three makes a serving), or interspersed with bits of green pepper or scallion. As the meat is broiled or grilled, it is dipped into a sweetened soy-based sauce. The servings are tantalizingly small, but one can have as many as one wants.

Chicken innards seem just as popular as the meat; gizzards, livers and hearts may be ordered. The possibilities grow. There is blanched chicken skin, grilled and served with a sprinkling of salt and pepper; there are chicken meatballs and chicken wings; and, for those who want them, other small birds, such as sparrows. If you are hungry enough for a full meal, you can order any of these served on a bowl of rice *(yakitori donburi)* with tea and pickles on the side.

You may serve the simple *yakitori* described below either with drinks or as a meal. A note about the skewers: most oriental shops sell 6–8 inch bamboo skewers. They should be soaked in water for 30 minutes–1 hour before being used. All the meat should be placed at one end and it is that end that should be set directly over or under the heat source. You could use metal skewers instead—the best kind are somewhat flattened, like swords, because the meat does not roll around on them when it is turned. In Japan the small *yakitori* sticks are a little like lollipops. You pull the meat off with your mouth. If longer, metal skewers are used, it would be best to push the meat off onto a plate before serving it.

The chicken can be skewered well ahead of time, covered and refrigerated. You may cook this dish outdoors over charcoal or indoors under your oven broiler.

Serves 4 as a main course or up to 8 with drinks

---

4 medium chicken legs (thighs and
   drumsticks), boned (see page 55)

1 large green bell pepper

8 tablespoons Japanese soy sauce (shoyu)

4 tablespoons sake

3 tablespoons sugar

Cut the boned chicken leg meat into 1-inch chunks. If some skin separates from the meat, discard it. Leave any skin that clings naturally. Cut the green pepper in half and discard the seeds. Cut it into 1-inch squares.

Thread 2 pieces of meat onto a skewer, followed by a piece of pepper.

If you are preparing bamboo skewers, Japanese-style, push the meat to one end and keep alternating 2 pieces of meat with a piece of pepper until you have loaded about 3 inches of each skewer. If you are using long metal skewers, you can thread their whole length, leaving each end empty. Use up all the meat in this way, filling up as many skewers as required. Cover well and refrigerate until needed.

Meanwhile, combine the soy sauce, *sake* and sugar in a small pan and bring to the boil. Lower the heat and cook gently until the sugar has dissolved.

Preheat an oven broiler or an out-door charcoal grill. Rest the skewers 4–5 inches from the source of heat and grill for 4–5 minutes on each side or until the meat is three quarters cooked. Brush the sauce over the meat and green peppers and grill briefly on both sides until the meat is almost done. Brush with the sauce a second time and grill for another 30 seconds on each side. Serve hot. If you are serving this *yakitori* with drinks and have cooked the meat on long skewers (and have now pushed it off them), stick toothpicks into the pieces of meat so that they may be picked up easily.

Indonesia

SPICY CHICKEN KEBABS WITH A PEANUT SAUCE

SATAY AYAM

*I*t is believed that *satays,* or tiny bits of meat threaded onto fine bamboo skewers and grilled, spread throughout much of East Asia from Java. Before they reached Java, their origins can surely be traced to the kebabs of India, and beyond India to the Middle East. *Satays* take different forms in different parts of the vast Indonesian archipelago. In Jogyakarta, for example, they tend to be rather sweet, eaten as they are with ritual dips in a thick, syrupy, sweet soy sauce known as *kecap manis.* Crushed peanuts or sliced shallots and an occasional hot chili may be added to the *kecap.* As you travel west, the sweetness gives way to greater pungency and nuttiness.

Here follows the recipe for one of my favorite Indonesian *satays.* The peanut sauce is exactly the same as the dressing for the *gado-gado* (Salad of Assorted Vegetables with a Delicious Peanut Dressing, page 207). It needs to be heated, beaten lightly and then poured over the grilled kebabs. You may serve these kebabs as a first course, all by themselves, or as main dish along with rice, a vegetable or salad and perhaps some crisp Shrimp Wafers (page 76).

continued

As in the recipe for Chicken Bits on a Skewer (page 126), I prefer to use boned and skinned chicken legs as the meat is more moist. You may, however, use boned and skinned chicken breast. I generally find it easier to use flat metal skewers, but if you wish to use the more traditional bamboo *satay* skewers, soak them in water for 30-minutes–1 hour before threading the meat onto them. *Serves 4*

4 medium chicken legs (thighs and drumsticks, boned and skinned; (see page 55) or 1 lb chicken breast, boned and skinned

1 garlic clove

1-inch cube fresh ginger

½ large shallot (or ¾-inch cube of onion)

4 teaspoons Chinese light soy sauce

1 tablespoon lime or lemon juice

1 teaspoon ground coriander seeds

½ teaspoon sugar

¼ teaspoon ground red (cayenne) pepper

Peanut Dressing

Cut the boned and skinned chicken into 1-inch cubes.

Peel the garlic and crush it to a pulp. Peel the ginger and grate it as finely as possible. Peel the shallot and chop it finely. In a medium-sized bowl, combine the garlic, ginger, shallot, soy sauce, lime juice, coriander, sugar and ground red pepper and mix well. Put in the chicken and rub the marinade over the meat. Cover and refrigerate for 2–24 hours. (Bring the chicken to room temperature before grilling.) Make the Peanut Dressing.

Preheat an oven broiler or an outdoor charcoal grill. Use bamboo skewers solely for an outdoor grill or for an oven broiler if you can ensure that the heat will hit only the upper 3–4 inches of the skewer (otherwise the exposed bamboo may burn). If using them, thread about 3 inches of chicken pieces onto one end of a bamboo skewer. Fill in this way as many skewers as needed. If you are using long metal skewers, use 4 and divide the meat evenly between them.

If you are broiling indoors, balance the skewer ends on the raised edges of a grill rack and place them about 4 inches from the heat source. If grilling over charcoal, balance the skewers about 4 inches from the heat source. Grill for about 5 minutes on each side or until the meat is browned.

Heat the Peanut Dressing and beat it lightly. Place the bamboo skewers (if using) directly on individual plates. Pour a few tablespoons of the dressing over each portion and serve. If you are using metal skewers, remove the meat with the help of a fork and divide it among 4 plates. Spoon a few tablespoons of dressing over each serving.

SPICY STIR-FRIED CHICKEN WITH LEMONGRASS

Vietnam

From the Nhà Hàng Nôi Nhà Bè Restaurant in Hô Chí Minh City

GÀ XÀO XAᶻ ỐT

This was one of the quick, very flavorful, stir-fried dishes served to me in a floating restaurant on Saigon River. It is important to let the chicken sit in its marinade for at least an hour and that the chicken (while still on the bone) be cut into fairly small, bite-sized pieces. As chicken bones, especially those in the leg, have a tendency to splinter, it is best to let the butcher cut up the chicken for you. *Serves 4*

FOR THE MARINADE

1 stick fresh or 2 tablespoons dried sliced lemongrass

2 lb chicken parts, cut into small pieces

1 large garlic clove

½-inch cube fresh ginger

1 tablespoon sugar

1½ teaspoons tomato paste

½ teaspoon salt

¼ teaspoon ground red (cayenne) pepper

¼ teaspoon ground turmeric

YOU ALSO NEED

5–6 garlic cloves

3 tablespoons vegetable oil

1 tablespoon fish sauce or salt to taste

4–8 tablespoons Chicken Stock, homemade (see page 77) or canned

1 large onion

First prepare the marinade. If you are using fresh lemongrass, cut it crosswise into very thin slices, starting at the bulbous bottom end and going up about 6 inches. Discard the strawlike top. If you are using dried sliced lemongrass, soak it in 4 tablespoons hot water for 1 hour.

Put the chicken pieces in a bowl. Add the fresh lemongrass, if you are using it. If you are using dried lemongrass, remove it from its soaking liquid and add it to the chicken. (Save the soaking liquid.) Peel the large garlic clove and crush it well. Peel the ginger and grate it finely. Add the garlic, ginger, sugar, tomato paste, salt, ground red pepper and turmeric to the chicken. Mix thoroughly. Cover and refrigerate for 1–24 hours.

Peel and finely chop the remaining 5–6 garlic cloves. Put the oil in a wok or large frying pan and set it over a high heat. When it is hot, put in the garlic. Stir and fry for 30 seconds or until the garlic is golden. Add the chicken and all its marinade. Stir and fry for 5–6 minutes or until the chicken browns a little. Then add the fish sauce and either the lemongrass soaking liquid or 4 tablespoons stock. Stir once and cover. Cook on a high heat for 5 minutes. Lift the lid and stir, and then add another 4 tablespoons stock. Cover, turn the heat to low and cook for 5 more minutes.

While the chicken cooks, peel the onion and cut them into ¾-inch dice. Separate the onion layers within the diced pieces. Remove the lid from the wok containing the chicken and turn the heat to high. Put in the onion, and stir and fry for 1 minute. Lift the chicken out of its oil and serve.

Thailand

From Pieng Chom Darbanand at the Imperial Hotel, Bangkok

GROUND CHICKEN STIR-FRIED WITH BASIL

KAI PAD BAI KAPROW

Here is an exquisite, quick-cooking dish that is made with fresh holy basil (*bai kaprow*). As I cannot always obtain it, I use ordinary basil and find that it makes a superb substitute. The green herb is used in two ways: it is stir-fried with the chicken and it is also shallow-fried until crisp and used as a generous topping. The result is uncommonly good. (If red chilies are unavailable, increase the number of green chilies accordingly.)   *Serves 4*

¼ lb (2 lightly packed quarts) fresh holy basil (bai kaprow) leaves or ordinary basil (net weight without stems)

Vegetable oil for shallow-frying

5 garlic cloves

7 medium shallots (or 1 medium onion)

2 fresh hot green chilies or to taste

2 fresh hot red chilies or to taste

1-inch cube fresh ginger

1 lb ground chicken (from boned and skinned breast or legs or both)

5 teaspoons fish sauce or salt to taste

1½ teaspoons dark brown sugar

Break off and discard the stems of the basil leaves. Wash the leaves and pat them dry. Divide them into two equal parts. Chop one part very coarsely and then set both parts aside.

Pour the oil to a depth of ½ inch into a medium-sized frying pan and set it over a medium-high heat. Put a plate lined with paper toweling near your stove. Have ready a splatter screen or an upturned sieve to cover the pan as soon as you have put in the leaves; this will prevent your being splashed with hot oil. When the oil is hot, place a smallish handful of whole leaves into the frying pan. Cover immediately with the screen or sieve. As soon as the intense sizzling has died down (this takes only seconds), remove the cover and stir the leaves once or twice. They will turn crisp very quickly. Remove them with a slotted spoon and spread them out on the paper toweling to drain. Fry all the whole basil leaves in this way. Replace the paper toweling under the basil leaves several times to prevent the crisp leaves from becoming soggy.

Peel the garlic cloves and chop them finely. Peel and finely slice the shallots. Cut the green and red chilies into fine rounds. Peel the ginger and grate it finely. Once the oil used for frying the basil leaves has cooled a little, strain it and save it.

Just before serving, put 4 tablespoons of this oil in a large frying pan or wok and set it over a medium-high heat. When it is hot, put in the garlic and shallots. Stir and fry for about 2 minutes or until the shallots are a medium brown. Add the chilies and ginger and give a few vigorous stirs. Now turn the heat to high and put in the chopped basil. Stir once and add the ground chicken. Stir and fry for about 3 minutes, breaking up the chicken lumps as you do so. The chicken should turn white all the way through. Add the fish sauce and sugar. Mix, then transfer to a serving dish. Top with the crisp basil leaves and serve.

CHICKEN STIR-FRIED WITH CELERY

Hong Kong

From the American Restaurant in Wanchai

JIANCAI JIDING

Some of the best food that I have eaten in Hong Kong has been at a restaurant that calls itself, strangely enough, the American Restaurant. It specializes in northern food, and its offerings, particularly its breads, are quite unbeatable.

Not all the chefs in the kitchen, however, are from the north. After feeding the clients superlative Beijing-style food, the chefs settle down to a meal of their own that is often a mixture of northern and their own Cantonese food. Here is a Cantonese dish that I caught the staff eating one day.   *Serves 2–4*

continued

10 oz. chicken breast, boned and skinned

1 egg white

3 teaspoons cornstarch

¼ teaspoon salt

6 tablespoons Chicken Stock, homemade
(see page 77) or canned

½ dried hot red chili

1 tablespoon Chinese light soy sauce

2 teaspoons Chinese rice wine or dry
sherry

2 teaspoons lemon juice

1 garlic clove

About 4 celery stalks, preferably from the
middle of the bunch

2 tablespoons vegetable oil

Spread the chicken breast out and hit it with a mallet in order to flatten it. It should end up being about ¼ inch thick. Cut it into 1-inch squares. Combine the egg white, 2 teaspoons of the cornstarch and the salt in a small bowl. Beat lightly to mix. Toss the chicken in the egg mixture until it is well coated. Cover and set aside for 2 hours or longer.

Now prepare the sauce. Put the remaining teaspoon of cornstarch in a cup. Slowly add 5 tablespoons of the chicken stock, mixing well between each addition. Crumble in the red chili. Add the light soy sauce, rice wine and lemon juice. Mix and set aside.

Peel and finely chop the garlic. Cut the celery sticks crosswise into 1-inch pieces.

When the chicken has marinated for 2 hours, bring about 1½ inches water to a boil in a medium-sized frying pan or a wide shallow saucepan over a high heat. As soon as it starts bubbling, put in all the chicken, separating the pieces with a spoon. Let the pan sit over the heat for about 30 seconds. The chicken should turn white. (If the water returns to a boil before that, turn the heat to low.) Drain the chicken and set it aside—do not refrigerate.

Just before you are ready to serve, set a wok over a high heat. When it is hot, put in 1 tablespoon of the oil. When the oil has heated, put in half the chopped garlic. Stir once or twice and add the chicken. Stir and cook for about 1 minute. Remove the chicken and set it aside in a bowl.

Wash out the wok and dry it. Heat it again over a high heat. When it is hot, put in the remaining tablespoon of oil. When the oil has heated, put in the remaining chopped garlic. Stir once or twice and add the chopped celery. Stir it around for 30–40 seconds. Put in the remaining tablespoon of chicken stock and cover immediately. Turn the heat to low and cook for about 3 minutes or until the celery is just tender. Take the wok off the heat. Stir the sauce and put it into the wok. Put the wok over a low heat. Add the chicken. Stir and cook until the sauce has thickened. Serve immediately.

CHICKEN PATTIES WITH GINGER AND SESAME SEEDS

TAK KOGI SOPSANJOK

*T*hese delightfully seasoned chicken hamburgers are easy to prepare for light informal meals and picnics. While they may be broiled indoors in the oven or outdoors over charcoal, here I have cooked them in a frying pan.

Boned and skinned ground chicken is required for this dish. I get my butcher to grind a half-and-half combination of light and dark meat for me as that gives the best texture. These patties are normally served with Korean Dipping Sauce (page 241) and rice. You could, if you like, spoon a generous amount of the sauce over them and then slap them inside a hamburger bun. *Makes 5 patties*

1 scallion

1 large garlic clove

1-inch cube fresh ginger

1 lb ground chicken

1 tablespoon roasted sesame seeds (see page 299)

1 tablespoon sesame oil

1 tablespoon soy sauce (preferably Japanese —shoyu)

Freshly ground black pepper

¼–½ teaspoon ground red (cayenne) pepper

Korean Dipping Sauce (see page 241)

1–2 tablespoons vegetable oil

Cut the scallion crosswise into very fine rounds along its entire length, including the green section. Peel the garlic and crush it to a pulp. Peel the ginger and grate it very finely.

Put the chicken in a bowl. Add the scallion, garlic, ginger, roasted sesame seeds, sesame oil, soy sauce, black pepper and ground red pepper. Mix thoroughly and make 5 patties that are about 3½ inches in diameter. Put them in a single layer on a plate and cover with plastic wrap. Set the patties aside until you are ready to eat.

Prepare the Korean Dipping Sauce.

Just before eating, grease the bottom of a large nonstick frying pan very lightly with about 1 tablespoon of the vegetable oil and set it over a medium-high heat. When it is hot, put in the patties in a single layer. Cook for 1–1½ minutes or until they are medium-brown on one side. Turn the patties over and cook the second side the same way. Turn the heat to medium and cook both sides of the patties again for about 1 minute or a little more on each side so that they are nicely browned and cooked through. Pierce the center of one patty with the point of a sharp knife to check it. If it is no longer pink inside, it is ready. Serve hot.

ROAST CHICKEN WITH FIVE-SPICE POWDER

GÀ XỐI MỞ

*T*his dish, very popular in South Vietnam, is traditionally made by first roasting a whole marinated chicken over charcoal, just to dry it out, and then deep-frying it. Vietnamese with Western kitchens take the easy way out and simply roast the whole bird in the oven. That is what I have chosen to do.

Five-spice powder, a Chinese spice mixture, contains star anise, fennel, cloves, cinnamon and Szechuan peppercorns. It is sold by Chinese grocers in a powdered form. (For instructions on how to make your own, see page 286).   *Serves 4*

3½-lb whole roasting chicken
2 garlic cloves
½ smallish onion
2 tablespoons Chinese rice wine or dry sherry
2 tablespoons Chinese light soy sauce
2 tablespoons Chinese dark soy sauce
2 teaspoons sugar
1¼ teaspoons five-spice powder
2 tablespoons sesame oil
Soft lettuce leaves and fresh mint sprigs
Fish Sauce Seasoned with Lime Juice (see page 239)

Wash the chicken and pat it dry. Peel the garlic and onion and chop them finely. Combine the garlic, onion, wine, the two soy sauces, sugar and five-spice powder in a bowl. Stir until the sugar has dissolved. Put the chicken into the marinade and rub it generously inside and all over the outside. Pour any remaining marinade over the chicken and set aside for 2–3 hours. Turn the chicken around every 20 minutes so that it evenly absorbs the flavors and color of the marinade.

Preheat the oven to 425°F. Lift the chicken out of its marinade and place it, breast-side down, on a rack set in a roasting pan. Roast for 10 minutes. Brush the back with the marinade and turn the chicken over so that the breast is now facing upward. Brush the breast with the marinade and roast it for 15 minutes. Then brush the chicken with the marinade again, turn the heat down to 350°F, and continue to cook for 45 minutes, brushing with the marinade every 15 minutes or so. After this period, brush the chicken generously with the sesame oil and cook it for another 2–5 minutes or until the juices run clear when you pierce the flesh with a fork or skewer. Let the chicken rest for 10 minutes before carving.

Serve the roast chicken with lettuce leaves and mint sprigs as well as the Fish Sauce Seasoned with Lime Juice. Pour a little of the sauce over the chicken once it has been put on its serving plate. The leaves can either be nibbled or the lettuce can be used to make mint-and-chicken-filled parcels.

CHICKEN WITH A SWEET SAKE GLAZE

Japan

Adapted from a recipe of the École Technique Hôtelière Tsuj in Osaka

TORINIKU NO TERIYAKI

Under the guidance of Mr. Saito, I learned much at Professor Tsuji's cookery school in Osaka. To turn out simple dishes—like this *teriyaki*—trusted techniques are used with precision, and simple logical steps are followed methodically. For example, only chicken thighs are used in this receipe. Thigh meat is juicy and moist, much more so than breast meat. The thigh is boned, which allows the meat to be cooked evenly and quickly. It also allows the meat to be sliced after it is cooked so that it can be picked up easily with chopsticks. The chicken is marinated for an hour so that the flavors of the sauce can penetrate the meat. Even though chicken *teriyaki* is generally cooked on a grill, Mr. Saito favors another method. He browns the chicken first in a frying pan and then lets it cook very briefly in a moderately hot oven. The chicken is marvelous; it is moist, slightly sweet, slightly salty, crisp on the outside and meltingly tender inside. Once you have learned this method of preparing it, I am sure you will want to use this technique to cook chicken thighs with other seasonings of your choice.

The Japanese tend to eat small portions of meat. One thigh would be just enough for a single serving at a fine restaurant. It would sit alone on a plate in glorious splendor, garnished perhaps with a few bamboo shoots leaning against it, a few lime wedges and a few boiled pods of freshly plucked green soybeans. (You may substitute green beans—page 256—or carrots—page 255—as a garnish.) There should be Plain Japanese Rice (page 211) on the side. Keeping Western appetites in mind, I've allowed two thighs per person. You will need to cook them in a large frying pan, or in two batches. *Serves 4*

Sweet Glazing Sauce (see page 246)
8 chicken thighs, weighing 2 lb, boned (see page 55)
About 2 tablespoons vegetable oil

First make the Sweet Glazing Sauce. Put it in a bowl and let it cool.

Make sure that you do not pierce the skin when boning the chicken thighs. Put the boned and unskinned thighs in the bowl with the Sweet Glazing Sauce. Mix and set aside for 1 hour, turning the pieces over now and then so that they absorb the flavors and color evenly. Set a shelf in the top third of the oven. Preheat the oven to 400°F.

Fifteen minutes before you wish to eat, put the oil in a very large nonstick frying pan and set it over a medium-high heat. When it is hot, lift the chicken pieces out of their sauce. Put the sauce aside. Place the chicken pieces, in a single layer and skin-side down, in the frying pan. Cook for 5–6 minutes or until the skin is browned. Turn the chicken pieces over and cook them for another 30 seconds only. Lift the chicken pieces out with a slotted spoon and put them skin-side up in a single layer on a roasting rack set over a broiling tray. Bake in the oven on the prepared shelf for 8 minutes, basting the skin 3 times during this period with the Sweet Glazing Sauce.

Put the chicken pieces on a chopping board and cut each lengthwise into 3 segments. Reassemble each thigh into its original form and place 2 thighs in the center of each of 4 plates. Garnish as suggested above.

Thailand

CHICKEN WITH GARLIC AND BLACK PEPPER

KAI TOD KRATIUM PRIKTAI

At simple family meals this quick-cooking chicken is usually accompanied by plain rice and a soupy dish or a curry. I find that a green salad, with lots of fresh basil, mint and fresh coriander leaves thrown in, also goes very well with it. The chicken takes about 9 minutes to cook and is best made just before eating. The dipping sauce that accompanies it can be made several hours in advance.
Serves 2–4

4 chicken thighs, weighing about 1 lb, boned (see page 55)
1½–2 teaspoons coarsely ground black pepper
4 large garlic cloves
About ½ packed cup fresh coriander leaves
1½ tablespoons fish sauce
1 teaspoon sugar
¼ teaspoon ground red (cayenne) pepper (optional)
2 tablespoons vegetable oil
Sprigs of fresh herbs, such as mint, coriander and basil, to garnish (optional)
Fish Sauce Seasoned with Lime Juice and Chili (see page 238)

Make sure that you do not pierce the skin when boning the chicken thighs. Rub the chicken on both sides with the black pepper and set it aside.

Peel the garlic and crush it to a pulp. Finely chop the fresh coriander leaves. Combine the garlic, coriander leaves, fish sauce, sugar and ground red pepper and mix well. Rub this mixture over the chicken and let it marinate for 1 hour.

Put the oil in a nonstick frying pan and set it over a medium-high heat. When it is hot, put in the chicken pieces, skin-side down. Cook for about 5 minutes, or until the skin is brown and crisp. Turn the chicken over and reduce the heat to medium-low. Cook the second side for 3½–4 minutes, or until the chicken is just cooked through. Remove the pieces with a slotted spoon and place them on a chopping board, skin-side up. Cut each thigh with a sharp knife into 3 strips, reform it into the original shape and arrange on a serving plate. Garnish with fresh herbs, if desired, and serve with Fish Sauce Seasoned with Lime Juice and Chili.

HEARTY CHICKEN CURRY WITH POTATOES

Malaysia

From Puan Rashidah in Kuala Lumpur

LAUK AYAM

Malaysian curries are among the best in East Asia and Rashidah's, which are extra spicy and rich, are better than most. She prepared this for a casual lunch and served it with a local bread. It could be served with almost any bread, from crusty French or Italian loaves to *pita* breads and Indian *naans.* It may also be served with rice. This curry seems to get even better with time, so it can easily be made a day in advance and refrigerated. Use less than the recommended quantity of ground red pepper if you prefer a mild curry.   *Serves 6*

6–8 cardamom pods

6 whole cloves

2 whole star anise

2 2-inch sticks cinnamon

2 tablespoons whole fennel seeds

1½ tablespoons whole cumin seeds

4 tablespoons ground coriander seeds

1½–2 teaspoons ground red (cayenne) pepper or to taste

1 tablespoon paprika

4 1-inch cubes fresh ginger

3 large garlic cloves

4 medium onions

4 lb chicken pieces (preferably legs)

3–4 medium potatoes

¾ cup vegetable oil

1 tablespoon salt

1 cup coconut milk (see page 282)

Large handful fresh mint leaves

continued

Put the cardamom pods, cloves, star anise, cinnamon, fennel and cumin into the container of a food processor fitted with the metal blade. Grind as finely as possible. Empty into a bowl. Add the coriander, ground red pepper, paprika and 8 tablespoons water. Mix to a thick paste.

Peel the ginger, garlic and 3 of the onions. Chop them coarsely. Peel and finely slice the fourth onion; set this aside. Combine the chopped onions, ginger and garlic in an electric blender, together with about 4 tablespoons water. Blend until you have a smooth paste.

Skin the chicken and cut it into serving pieces. (A whole leg should be cut into thigh and drumstick; a breast should be quartered.) Peel the potatoes and cut them into 1-inch cubes.

Put the cut potatoes into a bowl of water.

Pour the oil in a large wide pan and set it over a medium-high heat. When the oil is hot, add the sliced onion. Stir and fry until the onion is golden brown. Put in the paste from the blender and the spice paste from the bowl. Stir and fry for 10–12 minutes or until the mixture is well fried and dark in color. Put in 3 cups water, the chicken, the drained potatoes and salt. Stir and bring to a simmer. Cover, lower the heat and simmer gently for 30 minutes or until the chicken is tender. Stir the coconut milk and pour it in. Stir and cook for another minute. Coarsely chop the mint leaves and stir them in. The oil floating on the top of the curry may be removed before serving.

Indonesia

STUFFED WHOLE CHICKEN IN A PARCEL

BETUTU AYAM

Many years ago a large banana-leaf package was unwrapped before me on the beach in Bali to reveal a whole cooked chicken, beautifully red and aromatic from all the spices still clinging to it. The chicken was heavenly. As fresh banana leaves are not always available in New York, I use the more prosaic aluminum foil. The chicken still tastes very good. If you cannot get any lemongrass use 1½ tablespoons grated lemon rind, adding it to the blender when mixing the ingredients.

Serves 4

Top: *Stuffed Whole Chicken in a Parcel (this page);* **bottom:** *Spicy Chicken Kebabs with a Peanut Sauce (page 127)*

continued

1 3 8   MADHUR JAFFREY'S FAR EASTERN COOKERY

1 stick fresh or 2 tablespoons dried sliced lemongrass or lemon rind (see above)

4 whole dried hot red chilies

4½ tablespoons lime or lemon juice

1 tablespoon plus 1 teaspoon dark brown sugar

2 teaspoons salt

½ teaspoon ground turmeric

¼ teaspoon ground red (cayenne) pepper

3½-lb whole roasting chicken

2 medium red bell peppers

6–7 medium shallots (or 1 medium onion)

1½-inch cube fresh ginger

8 garlic cloves

12 candlenuts or 24 cashew nuts

1½ teaspoons coarsely ground black pepper

5 tablespoons vegetable oil

If you are using fresh lemongrass, cut it crosswise into the thinnest possible slices, starting at the root end and going up about 6 inches. Discard the strawlike top. Crumble the dried red chilies into a small bowl. Add 5 tablespoons water, and set aside for 30 minutes. If you are using dried lemongrass, add it to the water along with the chilies.

Meanwhile, combine 3 tablespoons of the lime juice, 1 tablespoon sugar, 1 teaspoon of the salt, the turmeric and the ground red pepper in a small bowl, and mix.

Put the chicken, breast down, in a large bowl or deep dish. Cut 4 deep diagonal slits on the back, 2 on each side. Rub some of the lime juice mixture into the slits and all over the back. Turn the chicken over. Cut 2 diagonal slits on each side of the breast, 2 slits on the wings, 2 slits on each side of both thighs and 2 slits on each side of both drumsticks. Rub the remaining marinade over the rest of the chicken, working it deeply into all the slits. Set aside for 40 minutes–1 hour.

Coarsely chop the red bell peppers, discarding all the seeds. Peel and coarsely chop the shallots, ginger, and garlic. Coarsely chop the nuts. In an electric blender, combine the red bell pepper, shallots, ginger, garlic, nuts and the remaining 1½ tablespoons lime juice. Blend until smooth. Add the remaining teaspoon of salt, 1 teaspoon sugar and the black pepper as well as the fresh or soaked dried lemongrass and red chilies and their soaking liquid. Blend again.

Put the oil in a medium-sized non-stick frying pan and set it over a medium-high heat. When the oil is hot, put in the paste from the blender. Stir and fry for about 15 minutes or until the oil separates from the spices and the paste is a dark reddish brown.

Preheat the oven to 350°F.

Spread out a large piece of heavy-duty aluminum foil about 30 inches long and put the chicken, breast down, in the center. Rub about a quarter of the fried spice mixture onto the back of the chicken. Turn the bird over and rub another quarter of the spice mixture over the front. Stuff the remaining spice mixture inside the chicken. Now fold the foil over the bird, crimping the edges together at least 2 inches above the bottom of the parcel to prevent leakage of juices. Put the chicken parcel in a baking pan and bake in the oven for 1¾ hours.

Open the parcel carefully and pour out the collected liquid into a small pot. Spoon off the fat. Take all the stuffing out of the bird and add it to the pot of liquid. Stir to mix, heating it if necessary. Put the whole chicken in a dish, pour the hot sauce over it and serve.

SPICY CHICKEN STEW WITH CARROTS AND POTATOES

Korea

From Sang Kyung Lee

TAK TORI TANG

*T*his lightly spiced, hearty and warming stew gets its flavors from Hot Fermented Bean Paste (see page 240), an inspired mixture of fermented beans and red chilies, as well as from soy sauce and sesame seeds. It has a thinnish sauce and is best eaten with plain rice. I skin the chicken pieces before I stew them. The Koreans tend to leave the skin on. You may do whichever you prefer.
     Serves 4–6

3½ lb chicken pieces (preferably legs—
     thighs and drumsticks)

4 tablespoons Japanese soy sauce (shoyu)

2 tablespoons sugar

2½ tablespoons Hot Fermented Bean Paste
     or to taste

3–4 medium potatoes

4 carrots

4 scallions

½ medium red bell pepper

½ medium green bell pepper

Salt (optional)

1 tablespoon roasted sesame seeds
     (see page 299)

Freshly ground black pepper

Combine the chicken, soy sauce and sugar in a large wide pan. Put the Hot Fermented Bean Paste in a bowl and slowly add 2 cups water, mixing as you go. Add this combination to the chicken and bring it to a boil. Cover, turn the heat to medium-low and simmer for 10 minutes.

Meanwhile, peel the potatoes and cut them into 1½-inch cubes. Peel the carrots and cut them crosswise into 2-inch lengths. Cut the scallions into 2-inch lengths. Cut the red and green bell peppers into ½-inch squares, discarding the seeds.

When the chicken has simmered for 10 minutes, put in the potatoes, carrots and scallions. Stir gently and bring to a boil. Cover, turn the heat to medium-low and simmer for 15–20 minutes or until the chicken and potatoes are tender, stirring occasionally. Taste and add salt if you think it is needed. Put in the red and green bell peppers. Stir and cook for 1–2 minutes. Lift out all the solid ingredients with a slotted spoon and put them into a serving bowl. Boil the sauce for a short time in order to reduce it a little and then pour it over the chicken. Top with the roasted sesame seeds and some freshly ground black pepper.

Malaysia

*From the Hyatt
Saujana's Sri
Melaka
Restaurant in
Kuala Lumpur*

CHICKEN WITH BAMBOO SHOOTS AND MUSHROOMS IN BLACK BEAN SAUCE

AYAM PONGTAY

The food of the Straits Chinese—the Chinese who migrated to the Straits settlements of Penang, Malacca and Singapore and who married local Malay women—has become very popular of late in this region of Southeast Asia. Known as the cooking of the Nonyas (the Straits Chinese women), it can now be found in elegant trendy restaurants such as the Sri Melaka in Kuala Lumpur.

Ayam pongtay is a Nonya classic. Do not be fooled by its simple ingredients. Subtle, gentle, full of rich flavor and absolutely addictive, it is, to my mind, one of Southeast Asia's finest dishes.

Ingredients are, of course, important. You need chunky tender bamboo shoots, which are available in cans. Soft, rounded, cone-shaped "tips," usually about 1½–2 inches long, are ideal, if you can find them. The best mushrooms to use for this recipe are dried Chinese mushrooms. In a pinch you could use fresh button mushroom caps which do not, of course, need to be soaked. Sauté them lightly in oil and put them into the pan 10 minutes before the end of cooking time. Instead of using the mushroom-soaking liquid for the cooking use 2½ cups water or light chicken stock. As a substitute for black bean sauce you can use 2½ tablespoons canned or dried salted black beans, washed and mashed with 1 tablespoon oyster sauce. *Serves 4*

10–12 large dried Chinese mushrooms (the thicker the caps, the better the quality)

8–10 shallots (or 1 large onion)

6 garlic cloves

3 tablespoons black bean sauce

2 lb chicken pieces (preferably legs)

3 tablespoons vegetable oil

10–12 chunky pieces good-quality canned bamboo shoots

1½ teaspoons dark soy sauce

1½ teaspoons molasses

Quickly rinse the dried mushrooms in cold water and then soak them in 2½ cups hot water for 30 minutes or until the caps are soft. Lift the mushrooms out and save the soaking liquid. Cut off the hard stems and discard them. Strain the soaking liquid through a clean cloth.

Peel the shallots and garlic and chop them coarsely. Put them into an electric blender along with 3 tablespoons water and the black bean sauce. Blend thoroughly.

Peel off the chicken skin and cut the whole legs into 4 pieces: divide them into thighs and drumsticks and then divide each thigh and drumstick in half using a cleaver or heavy knife to cut through the bone. Alternatively, ask your butcher to do this for you. If you are using chicken breasts, cut each in quarters.

Put the oil in a wide, heavy frying pan and set it over a medium-high heat. When the oil is hot, put in the paste from the blender. Stir and fry for 2–3 minutes or until it has reduced a little and has a slightly fried look. Put in the chicken, bamboo shoots, mushroom caps and strained mushroom-soaking liquid. Stir and bring to the boil. Cover and cook over medium heat for 15 minutes. Remove the lid, turn the heat to high and cook for another 6 minutes or until the sauce is reduced and thick. Then combine the soy sauce and molasses and add the mixture to the pan. Stir well and serve.

Hong Kong
From Mrs. Fung

COLD CHICKEN WITH SESAME AND CHILI SAUCE

MALAJI

Known also as Bon Bon Chicken (from the sound of the pounding once required to shred the chicken) and Strange Taste Chicken (it has the highly aromatic Szechuan peppercorns in it), this spicy dish from the Szechuan province of China is just superb. It is generally served as a first course, though you could have it for lunch with a simple salad.

It is the Szechuan peppercorns that give the dish its special flavor. Even though you could, in a pinch, substitute black peppercorns, here is a spice that you should get to know. Pick up some Szechuan peppercorns when you are next in a Chinese grocery or else send for them by mail order. You will find yourself using them in salads, over eggs, over oily fish (such as mackerel) and in hearty meat stews.

In Hong Kong a whole chicken is steamed, plunged into cold water and then shredded. I simply poach boned and skinned chicken breasts in order to make the preparation of this dish very easy. The sesame paste is sold by Asian, Chinese and Greek grocers, as well as by health food shops. (It is sometimes labeled as *tahini*.) Please note that the stalks of fresh coriander are used in this recipe as well as its leaves. This dish is usually served at room temperature, not icy cold.

Serves 4–6

continued

FOR THE SAUCE

1-inch cube fresh ginger

1 garlic clove

2 tablespoons sesame paste (tahini)

1 tablespoon sesame oil

1 teaspoon sugar

2½ teaspoons Chili Oil (see page 237)

4 teaspoons Chinese light soy sauce

½ teaspoon roasted and ground Szechuan peppercorns (see page 302) or coarsely ground black peppercorns

YOU ALSO NEED

14 oz chicken breasts, boned and skinned

Salt

1 scallion

⅛-inch slice fresh ginger

1 stick celery

1½ oz fresh coriander (stalks and leaves)

First make the sauce. Peel the cube of ginger and grate it finely. Peel the garlic and crush it to a pulp. Combine the ginger, garlic, sesame paste, sesame oil, sugar, chili oil, soy sauce and roasted and ground Szechuan (or black) peppercorns. Mix well.

Cut the chicken breasts lengthwise into ½-inch-wide strips. Put the strips into a medium-sized frying pan. Pour in just enough water to cover by ¼ inch. Add a generous pinch of salt and put in the scallion and the slice of ginger. Bring to a boil, then turn the heat to low immediately and simmer very gently, turning the pieces over, until the meat becomes white all the way through—this happens very quickly, so keep watching it. Remove the chicken with a slotted spoon and rinse it under cold running water. (Save the poaching liquid.) Using both hands, pull the chicken into long shreds; they do not have to be very fine.

Cut the celery into very fine dice. Cut the coriander stalks crosswise into very fine pieces. Coarsely chop the coriander leaves, cover with plastic wrap and set aside. Add 3 tablespoons of the poaching liquid to the sesame sauce. Stir to mix.

To serve, combine the chicken, celery, diced coriander stalks and sesame sauce and mix well. Put the mixture in a serving dish and sprinkle the chopped coriander leaves over the top.

RED CHICKEN CURRY

KAENG PET KAI

The people of this world can probably be divided into those who like chicken legs and those who like chicken breasts. For curries I prefer dark meat as it remains more moist; that is what I have used in this recipe. The meat needs to be boned and skinned. My butcher very kindly does this for me but you could do it yourself at home. Just follow the simple directions given on page 55. If you wish to use boned and skinned breast meat, buy 1¼ lb, dice it and poach it in the coconut milk on *low* heat for just 5 minutes. This way it will remain soft and tender.

This dish is absolutely the best of Thai curries. You may use the recipe to cook chunks of fish or shrimps as well as chicken—simply adjust the cooking time so that the fish does not fall apart or turn rubbery.

Most Thai curries are made with a basic paste of ground spices. Canned and bottled Thai curry pastes are sold by many Asian grocers, but their quality varies. If you wish to try them, look for red curry paste, but it is best to make your own (see the recipe on page 244).   *Serves 4*

1¾ cups coconut milk (see page 282)

4 medium whole chicken legs (thighs and drumsticks), boned

½ teaspoon salt

4 tablespoons vegetable oil

4 tablespoons Red Curry Paste

1–1½ tablespoons fish sauce or salt to taste

1 teaspoon dark brown sugar

4 fresh or dried kaffir lime leaves or 2 teaspoons finely julienned lemon rind

15–20 fresh sweet basil leaves (bai horapha) or ordinary basil or mint leaves

If you are using fresh coconut milk, let it stand until the cream rises to the top. Whether using fresh or canned milk, skim off 4 tablespoons of the thick cream and set it aside. Stir the rest of the milk to mix.

Skin the boned chicken legs and cut the flesh into 1-inch cubes.

Put the thin coconut milk (not the cream) into a medium-sized frying pan. Add the salt and mix. Now put in the chicken pieces and bring the milk to a boil. Stir and cook on medium-high heat for about 20 minutes or until the chicken is just done. Remove from the heat and set aside.

Put the oil and the reserved coconut cream in a heavy wok or wide heavy pan. Bring it to a boil. Put in the curry paste and stir and fry on a medium-high heat until the oil separates and the paste is lightly browned. Lower the heat and add the fish sauce and sugar. Stir to mix. Now put in the chicken and the coconut milk it was simmered in. Bring to the boil. Simmer on a low heat for a minute. (All this can be done several hours ahead of time.)

continued

To serve, proceed as follow. If you are using fresh kaffir lime leaves, remove the center vein and cut the leaves crosswise into very fine, hair-thin strips. If you are using dried leaves, you will need to soak them in a little water for 30 minutes first. Break the basil (or mint) leaves off their stems and discard the stems. Put the hot curry into a serving dish. Scatter the basil (or mint) leaves over the chicken and then, with the back of the spoon, submerge them slightly in the sauce. Scatter the kaffir lime leaves (or julienned lemon rind) over the top.

Hong Kong
From the Shanghai Club

FRIED CHICKEN WITH SCALLION SAUCE

YOUPI ZIJI

Some of the best Shanghai-style food can be found today at the Shanghai Club in Hong Kong. Here is one of its recipes. A whole chicken is opened up at the breast bone, marinated with (among other things) Szechuan peppercorns, and then deep-fried, beak, feet and all. The crisply fried bird is then cut up, reassembled to look like itself, head chirpily upright, and doused with an unusual sauce, chock-full of fresh herbs and seasonings. The dish is uncommonly good.

I have simplified it somewhat here. I am assuming that you, like me, have difficulty in obtaining a chicken with head and feet and that, if you did, your heart might yearn for the safer look you know and understand! I have used chicken pieces as they are easier to fry in hot oil. If you prefer, you can broil them and then smother them with the sauce.

If you can find Chinese celery at a Chinese grocer's, do buy it. Only the stems are used here. If you cannot obtain it, ordinary celery, especially its upper portion with the generally unused thin stems, makes a good substitute. This recipe requires many stalks and stems of herbs, items that might normally be thrown away. *Serves 4*

FOR THE MARINADE

1-inch cube fresh ginger

1 scallion

3 lb chicken pieces (preferably legs—thighs and drumsticks)

2 teaspoons roasted and ground Szechuan peppercorns (see page 302)

2 tablespoons Chinese light soy sauce

½ teaspoon sugar

FOR THE SAUCE

3 garlic cloves

2 scallions

Few stalks Chinese celery or 1 stalk ordinary celery

Few stems fresh coriander or parsley

1-inch cube fresh ginger

2 tablespoons Chinese light soy sauce

2 teaspoons distilled white vinegar

4 tablespoons chicken stock

1 tablespoon tomato ketchup

½ teaspoon sugar

2 tablespoons sesame oil

YOU ALSO NEED

About 3 tablespoons cornstarch

Oil for deep-frying

First prepare the marinade. Peel the ginger and grate it as finely as possible. Cut the scallion crosswise into very fine rounds. Divide the whole chicken legs into thighs and drumsticks. If you are using chicken breasts, cut each breast in quarters. Put the chicken in a bowl. Prick the areas without skin with the point of a sharp knife. Sprinkle the ground roasted Szechuan peppercorns, ginger, scallion, soy sauce and sugar over the chicken. Rub this marinade in as well as you can with your hands. Cover and set aside for 2–4 hours, refrigerating if necessary.

Meanwhile, combine the ingredients for the sauce in 2 separate bowls. Peel the garlic and chop it as finely as possible. Cut the scallions crosswise into the finest possible rounds. If you are using Chinese celery, cut its stems into very fine rounds. If using ordinary celery, cut it into minute dice (you need about 3 tablespoons). Hold several stems of coriander together and cut crosswise into minute pieces (you need about 1 tablespoon). Peel the ginger and cut it into paper-thin slices. Stacking a few slices at a time together, cut the slices first into thin slivers and then into minute dice. Combine the garlic, scallions, celery, coriander and ginger in a small bowl. Cover and set aside.

In another bowl combine the soy sauce, vinegar, stock, ketchup, sugar and sesame oil. Stir well to mix and set aside.

Lay out the chicken pieces in a single layer and dust both sides with the cornstarch. Pat the cornstarch in and set the chicken aside for 20 minutes.

Put the oil for deep-frying in a large wok or in a deep-fat fryer over a medium heat. When it is hot, put in the chicken pieces and fry them. If you are using a wok, turn them when necessary. Cook for about 15–20 minutes or until the chicken pieces are nicely browned on the outside and cooked all the way through. Drain them on paper toweling and put them in a serving dish. Mix together the 2 bowls of sauce ingredients and pour over the chicken. Serve at once.

DUCK BRAISED IN WINE

TEO CHEW-STYLE DUCK

Duck is good cooked in most ways but I find that braising—a much under-used technique for cooking this bird—brings out its flavors best. All of it remains moist; even the bones become eminently suckable. You may make this dish ahead of time and then reheat it. In fact I prefer to do this as it is much easier to degrease the sauce once it has been chilled. The duck is normally cooked whole in Malaysia. I quarter it only to make it easier to handle; you could ask the butcher to do this.

Served with stir-fried greens, such as spinach, and an elegant rice dish, this duck becomes decidedly festive.   *Serves 4*

4-lb duck, quartered

¼ teaspoon five-spice powder (optional; see page 286)

2 tablespoons vegetable oil

3 garlic cloves

6 scallions

2 cups Chinese rice wine or dry sherry

4 tablespoons Chinese dark soy sauce

1 tablespoon Chinese light soy sauce

3½ tablespoons sugar

3-inch cinnamon stick

½ teaspoon Szechuan or black peppercorns

3 whole star anise

8–10 slices fresh or dried galangal or fresh ginger

Examine your duck. If parts of it near the neck or tail seem like nothing but skin or fat, cut them off. Wash the duck and pat it dry as best you can. Dust the five-spice powder over it on both sides.

Put the oil in a large frying pan and set it over a high heat. When the oil is hot, put in as many duck pieces as it will hold easily, skin-side down. (The aim here is to sear the skin.) Turn the pieces around so all the skin gets browned. Remove the browned pieces of duck with a slotted spoon. Brown all the duck pieces in this way.

Peel the garlic cloves and mash them lightly.

Lay the scallions over the bottom of a wide pan large enough to hold the duck easily, preferably in one layer. Now put the duck pieces on top of the scallions, skin-side down. Pour the wine and 2½ cups water over the duck. Add the garlic and all the remaining ingredients, and bring to a simmer. Cover and simmer gently for 45 minutes. Turn the duck pieces over and simmer, covered, for another 45 minutes. Remove the cover and turn the heat up to medium. Turn the duck pieces over again and continue to cook for 6–7 minutes. Turn the duck pieces over a third time and cook for another 6–7 minutes. Remove them carefully and put them on a plate to cool.

Strain the duck broth. (You should have about 2½ cups.) Remove the grease from the top if you wish to eat immediately. If you plan to eat the duck the next day, cover the duck pieces well after they have cooled and refrigerate them. Cool the broth and put it in a covered container. Refrigerate that as well.

To serve, degrease the duck broth and put into a large pan. Add the duck pieces, cover the pan and heat through. Lift the duck pieces out and arrange them on a plate. Pour just a little of the broth over the duck. The rest of the broth can be handed around separately in a sauce boat.

SAVORY EGG CUSTARD WITH SHRIMPS AND MUSHROOMS

Korea

With help from Mrs. Han Chung Kyu

KERAN CHIM

Savory egg custards, quivering, soft and soothing, are eaten in China, Japan and Korea. In Japan, where they are called *chawanmushi*, they are steamed in individual cups (sold in most Japanese food shops) and served as a soup course. In Korea, where most dishes at a meal (except rice) are communal, egg custard is eaten from a large bowl in the center of the table. In the West, individual servings are easiest. Old-fashioned egg coddlers are ideal for cooking single portions.

To steam *keran chim* properly, always place the custard dish on a rack or trivet. Use plain water if a very gentle flavor is desired and serve highly seasoned pickles as a balance. I prefer the heartier flavor of Chicken Stock (see page 77) or clam broth. The water should simmer gently to prevent bubbles from forming in the custard. Do not overcook it or the custard might separate. The custard should be cooked just before it is eaten. All the ingredients can, however, be prepared ahead of time but *not* mixed. The cooking time is 13–25 minutes, depending on the size of the dish you use. The Koreans use about 4–5 fresh oyster mushrooms, but as they are hard to come by, I have used ordinary mushrooms.   *Serves 4–5*

1 garlic clove
3 scallions
6–8 medium mushrooms
¼ lb medium shrimps
5 large eggs
2½ cups chicken stock, homemade or
   canned, or water

1 tablespoon sesame oil
¾ teaspoon salt (omit if stock is salted)
4 teaspoons Japanese soy sauce (shoyu)
1 tablespoon roasted sesame seeds
   (see page 299)

continued

Peel the garlic and crush it to a pulp. Cut the scallions into very fine rounds along their entire length, including the green section. Slice the mushrooms finely. Peel and devein the shrimps, wash them and pat them dry. Cut the shrimps crosswise into ½-inch sections. Beat the eggs lightly in a bowl. Add the chicken stock (or water), the sesame oil, salt and soy sauce. Mix and then strain to make sure that the egg whites and yolks are thoroughly blended.

Set some water to heat in a wok, large saucepan or steamer wide enough to hold a custard bowl or individual egg coddlers easily. (Remember that the bowl in which you cook will also be your serving bowl). Bring the water to a simmer. Set a rack or trivet on the bottom of your steamer.

Stir the egg mixture again and add to it the garlic, scallions, mushrooms and shrimps. Pour the mixture into the custard bowl or spoon evenly into the coddlers. Sprinkle sesame seeds over the top and cover. (You could cover the bowl with a plate or the individual coddlers, if using, with foil.) Stand the bowl or coddlers on the rack. The simmering water should come three quarters of the way up the sides of the bowl or coddlers, so add more if necessary. Cover the steaming pan and simmer gently for 13–25 minutes. Check whether the custard is set by inserting a knife into it. The knife should come out clean. If it does not, cook for another minute or so. Remove carefully from the water and serve.

Malaysia

EGG CURRY

GULAI TELOR

*H*ere is one of my favorite egg curries. It is hot and spicy, and quite typical of Malaysian food. Served with plain rice and a salad, it is perfect for a Sunday lunch. I have even been known to serve it with crusty bread or with thick toast. In Malaysia the spices are pounded very finely on stone. Since I can never quite manage to get the same effect in a blender, I strain the coarse particles out of the curry sauce before putting the eggs into it.

A note about the hotness of this dish: in Malaysia, it is prepared with 20–30 dried red chilies. It *is* hot *and* good. I tone it down by using 10–15 chilies and I would describe my dish as fairly hot. You may use as few as 2 chilies, if you want it very mild. The fresh red and green chilies added at the end are more of a garnish than anything else. They give the dish a Malaysian look. If fresh red chilies are unavailable, simply use twice as many green ones. You may use slivers cut from fresh red and green bell peppers, if you prefer. If you cannot get lemongrass, use 1 tablespoon grated lemon rind, adding it to the curry at the same time as the tomato. This curry may be made a day in advance and reheated.   *Serves 6–8*

Bottom: *Egg Curry (this page);* **top:** *Savory Egg Custard with Shrimps and Mushrooms (page 149)*

continued

2–15 whole dried hot red chilies

½ teaspoon whole black peppercorns

2 tablespoons whole coriander seeds

1 stick fresh or 3 tablespoons dried sliced lemongrass or lemon rind (see above)

1½-inch cube fresh or 8 large slices dried galangal (optional)

1½-inch cube fresh ginger

¾ teaspoon ground turmeric

18 eggs

8 medium shallots (or 1 large onion)

5 garlic cloves

9 tablespoons vegetable oil

1 quart coconut milk (see page 282)

3 tablespoons tamarind paste (see page 303) or 2 tablespoons lime juice

2½ teaspoons salt

1 teaspoon sugar

2 medium or 4 plum tomatoes

4 fresh hot green chilies

4 fresh hot red chilies

Few sprigs fresh mint

Crumble the dried red chilies and put them in a bowl. Add the peppercorns, coriander seeds, dried lemongrass (if you are using it) and dried galangal (if you are using it). Add about 1½ cups hot water and leave to soak for at least 1 hour.

If you are using fresh lemongrass, slice it crosswise very finely, starting at the root end and going up about 6 inches. Discard the strawlike top. If you are using fresh galangal, peel it and chop it coarsely. Peel the ginger and chop it coarsely.

Combine all the soaked seasonings, their soaking liquid, the fresh lemon grass and fresh galangal (if you are using them), the ginger and the tur-

meric in an electric blender. Blend thoroughly, adding another few tablespoons of water if needed to make a pastelike consistency, and stopping the machine to stir with a spatula if required.

Put all the eggs in a large pan. Cover well with water and bring to the boil. Turn the heat to very low and simmer until the eggs are hard-boiled (about 12 minutes). Shell them under cold running water.

Peel the shallots and slice them finely. Peel the garlic and slice it finely.

Put the oil in a large, wide, preferably nonstick pan and set it over a medium-high heat. When the oil is hot, put in the shallots and garlic. Stir and fry until they are golden. Pour in the paste from the blender. Stir and fry for about 10 minutes or until the oil separates from it and the paste turns dark. Stir the coconut milk and pour it in. Add the tamarind paste (or lime juice), salt and sugar. Mix well and taste; adjust the seasoning if necessary. Bring to a simmer, stirring as you go. As soon as the sauce begins to bubble, turn off the heat. Strain it through a sieve, pushing out as much liquid as possible. Put the sauce back in the pan and add the hard-boiled eggs. (This much of the dish can be prepared a day ahead of time and refrigerated.)

If the tomatoes are small, cut them into wedges; if they are large, cut them into 1-inch dice. Wash the fresh chilies and mint sprigs. Remove the coarse stems from the mint sprigs. Just before serving, bring the egg curry to a simmer. Put in the tomatoes and stir a few times. Let the sauce come to a simmer again. Empty the curry into a serving bowl. Garnish with the fresh chilies and the mint sprigs.

Fish and Seafood

WHOLE BROILED FISH, SOUR AND SPICY

IKAN PANGGANG

*I*t was a warm day. A fire of coconut shells had been lit under a spreading star fruit tree to grill the fish. I was in the seafront town of Padang in Western Sumatra but the fish we were to eat was *gurami,* a freshwater creature. It had already been bathed in two marinades—one of lime juice and salt and the other of coconut milk and hot spices. Then it was put between the twin racks of a hinged grilling contraption and cooked slowly about 6 inches above the fire with frequent and lavish bastings of the marinade. The basting brush was unusual: it consisted of a stick of lemongrass whose bulbous end had been lightly mashed, so that it basted the fish and flavored it at the same time.

This fish may be either grilled outdoors over charcoal or broiled indoors. If you are broiling indoors, it is important to keep the fish far enough from the heat so that it cooks without charring on the outside. Alternatively, you could brown the fish on both sides and then put it into the oven at 350°F for 10–15 minutes or until it has cooked through.

Whether cooking outdoors or indoors, it helps to have a hinged double-racked "holder," which makes turning the fish much easier. Mine is rectangular and can hold two medium-sized fish. Such gadgets are available from kitchen supply shops, but if you cannot obtain one, just oil your grill rack well and place the fish directly on it.

The quantities in this recipe may easily be doubled.   *Serves 2–3*

1¼-lb whole fish (such as red snapper,
    small salmon, trout, salmon trout,
    bass, sole or porgy), scaled and cleaned
¾ teaspoon salt
3 tablespoons lime or lemon juice
½-inch cube fresh or 3 slices dried
    galangal
1 stick fresh or 1 tablespoon dried sliced
    lemongrass
2–3 whole dried hot red chilies

4–5 medium shallots (or 1 small onion)
½ large red bell pepper
½-inch cube fresh ginger
3 garlic cloves
¼ teaspoon ground turmeric
1 cup coconut milk (see page 282)
2 tablespoons vegetable oil (approximately)
Lime wedges to serve

Cut 3 or 4 deep slightly diagonal slits across both sides of the fish. Rub ½ teaspoon of the salt and 1 tablespoon of the lime juice over the entire fish, working the mixture well into the slits and the stomach cavity. Set aside for 20–30 minutes.

Meanwhile, if you are using dried galangal and dried lemongrass, put these into a cup with 4 tablespoons water. Crumble the dried red chilies into the water as well. Set aside for 20–30 minutes. If you are using fresh galangal, peel and coarsely chop it. If you are using fresh lemongrass, cut off about ¼ inch of its bottom tip and then lightly crush about 1 inch of the bulbous bottom to open it up like a brush.

Peel the shallots and chop them coarsely. Coarsely dice the red bell pepper, discarding all the seeds. Peel the ginger and garlic and chop them coarsely.

Put the soaked spices and their soaking liquid, the shallots, red bell pepper, ginger, garlic, turmeric and the remaining 2 tablespoons lime juice and ¼ teaspoon salt into an electric blender. If you are using fresh galangal add it too. Blend until smooth.

Preheat an outdoor charcoal grill or an oven broiler. Put the spice paste into a wide shallow dish large enough to hold the fish. Stir the coconut milk, add it to the paste and stir to mix. Put the fish into the dish. Spoon some marinade over it, making sure that it penetrates all the slits and cavities. Set aside for 10 minutes, turning the fish over a few times during this period.

Brush the grill rack lightly with oil to help prevent the fish from sticking. Remove the fish from the marinade and place it on the rack about 5–6 inches from the heat source. Baste the fish frequently and generously with the marinade using the lemongrass brush, if you have it. Turn the fish every 5 minutes or so if you can. Cook for about 20–30 minutes or until the fish has cooked through. It should be nicely browned on the outside but still soft and tender inside. Do not baste during the last 5 minutes so that the spices can form a nice crust. Serve with lime wedges.

MONKFISH WITH DILL

CHA^z CÁ

There is a street in Hanoi, Cha² Cá Street, that is named after this famous dish. Here fresh, firm river rish is marinated with turmeric and tamarind, grilled over charcoal or wood and then brought to the table. The diners take over and cook it briefly again, tossing it with a mound of fresh dill and scallions.

At the suggestion of Vietnamese living in the West, I have used monkfish as a substitute for the fish used in Vietnam though I find that tilefish works equally well. This dish is traditionally eaten with thin fresh rice noodles, which we in the West can find only at some Chinese and Far Eastern grocers'. (Look for rice vermicelli noodles.) Ground fried galangal is also needed for this recipe. Since I have not suggested that you use this form of galangal for any other dish in this book, I suggest that you take just a little of the dried sliced galangal and whir it to a powder in a clean coffee grinder or food processor. Of course, if you *can* get ground galangal (sometimes called Laos powder), do use it.

The way to eat this is as follows: you prepare one mouthful at a time by first putting a few noodles in your bowl. On top of the noodles goes the dilled fish, which you may or may not dip first in the anchovy-lime sauce or the Fish Sauce with Vinegar and Lime Juice. On top of this you put some fresh mint or coriander, the white part of scallions and some peanuts. You may spoon some more of any sauce you like on top of all this. You could also squeeze some lime juice over it. You then pick up this combination with chopsticks and eat.   *Serves 4*

1¼ lb monkfish or tilefish fillet
½ teaspoon ground turmeric
1 teaspoon anchovy paste
3½ tablespoons lime juice
½ teaspoon vinegar
½ teaspoon ground galangal
  (Laos powder)
1 tablespoon tamarind paste (see page 303)
  or ½ tablespoon lime juice mixed with
  ¼ teaspoon sugar
2 oz fresh dill
8–10 scallions

Several sprigs fresh mint
Several sprigs fresh coriander
10–12 canned anchovy fillets
8 oz dried fine rice noodles (rice vermicelli)
1 tablespoon lard or vegetable oil
Few tablespoons fish sauce
Fish Sauce with Vinegar and Lime Juice
  (see page 238)
Roasted Peanuts (see page 247)
Lime wedges
About 2 tablespoons vegetable oil

Wash the fish and pat it dry. Cut it into 1-inch chunks. In a wide shallow dish mix together the turmeric, anchovy paste, 2 tablespoons of the lime juice, the vinegar, galangal and tamarind paste (or lime juice and sugar). Put in the fish and rub the mixture over it. Cover the dish and refrigerate for 2–3 hours.

Wash the dill and pat it dry. Trim away all the coarse stalks. You should have only very fine sprigs left. Put these on one side of a large plate. Separate the green and white sections of the scallions. Cut the green sections into 2-inch lengths and put these beside the dill. Cut the white part of the scallions into very fine rings and put these into a small bowl. Wash and pat dry the sprigs of mint and coriander. Put each herb into a separate bowl.

Next make the anchovy-lime sauce. Wipe the oil off the anchovies and put them in a blender along with the remaining 1½ tablespoons lime juice. Blend until smooth, and then put the mixture in a small bowl.

Soak the noodles for 2 hours in cold water. Drain them and then drop them into boiling water for a minute or less, until they are just tender. Rinse under cold running water. Drain them again and put them into a serving bowl.

If you wish to cook at the table, put an electric frying pan in the center. Put the lard in a small bowl and place this next to it. Put the fish sauce in another small bowl also next to the frying pan. Near the lard put the plate of dill and scallion greens. Arrange the bowls of mint, coriander, scallion whites and anchovy-lime sauce on the table. Set out the cold noodles, the Fish Sauce with Vinegar and Lime Juice, the Roasted Peanuts and lime wedges as well.

Preheat an oven broiler or an outdoor grill. When it is hot, brush the fish lightly with the vegetable oil and broil or grill it about 5 inches from the heat source for 4–5 minutes on the first side and about 3 minutes on the opposite side. Now bring the fish to the table if you aim to continue the cooking there, or complete the cooking in the kitchen. Heat the lard or oil in the frying pan. When it is hot, put in the fish. Stir it once and then pile in all the dill and scallion greens. Moisten with a tablespoon or so of fish sauce and stir. The fish is now ready to be eaten with the various herbs, sauces and seasonings as described above.

Fish Fillets with Black Bean Sauce

DOUSHI YI

Here is southern Chinese food in its simplest and most divine form. I love salted black beans whenever they make an appearance, but have always had trouble stir-frying delicate fish fillets as they have such a frightening tendency to crumble. I now have to worry no more: having learned the trick from Chinese masters, I realize how easy the technique really is.

When the fish is put in a marinade of egg white and cornstarch, there has to be sufficent cornstarch to hold the fish together when it is cooked. The fish also has to be allowed to sit in this marinade for at least 2 hours. I frequently leave it to marinate in the morning and cook it in the evening. The fish also needs to be precooked, very briefly, in water. This has to be done tenderly, just before it is put in its sauce. For those who like fish, I cannot recommend a better way to prepare it. It is light, delicate and full of flavor.   *Serves 3–4*

FOR THE MARINADE

14–15 oz flat white fish fillets (such as flounder or sole)
¼ teaspoon salt
1 tablespoon Chinese rice wine or dry sherry
Freshly ground black pepper
1 egg white
4 teaspoons cornstarch
2 teaspoons sesame oil

FOR THE SAUCE

1 teaspoon cornstarch
½ cup Chicken Stock, homemade (see page 77) or canned
2 teaspoons Chinese rice wine or dry sherry
¼ teaspoon salt
2 tablespoons sesame oil
Freshly ground black pepper
1 whole dried hot red chili

YOU ALSO NEED

1½ tablespoons salted black beans
2 garlic cloves
1-inch cube fresh ginger
2 scallions
3 tablespoons vegetable oil

Cut each fish fillet in half lengthwise. Then cut it crosswise into 2-inch-wide strips. Next marinate the fish. Put it in a wide bowl and add the salt, rice wine and black pepper. Stir gently to mix. Beat the egg white lightly (not to a froth) and add that as well as the 4 teaspoons cornstarch and 2 teaspoons sesame oil. Mix. Cover with plastic wrap and refrigerate for 2 hours or longer.

Now make the sauce. Put the 1 teaspoon cornstarch in a cup. Slowly add the stock, mixing as you go. Add the rice wine, salt, sesame oil and black pepper. Crumble in the dried red chili. Set aside.

Rinse the black beans and chop them coarsely. Peel the garlic and ginger and chop them finely. Cut the scallions crosswise into very fine rounds along their entire length, including the green section.

Just before eating, put about ¾ inch water into a large, preferably nonstick frying pan and bring it to a boil. Turn the heat down to a bare simmer. Put the fish into the water, separating the pieces very gently and spreading them around in the pan. Even before the water comes to a simmer again, the fish pieces will turn nearly white. Remove them gently with a slotted spoon and put them on a plate.

Discard the water in the frying pan and wipe the pan dry. Put 2 tablespoons of the vegetable oil in the frying pan and set it over a medium-high heat. When the oil is hot, put in the garlic, ginger and black beans. Stir once or twice or until the garlic turns golden. Take the pan off the heat, stir the sauce and pour it in. Put the pan back on a medium-low heat and stir gently until the sauce thickens. Put the fish gently back in and spread it out in the pan. Spoon the sauce over the fish, turning over the pieces carefully just once. Slide the contents of the pan onto a warm serving plate. Scatter the scallions over the top. Quickly put the remaining tablespoon of oil into a small pan and heat it. Pour the hot oil over the onions to wilt them slightly and to make the fish glisten. Serve immediately.

FISH STEAMED WITH LEMONGRASS

TOM SOM PLA

I am sure you must have eaten Cantonese-style steamed fish. Cooked with a fine julienne of ginger and sliced scallions, it is light, succulent and delicious. The Thais, influenced by the Chinese, keep to the same basic concept but add some of their own aromatic seasonings—galangal, kaffir lime leaves, fresh coriander leaves and lemongrass. Fish sauce replaces soy sauce and fresh green chilies are added if a little heat is required. No oil is called for, so this dish is perfect for dieters. If you cannot get lemongrass use 1 tablespoon finely grated lemon rind, scattering it over the fish at the same time as the lemongrass, just before steaming.

Almost any whole fish can be used, such as red snapper, sole, flounder, trout or even small salmon. What *is* important is that it be very fresh. It should be gutted and its scales, gills and fins removed. In the Far East the head is always left on a steamed whole fish (the cheeks are a great delicacy), but if you cannot bear to look at it you could ask your fishmonger to remove it. The fish should be of a size that can fit into your wok or steaming pan. The fish is laid out on a large serving plate (to catch the precious juices) and the plate is then balanced on a rack over boiling water, the level of which should be ¾ inch below the plate. The pan or wok is then covered and the fish steams, lying happily on its plate, until it is done. Any desire to lift the lid and peep inside is best resisted as precious aromas can vanish with the steam. (For suggestions on steaming equipment, see page 59.) If you do not wish to cook a whole fish, you may cook fillets or steaks by the same method.

How long do you steam the fish? This depends largely on its thickness. Steaks or fillets about ½ inch thick can be done in 7–10 minutes; those which are ¾–1 inch thick may take 10–13 minutes. A whole flat fish, such as sole, weighing 1½ lb should take about 15 minutes while a 1½-lb bass should be allowed 20 minutes because of its thickness. You may, of course, peep at the fish toward the very end of the cooking. Look quickly, deep down into one of the cut slits, if the fish is whole. If it is white all the way through, it is ready. For a fillet or steak, poke the flesh gently with the point of a sharp knife. If it is white all the way through, it is done. *Serves 2–4*

¾-inch cube fresh or 6 large slices dried
   galangal
1 stick fresh or 1 tablespoon dried sliced
   lemongrass or lemon rind (see above)
1-inch cube fresh ginger
1 fresh hot green chili (optional)
3 medium shallots (or ½ small onion)
½ cup fresh coriander leaves
1½-lb whole fish, cleaned and scaled, or
   1 lb fish fillets or steaks (such as sole,
   haddock, cod, salmon or halibut)
4 teaspoons fish sauce or salt to taste
4–5 fresh or dried kaffir lime leaves
1 fresh hot red chili or equivalent-sized
   piece red bell pepper

If you are using fresh galangal, peel it and cut it into fine slivers. If you are using dried galangal, soak the slices in 4 tablespoons hot water in a cup for 30 minutes. If you are using fresh lemongrass, cut off and discard the strawlike top, leaving about 6 inches of the bottom. Hit the bulbous bottom with a hammer or other heavy object in order to crush it lightly. If you are using dried lemongrass instead, add it to the dried galangal in the cup or soak it separately in enough water to cover. Peel the ginger and cut it into very fine slivers. Cut the green chili into very fine rounds. Peel the shallots and cut them into fine slivers. Wash the fresh coriander leaves, pat them dry and chop them coarsely. Set aside a generous tablespoon for garnishing; the rest is for steaming.

If you are preparing a whole fish, wash it well and pat it dry. With a sharp knife, cut deep, slightly diagonal slits across the body on both sides of the fish. These slits should be made 1½ inches apart and go three quarters of the way down to the bone.

If you are using dried galangal and lemongrass, drain them, reserving the soaking liquid.

On an oval or rectangular plate large enough to hold the fish and fit inside your steaming pan, scatter a third of the galangal (fresh or dried), a third of the dried lemongrass (if you are using it) and a third each of the green chili, shallots and coriander which you have reserved for steaming. Place the fish (whole, fillets or steaks) over these seasonings. Scatter the remaining galangal, dried lemongrass, ginger, green chili, shallots and coriander reserved for steaming over the fish. Pour the fish sauce and the liquid from the soaked spices (if any) over the fish as well. Top the fish with kaffir lime leaves, which, if fresh, should first be torn in two and the central vein removed, and add the fresh lemongrass, if you are using it.

Set water about ¾ inch below a rack in a wok or steamer to heat. When the water comes to a rolling boil, put on long oven gloves to protect you from the steam and carefully lower the plate of fish onto the rack. Cover. Let the steam build up over a high heat for 2 minutes. Turn the heat to medium-high and cook for another 5–18 minutes (see the introduction to this recipe) or until the fish is just done.

Meanwhile, cut the red chili into fine long slivers. Lift the fish plate carefully out of the pan, again wearing oven gloves. Hold the plate level so that the precious juices do not spill over the edge. Sprinkle the fish with the red chili slivers and the green coriander leaves reserved for garnishing. Serve at once.

FISH POACHED IN AROMATIC TAMARIND BROTH

KAENG SOM

When I want a light meal, I have this poached fish with plain rice and then follow it with a green salad. The Thais, of course, serve this soupy dish as a main course along with rich coconut-based curries, stir-fried meats, rice and salads.

You could buy almost any filleted fish that you fancy. Moderately priced fillets, such as those from cod, halibut and haddock, are perfectly suited to this dish, though you could also use tile, sole, bass or red snapper. It is important to buy *thick* fillets or the thicker end of large fillets as they hold their shape best; about 1 inch is a suitable thickness.   *Serves 3–4*

3 medium shallots (or ½ small onion)

1½-inch cube fresh ginger

*2 oz fresh coriander (preferably with roots
    still attached)*

1 teaspoon shrimp or anchovy paste

*3 cups Chicken Stock, homemade
    (see page 77) or canned*

*1 tablespoon tamarind paste (see page 303)
    or 2 teaspoons lime juice*

1 teaspoon dark brown sugar

¼–½ teaspoon salt

1 lb thick white fish fillets

1 scallion

Peel the shallots and chop them coarsely. Peel the ginger and chop two thirds of it coarsely. Cut the remaining third into very fine julienne strips—as thin as you can manage—and set these aside. Cut the roots off the fresh coriander and chop them coarsely. In an electric blender combine the chopped coriander roots, the chopped shallots, the chopped ginger, shrimp paste and 3 tablespoons water. Blend until you have a puree.

Put the stock into a medium-sized frying pan. Add the puree from the blender as well as the tamarind paste (or lime juice), sugar and salt. Bring to a simmer, and simmer gently for 5 minutes. Taste and adjust the seasoning, if necessary.

Meanwhile, cut the fish into 3–4-inch squares. Cut the scallion crosswise into very fine rounds. Put the fish in a single layer into the poaching liquid. Bring the liquid to a simmer again. Cook gently for 1 minute. Turn the fish pieces over carefully. Cook gently for another 5–8 minutes, basting the top of the fish frequently, until it is cooked through. With a wide spatula, pick up the fish pieces carefully and put them in a wide serving bowl. Pour the poaching liquid over the fish. Scatter the sliced scallion, some coriander leaves and the reserved julienned ginger over the top and serve.

West Sumatran Fish Curry with Coconut Milk

Indonesia

From the Sanuar Family in Pandai Sikat

GULAI IKAN

This dish calls for rather a lot of coconut milk so I nearly always use a good canned variety. It does behave slightly differently from fresh milk and I have therefore had to change Mrs. Sanuar's recipe slightly. I do hope that this will meet with her approval, as she sits in her beautifully carved *minangkabau* house, with its roof curving up at the ends like a water buffalo's horns.

For this recipe you need steaks from a firm-fleshed white fish such as tile, cod, haddock or bass. Salmon, though not white, would be wonderful, if expensive. The Sanuars use a large goldfish from their very own tank and either cook it whole or, rather casually, chop it in half. The souring agent used in Western Sumatra was not regular tamarind but *asem candis*, something that I knew already from India as *kokum*. This is the dried sour skin of a mangosteenlike fruit. It is generally added whole or in segments to a dish where it slowly imparts its sourness. If you can obtain this seasoning, put in about 3 pieces when you add the fish. Tamarind paste or lime juice make a good substitute.   *Serves 4*

5 cups coconut milk

8–12 whole dried hot red chilies

2 sticks fresh or 2 tablespoons dried sliced lemongrass

1½-inch cube fresh or 5–6 slices dried galangal

6 candlenuts or 12 cashew nuts

1 medium red bell pepper

8–10 medium shallots (or 1 large onion)

1-inch cube fresh ginger

3 garlic cloves

½ teaspoon ground turmeric

1 teaspoon paprika

2 lb fish steaks about 1 inch thick

1½ teaspoons salt

2½ tablespoons lime or lemon juice

4 tablespoons vegetable oil

4–5 fresh kaffir lime leaves or 3 × ½-inch piece lemon rind

10 fresh curry leaves or 3 dried bay leaves

15–20 fresh mint leaves

8–10 cherry tomatoes

FISH AND SEAFOOD   **1 6 3**

If the coconut milk is fresh, let it stand for a while until the cream has risen to the top. (In a can, the cream is nearly always at the top.)

Crumble the red chilies into a small bowl. Add the dried lemongrass and dried galangal, if you are using them, and the nuts. Add enough water just to cover and leave to soak for 1 hour. If you are using fresh lemongrass, cut about 6 inches off each stick, measuring from the bottom, and discard the rest. Crush the bulbous bottoms lightly with a hammer or other heavy object and set aside. If you are using fresh galangal, peel and coarsely chop it.

Remove the seeds from the red bell pepper and chop it coarsely. Peel the shallots, ginger and garlic and chop them coarsely. In an electric blender combine the soaked ingredients and their soaking liquid, the fresh galangal (if you are using it), the red bell pepper, shallots, ginger, garlic, turmeric and paprika. Blend thoroughly, adding another 1–2 tablespoons water if it seems necessary.

Rub the fish steaks with ½ teaspoon of the salt and 1 tablespoon of the lime juice. Set aside.

Spoon off the thick coconut cream that has risen to the top and set it aside. Add enough water to the remaining thin coconut milk to make about 1½ quarts.

Put the oil in a large, preferably nonstick frying pan and set it over a medium-high heat. When the oil is hot, put in the paste from the blender. Stir and fry until the paste turns dark red and separates from the oil. (Turn the heat down a little, if necessary, while you do this.) Put in the thin coconut milk-water combination and the 2 whole sticks fresh lemongrass, if you are using it. Bring to the boil, scraping up any hardened juices stuck to the bottom of the pan. Turn the heat to low and simmer gently for 15 minutes. Remove the lemongrass and set it aside. Empty the contents of the pan into a sieve set over a bowl and push the sauce through. Return all but 4 tablespoons of the sieved sauce to the frying pan and bring it to a simmer. Put the lemongrass sticks back in along with the lime leaves (or lemon rind), curry leaves, mint, the remaining 1½ tablespoons lime juice and the remaining 1 teaspoon salt. Stir. Now place the fish steaks in a single layer in the pan and bring its contents to a simmer again over a medium-low heat. Cook gently for about 10 minutes or until the fish is done, spooning the hot sauce over the steaks frequently.

Put the thick coconut cream into a bowl and stir it well. Slowly add the 4 tablespoons of reserved sauce and mix it in. Pour this over the fish. Halve the tomatoes and add them to the pan. Cook until everything is just heated through, then serve.

FISH BRAISED IN TEA

CÁ KHO

Oily fish, such as mackerel and sardines, are amazingly good when they are braised over a long period. Their flesh turns meltingly tender but does not fall apart, while the braising juices add extra flavor. Tea bags are needed here. It is best to use a plain, dark tea that has not been made too aromatic with added seasonings.

The mackerel is served at room temperature or cold with some of its juices poured over it. You may eat it with a green salad that contains fresh herbs such as basil, coriander and mint. You may also serve this fish in much the same way that you might serve canned sardines—on toast with sliced tomatoes, or arranged over salad greens as a first course.

Serves 4 as a first course or 2 as a main course

1½-lb whole mackerel, cleaned, gills removed

1-inch cube fresh ginger

1 tablespoon Chinese dark soy sauce

2 tablespoons fish sauce

2 tea bags

1 tablespoon sugar

Cut the mackerel crosswise into 3-inch sections. The head may be left on the fish or discarded. Wash the mackerel pieces and put them into a medium-sized pan. Cover with about 1 quart water and add all the other ingredients. (The ginger does not need to be peeled.) Bring to a boil. Turn the heat down to medium-low and simmer, uncovered, for 1½ hours. You should now have about ¾ cup of sauce left at the bottom. Leave the fish to cool in the sauce. When you are ready to serve, lift the fish out of its liquid. Skin it, if you like, and open the pieces like a book, removing the center bone. Pour just a little sauce over the top.

BROILED MACKEREL (OR SALMON) WITH SWEET SOY SAUCE

SAKE NO TERIYAKI

You may cook mackerel or salmon fillets in this way—or even whole eels that have been split open. All you need is Sweet Glazing Sauce and some skewers. The Japanese like to skewer their fish before it is grilled. The reason is simple, and practical enough: it is much easier to turn the fish over with the help of skewers. If you want both sides browned and glistening with the glaze of the sauce, there is no better way to do it. And it is the only way to make the skin crisp.

There are a few pointers here that might prove useful. In order to prevent the fish from falling off the skewers while it is being cooked, the skewering must always be done against the grain. Push the skewers into the flesh just under the skin. Also, let the skewers fan out so that the handles are all close together but the tips are quite separated. This way you will be able to hold all the handles with one hand when the fish needs to be turned.

The Japanese also like to salt fatty fish before setting it to grill. This draws out excess water and firms up the flesh. You may grill this fish over charcoal outdoors or cook it indoors under your oven broiler.   *Serves 4*

2 tablespoons coarse sea salt or kosher salt

1½–2 lb unskinned mackerel or salmon fillets

Sweet Glazing Sauce (see page 246), cooled

A little vegetable oil

Ginger Shreds in Sweet Vinegar (see page 245)

From the height of about 1 foot, sprinkle half the salt on one side of the fish pieces. (This ensures an even sprinkling of salt.) Turn the fish over and do the same on the other side. Set aside for 15 minutes and then wash the salt off. Pat the fish dry and put it into a large bowl. Pour the Sweet Glazing Sauce over it. Mix well so that the sauce covers both sides of the fish. Leave it to marinate for 1 hour.

Preheat an oven broiler or an outdoor charcoal grill. If you can control the heat, keep it at medium-high. Lift the fish pieces out of the marinade. (Save the marinade sauce.) Put between 3 and 5 skewers into each piece of fish, depending on its size, going against the grain and keeping the skewers just under the skin (see page 58).

Lightly oil the grill rack so that the fish will not stick to it. Arrange the grill rack so that it is about 5 inches from the heat source. Grill the fish, skin-side down, until it is medium brown. Turn the fish over carefully and grill it until the second side is light brown. Brush this second side with

Broiled Mackerel with Sweet Soy Sauce (this page); and Ginger Shreds in Sweet Vinegar (page 245)

some of the remaining marinade and continue to grill until the fish is glazed and brown. Turn the fish over very carefully, brush with the marinade and grill until this side is glazed and brown. To serve, lift the fish very carefully onto a plate and hand the Ginger Shreds around separately.

Vietnam

From the Đặc Sả n Restaurant in Hồ Chí Minh City

STEAMED FISH WITH GINGER AND COCONUT MILK

CÁ LÓC HẤP

Here is another steamed fish with deliciously contrasting tastes. There is oyster sauce and coconut milk, fried garlic and fresh ginger, scallions and mushrooms, all lending their flavors to the fish. You may, of course, eat the fish with plain rice, but to eat it the traditional Vietnamese way you will need:

1. A plate containing cucumber slices, sprigs of fresh mint, basil and coriander leaves as well as whole lettuce leaves.

2. A plate holding sheets of rice paper (see 298) cut in half and a bowl of water. (If you cannot get rice paper, use lettuce leaves alone to wrap the fish.)

3. Fish Sauce Seasoned with Vinegar (page 239).

To eat, you put a lettuce leaf onto a piece of rice paper. It should protrude on one side. Then, with chopsticks, take pieces of fish and cucumber and sprigs of herbs and put them on the lettuce. Wrap up or roll up the bundle and dip it into the sauce. If you find the rice paper a little too dry and crunchy for your taste, you can dip each sheet into a bowl of water immediately before assembling the "package." This will make the rice paper more malleable.

For general steaming directions, see page 59. *Serves 3–4*

1½-lb whole fish (such as red snapper, sole, or small salmon, trout, or striped bass) scaled and cleaned

½ teaspoon salt

Freshly ground black pepper

1 teaspoon dark brown sugar

3 garlic cloves

1 large onion

Vegetable oil for shallow-frying

1-inch cube fresh ginger

2 scallions

4 medium mushrooms

1½ tablespoons oyster sauce

6 tablespoons coconut milk (see page 282)

4–5 tablespoons Roasted Peanuts (see page 247), crushed

Wash the fish and pat it dry. Using a sharp knife, cut deep, slightly diagonal slits across the body of the fish on both sides, about 1½ inches apart. Put the fish on an oval or rectangular plate of a size that will fit into your steaming utensil. Rub the fish inside and outside with the salt, pepper and sugar.

Peel the garlic and cut it into fine slivers. Peel and finely slice the onion.

Put about ½ inch of oil in a frying pan and set it over a medium-low heat. While you are waiting for the oil to get hot, set a sieve over a bowl and place it near the burner. Spread some paper toweling on a large plate and place that nearby also. When the oil is hot, put in the garlic slivers. Stir and fry until they are golden. Empty the oil and garlic into the sieve. Spread the drained garlic over part of the paper toweling. Put the oil in the bowl back into your frying pan and heat it again on a medium heat. Set the sieve back on the bowl. When the oil is hot, put in the onion slices. Stir and fry until they are golden brown and crisp. Empty them into the sieve; then, when they are well drained, spread them on the unused part of the paper toweling.

Peel the ginger and cut it into fine slices. Stacking a few slices together at a time, cut the ginger into fine slivers. Cut the scallions crosswise into very fine rounds along their entire length. Slice the mushrooms thinly.

Combine the oyster sauce with 2 tablespoons of the coconut milk and pour the mixture evenly over the fish. Scatter the ginger, scallions and mushrooms as well as the fried garlic and half the fried onions over the top.

If steaming is a technique that is new to you, follow the instructions on page 55. Bring some water to a boil in a wok or steamer, remembering that it should be ¾ inch below the plate. Place the fish plate on the rack in the steamer. Cover and let the steam build up over a high heat for 2 minutes. Turn the heat down to medium-high and steam for another 18 minutes or until the fish is just done. Remove the cover and spoon some of the sauce from the fish into a bowl. Carefully lift the fish plate out of the steamer. Add the remaining 4 tablespoons coconut milk to the sauce in the bowl. Mix well and pour it over the fish. Scatter the crushed peanuts and remaining fried onions over the fish and serve.

FISH, SHELLFISH AND BEAN CURD STEW

SAENGSUN CHIGAE

This is one of my family's favorite stews. It has a bit of everything in it and is deliciously spicy to boot. You can put in almost any fish that you like. Rather like a *bouillabaisse*, the ideal combination includes a whole white-fleshed fish cut crosswise into three or four pieces (including the head if you wish), a few mollusks (such as clams or mussels), chunks of bean curd (which happily absorbs the good sauce), dried mushrooms, sliced zucchini and just a few slices of beef for a more complex flavor.

There is one seasoning ingredient in it, however, that is hard to find but very easy to improvise. It is Hot Fermented Bean Paste *(kochu chang)* and contains, among other things, fermented soybean powder and ground red (cayenne) pepper. To make a rough equivalent at home I combine Japanese-style *miso* or fermented soybean paste—red or brown miso is available in most health food shops —with ground red pepper and a little sugar (see page 240). Hot Fermented Bean Paste is *very* hot. *My* paste is relatively mild, though you could add more ground red pepper to it for a more fiery dish.

It might interest you to know that the water used in this stew in Korea is that which is saved from the second washing of raw rice. Because it is not from the first washing, it is clean. It adds a little flavor and the starch in the water helps to thicken the sauce just very slightly.

The pots used for cooking these stews (or *chigaes*) are made of heavy clay and are taken directly from the fire to the table. They retain their heat for a long time, so the stew stays hot. I use a heavy casserole dish instead. This stew is generally served with rice.   *Serves 4*

10 dried Chinese mushrooms or fresh
    mushrooms
¼ lb lean tender beef
1 small zucchini
2 garlic cloves
1 tablespoon Japanese soy sauce (shoyu)
1 teaspoon sesame oil
4 tablespoons Hot Fermented Bean Paste
4 scallions
¼ medium green bell pepper

¼ medium red bell pepper
8 small clams
2½ cakes bean curd
1½-lb whole white fish (such as snapper or
    trout), scaled, cleaned and cut
    crosswise into 3–4 pieces, or 1 lb fish
    steaks from tilefish or scrod
2 teaspoons vegetable oil
Few celery leaves to garnish

continued

*Fish, Shellfish and
Bean Curd Stew
(this page)*

Soak the dried mushrooms in about 1¼ cups hot water and set aside for 30 minutes or until they are soft. Cut off the hard stems and slice the caps into 3–4 pieces. If you are using fresh mushrooms, first trim the ends of the stalks and wipe the caps with damp paper toweling. Thickly slice the mushrooms. Cut the beef into very thin slices, about 1 x 2 inches. Trim the zucchini and cut it crosswise into ⅓-inch-thick-rounds. Peel the garlic and chop it finely. In a bowl combine the mushrooms, beef, zucchini, garlic, soy sauce, sesame oil and Hot Fermented Bean Paste. Mix and set aside.

Cut the scallions into 2-inch lengths. Cut the peppers into ½-inch squares and discard the seeds. Scrub the clams well with a stiff brush under cold running water. Cut the bean curd into 1-inch cubes. Wash the fish and pat dry.

In a large, wide, flameproof casserole that can be brought to the table, heat the oil over a medium-high heat. When it is hot, put in the meat mixture. Stir and fry for 2 minutes. Pour in 3¾ cups water and bring to a simmer, scraping off all the cooked meat juices stuck to the bottom of the casserole. Put in the fish pieces, scallions and peppers. Bring to a simmer. Cover and simmer for 5 minutes. Add the bean curd and clams, scattering them about and submerging them in the liquid as gently as possible. Bring to a simmer again. Cover and cook on medium-low heat for another 5 minutes or until the clams open.

Coarsely chop the celery leaves. Scatter them over the stew and serve.

Japan

SHRIMP AND VEGETABLE FRITTERS

TEMPURA

The Japanese may have learned the technique of making deep-fried fritters from Portuguese missionaries in the late sixteenth century, but by now they have made this dish their own. Only the freshest fish and vegetables are used, the batter is exceedingly light, and the dipping sauce is a glorious, almost drinkable mixture of stock, soy sauce, sweet *sake* and grated white radish.

In Japan the best way to eat *tempura* is at a *tempura* bar. You sit at a counter behind which the chefs work right before your eyes. One item at a time is dipped in batter, fried and placed in your paper-lined basket. You eat it immediately while it is still crunchy and hot, dipping it quickly into its dipping sauce or into the tiny bowls of salt and lemon juice on the counter. Warm *sake* or cold beer flows freely.

On one of my visits to Osaka, Professor Shizuo Tsuji, one of Japan's leading food authorities, arranged for me to have what he regarded as the best *tempura* in Japan. That the restaurant was in another town did not worry him at all. He had me driven to Kobe, but only after making sure that a certain fresh shrimp from the local seas had not already been sold out. He sent two of his leading chefs, Mr. Hatta and Mr. Saito, with me to extend his hospitality and to make sure that all my questions would be answered.

I had had *tempura* all over Japan—in Tokyo, where the batter is golden yellow; in the markets of Kyoto, where they like to build up the batter in a more-than-generous layer around the food (according to Professor Tsuji, "The common man goes for the crunch more than for the food it covers"); in Osaka, which is famed for its pale, almost white, batter; and now I was to try it in Kobe.

The *tempura* here just could not be improved upon. The shrimps we were served are sold live. This restaurant has first choice in the market, the shrimps being selected for their size and color. They had a very fresh sea flavor. We also had rolled white fish (*kisu*) fillets, minnows (all lumped into a ball), a moss-eating trout (*ayu*), octopus pieces, sea eels, baby shrimps and vegetables such as baby eggplants, lotus root slices, mushroom caps and green chilies. We ended with a *miso* soup, rice and pickles, to be followed by an exotic (and expensive) fruit, sweet prickly pears from Colombia.

Tempura, for the average person, is a simpler affair: one or two shrimps (they are very expensive in Japan), a few green beans and a few slices of sweet potato, eggplant and lotus root. A small Japanese salad is generally served beforehand and soup, rice and pickles at the end. All in all, it is very satisfying and good.

While I consider shrimps essential, you can add almost any other seasonal vegetable or leaf. Kyoto specializes in serving red maple leaves in the autumn. You might serve mint in the summer. Among the vegetables that can be dipped in batter and fried you have a choice of cauliflower, potatoes, green bell pepper, asparagus, mushrooms, sliced onions and broccoli.

The batter must be mixed only at the last moment, though all the ingredients for it may be measured and kept in readiness some time beforehand. It is important that the batter be left lumpy and not be overmixed. The flour and water are measured by volume here. After you have fried a batch of *tempura*, clean the oil of all debris using a slotted spoon. (In Japan this debris—little droplets of batter—is usually saved. It is then rinsed off and put into soup as tiny dumplings.)

If you are using *dashi-no-moto* instead of Japanese Soup Stock, use 2 tablespoons soy sauce in the dipping sauce.   *Serves 4*

12 medium shrimps

½ large green bell pepper

About 16 green beans

About ½ medium sweet potato

1 medium onion

8 medium mushrooms

1 cup Japanese Soup Stock (see page 78) or light unsalted Chicken Stock, homemade (see page 77) or canned

2½ tablespoons Japanese soy sauce (shoyu)

3 tablespoons sake

2 teaspoons sugar

3½ oz white radish

Salt

6 tablespoons lemon juice

Vegetable oil for deep-frying

1 egg yolk

1 cup ice-cold water

1 cup unbleached, all-purpose flour plus extra for dusting

continued

Prepare all the foods that are to be fried. Peel the shrimps but leave their tails on. The tails have a little water in them which must be pushed out. To do this, cut the very tip off each tail and then press the water out by pulling the blunt side of a knife along the tail. Devein the shrimps. Make a few strokes crosswise on the underbelly of each shrimp so that it does not curl up. Cut the green bell pepper lengthwise into ½-inch-wide strips, discarding the seeds. Trim the green beans, but leave them whole. Peel the sweet potato and cut it into slices, each about ⅛ inch thick. Put the slices in a bowl of water. Peel the onion and cut it in half lengthwise. Lay the onion halves on your work surface, cut side down. Push toothpicks vertically into the onion halves along their entire length at ¼-inch intervals so that they go all the way through. Cut the onion halves into slices downward between the toothpicks. The sticks will hold the onion slices together.

Next make the dipping sauce. Combine the stock, soy sauce, *sake* and sugar in a small pan and simmer gently for 1 minute or until the sugar dissolves. Divide the sauce among 4 bowls and keep them warm. Peel the radish and grate it finely. Put one small hillock of grated radish on each of 4 tiny saucers or into 4 tiny bowls. Prepare also a tiny bowl of salt and a tiny bowl of lemon juice for each diner.

In a wok or deep-fat fryer heat the oil to a temperature of 350–370°F. Drain the sweet potato and pat all the foods dry.

Make the batter. In a large bowl beat the egg yolk lightly and add the cold water to it. Mix lightly. Sift the flour and then dump it all at once into the bowl with the egg yolk and water. Stir lightly with a fork or chopsticks to mix.

Do not overmix. The batter should be lumpy and floury-looking.

Put the dusting flour on a plate. Dip the pepper strips first in the dusting flour, shaking off any excess, then dip them in the batter. Fry as many pieces as your wok or deep-fat fryer will hold easily in one layer for 2–3 minutes, turning once or twice, until the batter is golden. Remove with a slotted spoon. Drain once on paper toweling and serve. Fry all the vegetables in this way, removing the debris from the oil with a slotted spoon between each batch. Stir the batter lightly every now and then to keep it from separating. Fry the shrimps last.

Diners usually put some or all of the grated radish into the dipping sauce. They dip the food into the sauce or into the lemon juice and salt.

INSERTING TOOTHPICKS INTO AN ONION

a Peel the onion and cut it in half, lengthwise. Place the onion halves on your work surface cut side down and stick toothpicks along the length at ¼-inch intervals. Push the toothpicks all the way through the onion.

b Cut the onion crosswise between the toothpicks. The toothpicks will hold the onion slices together.

Shrimp and Vegetable Fritters (page 172)

PIQUANT SHRIMPS

GAMBAS PICANTES

Glenda Barretto, a very fine cook herself, has used her entrepreneurial skills to open some of Manila's most distinguished restaurants. The Nielson Tower is one of them. From 1937 to 1947 it was an airport terminal. Today it is the haunt of the city's movers and shakers in a different way—it feeds them. This dish, Spanish in its origins as are a great many other Filipino dishes, is served in the restaurant as an appetizer. I often serve it as a main course with rice and a simple vegetable. If you prefer a milder flavor, substitute 1½ tablespoons finely chopped green bell pepper for the chilies.   *Serves 4 as a main course or 6 as a first course*

1 lb medium shrimp
1 teaspoon paprika
5 garlic cloves
1–2 fresh hot green chilies
4 tablespoons olive oil
½ teaspoon salt
Freshly ground black pepper

Peel and devein the shrimps. Wash them, pat them dry and put them in a bowl. Add the paprika and toss.

Peel the garlic and chop it finely. Chop the chilies finely.

Put the oil in a wok or large frying pan and set it over a high heat. When the oil is hot, put in the garlic. Stir-fry for 30 seconds or until the garlic turns golden. Put in the shrimps and green chilies. Stir-fry over a high heat for 2–3 minutes or until the shrimps turn opaque all the way through. Add the salt and pepper. Toss again and serve.

SHRIMPS WITH ASPARAGUS

XIAN LUSUN CHAD XIAQIU

I serve this elegant Cantonese dish both as a main course and, in small portions, as a first course.   *Serves 3–4 as a main course or 6 as a first course*

½ lb medium shrimps

1 small egg white

2½ teaspoons cornstarch

2 teaspoons sesame oil

Salt

½ lb fresh asparagus (untrimmed weight)

3 tablespoons vegetable oil

¾-inch cube fresh ginger

1 garlic clove

1½ teaspoons oyster sauce

1 teaspoon Chinese light soy sauce

2 teaspoons Chinese rice wine or dry sherry

¼ teaspoon sugar

Peel and devein the shrimps. Wash well, pat them dry and put in a small bowl. Beat the egg white lightly and add to the bowl along with 2 teaspoons of the cornstarch, 1 teaspoon of the sesame oil and a pinch of salt. Mix well, cover and set aside for 30 minutes or longer, refrigerating if necessary.

Trim and discard the woody bottom ends of the asparagus spears. Peel the lower third of the spears and then cut them slightly diagonally along their entire length into 1½-inch-long pieces.

Bring about 3 cups water to a rolling boil in a medium-sized pan. Add ½ teaspoon salt and 1 tablespoon of the vegetable oil to the water. Stir. Put in the asparagus. Boil rapidly for 2–3 minutes or until the asparagus is just done but is still crisp and bright green. Drain and rinse under cold running water. Drain again and set aside.

Peel the ginger and garlic and chop each finely. Keep them separate.

In a small bowl combine the oyster sauce, soy sauce, and remaining 1 teaspoon sesame oil, the rice wine, sugar and 2 tablespoons water.

In a cup, mix remaining ½ teaspoon cornstarch with 1 tablespoon water.

Just before you are ready to eat, put the remaining 4 tablespoons vegetable oil in a wok or large frying pan and set it over high heat. When the oil is hot, put in the shrimps. Stir and fry for about 3 minutes or until they just turn opaque. Remove the shrimps with a slotted spoon and set them aside. Remove all but 1 tablespoon of the oil from the wok and heat over a medium heat again. When it is hot, put in the ginger. Stir once and add the garlic. Stir once or twice and put in the shrimps and asparagus. Stir once or twice and add the oyster sauce mixture. Stir a few times and take the wok off the heat. Give the cornstarch mixture a good stir, pour it into the center of the wok and stir to mix. Put the wok back on a low heat and cook briefly until the sauce has thickened, stirring as you do so. Serve immediately.

SPICY SHRIMP AND CUCUMBER CURRY

GULAI LABU

This curry is actually made with bottle gourd—a pale green vegetable shaped like a bowling pin. You can easily use cucumber instead as its taste is similar when cooked. The origins of this Malay dish probably lie in India—the use of ground coriander and fennel seeds as well as the final popping of seasonings in hot oil all testify to that. What I find utterly fascinating here is the use of white pepper. The original recipe calls for 1 tablespoon finely ground white pepper. This may sound unusual, and excessive, in the West. But if you travel in the regions where pepper has grown for thousands of years, such as Kerala in South India where black pepper may well have originated, you will find that the use of such large amounts is not at all uncommon. It makes the dish decidedly peppery. What must be kept in mind is that red chilies arrived in this part of the world only in the late fifteenth century.

If you cannot get ground fennel seeds, simply grind whole seeds in a clean coffee grinder or food processor.   *Serves 4–6*

¾ lb medium shrimps

3 Kirby cucumbers or 1½ regular
   cucumber

10 medium shallots (or 1 large onion)

6 garlic cloves

2 tablespoons ground coriander seeds

1 tablespoon ground fennel seeds

1 teaspoon ground white pepper or to taste

1 tablespoon ground cumin seeds

1 teaspoon ground turmeric

3–4 whole dried hot red chilies

¾–1 teaspoon salt

1 teaspoon sugar

1¾ cups thick coconut milk (see page 282)

4 tablespoons vegetable oil

1 teaspoon whole fennel seeds

Peel and devein the shrimps. Wash them and pat them dry. Peel the cucumber and cut it crosswise into ½-inch-thick rounds. Peel 7 of the shallots and chop them very finely. Peel and finely slice the remaining shallots. Peel the garlic cloves. Chop 4 of them very finely and cut the other 2 into fine slivers. Combine the sliced shallots and slivered garlic and set these aside.

In a medium-sized pan combine the chopped shallots, chopped garlic, ground coriander, ground fennel, white pepper, ground cumin, turmeric and 2½ cups water. Crumble in the red chilies. Stir and bring to a boil. Boil, uncovered, on a medium heat for about 5 minutes. Add the cucumber rounds, stir and bring to a simmer.

Cover and simmer gently for 5 minutes. Then add the shrimps, salt and sugar. Bring to a simmer again and simmer gently for about 1 minute, stirring the shrimps around in the sauce. Give the coconut milk a good stir and pour it in. Bring the mixture to a boil, then lower the heat and simmer for 1 minute, stirring now and then.

Put the oil in a very small pan or small frying pan and set it over a medium-high heat. When the oil is hot, put in the slivered shallots and garlic. Stir and fry until they turn a golden color. Add the whole fennel seeds. Stir once and quickly pour the contents of the pan (oil and seasoning) into the pan containing the curry. Cover the curry pan immediately to trap all the aromas.

SQUID SALAD

YAM PLA MUK

Squid is such an underused seafood. It is cheap and I happen to love it, so I cook it in as many different ways as I can. This is an easy salad that can be served as a main course in the summer and as an appetizer in the winter.   *Serves 4–6 as a main course or 8 as a first course*

2 lb squid, cleaned (see page 57)

7 medium shallots (or 1 medium onion)

4 tablespoons lime juice

3 tablespoons fish sauce or salt to taste

1 teaspoon sugar

¼ teaspon ground red (cayenne) pepper

6–8 tablespoons fresh coriander leaves

FOR THE GARNISHES

3–4 lettuce leaves

1½ Kirby cucumbers or 1 small regular cucumber

8–10 cherry tomatoes

Cut the tubelike bodies of the squid crosswise into ¼-inch-wide rings. Wash these rings and the tentacles and then put them in a pan with 4 tablespoons water. Bring to a simmer, cover, and simmer for about 3 minutes or until the pices of squid turn opaque. Drain them and put them in a bowl.

Peel and finely slice the shallots. Add these to the squid along with the lime juice, fish sauce, sugar, ground red pepper and coriander leaves. Toss well. Check the seasoning.

Just before serving, arrange the lettuce leaves on a serving plate. Peel the cucumber and slice it into thin rounds. Cut the tomatoes in half vertically. Put the squid salad on top of the lettuce and surround with the cucumber slices and tomato halves.

SQUID WITH TOMATOES

Philippines
From the Home of Dr. Fe Esleyer in Bacolod City, Negros

ADOBONG PUSIT

This easy dish, very Spanish in its heritage, is generally eaten with rice in the Philippines. I often serve it with pasta or enjoy it all by itself with a salad on the side when I want to eat lightly. It never ceases to amaze me that something as good should still be so cheap to make. Perhaps I should not speak too loudly!

I have used canned tomatoes in this recipe as they are always available and are usually redder and riper than anything I can get in the market. If you have access to good fresh tomatoes, use about 3 medium. Just drop them into boiling water for 15 seconds so that you can peel them easily.   *Serves 3–4*

1 lb squid, cleaned (see page 57)

4 garlic cloves

1 small onion

6 canned plum tomatoes, lightly drained

3 tablespoons olive oil

1 teaspoon vinegar

¾ teaspoon salt

Wash the squid and pat it dry. Cut the tubular bodies crosswise into ½-inch-wide rings. Cut the tentacles into 2 or 3 pieces. Peel the garlic and chop it finely. Peel the onion and chop it finely. Chop the tomatoes coarsely.

Put the oil in a medium-sized pan over a medium-high heat. When the oil is hot, put in the garlic. Stir once or twice and add the onions. Turn the heat to medium. Stir and cook for 1 minute. Then put in the tomatoes. Stir and cook on a medium-high heat for 2–3 minutes or until you have a thickish sauce. Turn the heat to high and put in the squid, vinegar and salt. Stir and cook just until the squid turns opaque—a matter of minutes.

SQUID IN BLACK SAUCE

SOTONG MASAK KICAP

The ingredients used in this recipe are simple and humble, but the dish, another Nonya classic, is exquisite. (Nonyas are women of mixed Chinese and Malay ancestry, born in the Straits settlements of Penang, Malacca or Singapore.) The black sauce used here is thick, smooth, very slightly sweet and made with mashed fermented soybeans. I find bottled black bean sauce to be fairly similar. If you cannot obtain it, use 1½ tablespoons canned or dried salted black beans, washed and mashed, mixed with 1 tablespoon oyster sauce. *Serves 4*

3 medium onions

1 lb squid, cleaned (see page 57)

4 tablespoons vegetable oil

2 tablespoons bottled black bean sauce

1 tablespoon Chinese light soy sauce

1½ teaspoons ground white pepper

FOR THE GARNISHES

The green section from 1 scallion, scallion cut into rings

2 tablespoons fresh coriander leaves (optional)

Few rings cut from a fresh hot red chili (optional)

Peel the onions and cut them in half lengthwise. Cut each half crosswise into ⅛-inch-thick slices. Wash the squid and pat it dry. Cut the tubular bodies of the squid crosswise into ¾-inch-wide rings. The tentacles may be left clumped together or separated into 2–3 clumps.

Put the oil in a frying pan and set it over a medium-high heat. When the oil is hot, put in the onions. Stir and fry them for about 4 minutes or until they are soft. Put in the squid, black bean sauce, soy sauce and white pepper. Stir and cook on the same heat for about 3 minutes or until the squid is opaque. Empty the contents of the pan into a serving dish. Garnish with the chopped green section of a scallion and, if you like, coriander leaves and hot red chili rings.

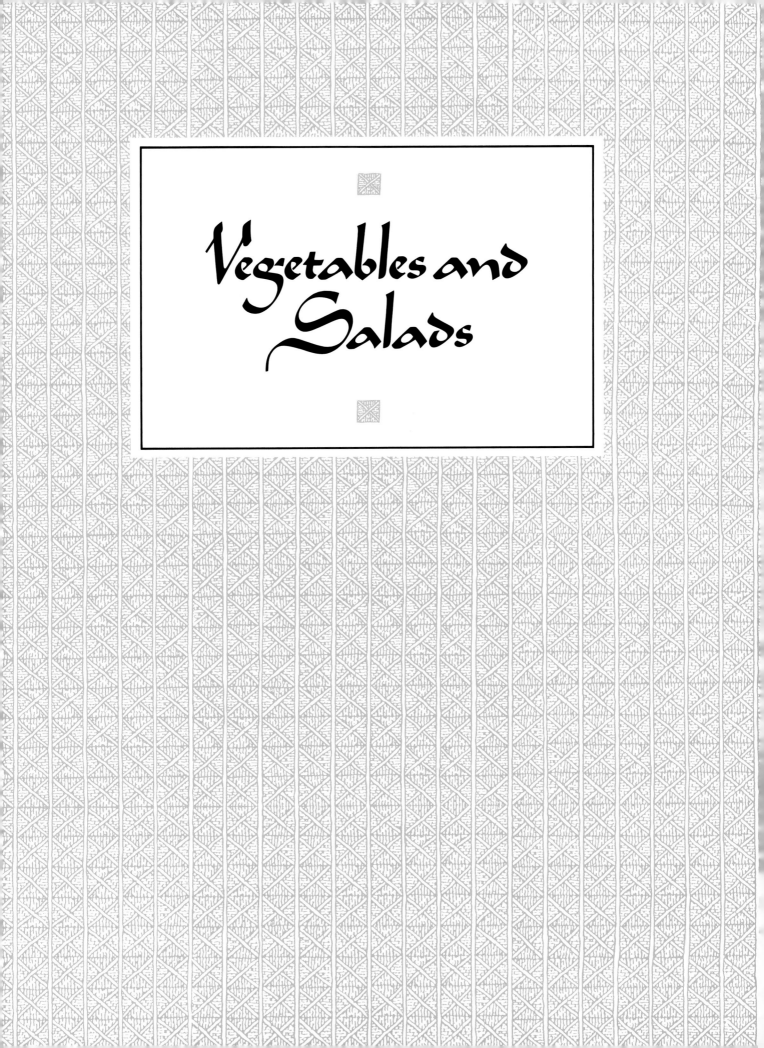

Vegetables and Salads

BEAN CURD WITH OYSTER SAUCE

HAOYOU DOUFU

This dish is made with fried bean curd. Bean curd turns spongy when fried and is better able to absorb sauces.   *Serves 4–6*

6–8 dried Chinese mushrooms or large
  fresh mushroom caps

1 lb firm bean curd

Oil for deep-frying

3 tablespoons oyster sauce

1 teaspoon Chinese light soy sauce

2 teaspoons Chinese dark soy sauce

2 teaspoons sugar

½ cup plus 1 tablespoon Chicken Stock,
  homemade (see page 77) or canned

1 teaspoon cornstarch

1 garlic clove

1 cup fresh peas (shelled) or frozen peas,
  defrosted

1 tablespoon sesame oil

Cover the dried mushrooms with warm water and leave to soak for 30 minutes or until soft. Remove them from the water and cut off the hard stems.

Cut the bean curd into slices about ½ × 1½ × 2 inches. Spread these between 2 layers of paper toweling to dry them off.

Put the oil in a wok or deep-fat fryer over a medium-high heat. (It should be about 2 inches deep in the center of the wok if you are using one.) When the oil is hot, fry the bean curd until golden brown on all sides. Remove it and leave to drain on a plate lined with paper toweling.

Combine the oyster sauce, light and dark soy sauces, sugar and ½ cup chicken stock in a small bowl. Stir to mix. Combine the cornstarch and the remaining 1 tablespoon chicken stock in a small cup. Peel the garlic and chop it finely.

Put 2 tablespoons of the frying oil in a wok or large frying pan. Set it over a high heat. When the oil is hot, put in the garlic. Stir and fry it for 30 seconds. Put in the Chinese mushrooms or fresh mushroom caps and continue to stir and fry for about 1 minute. Now add the bean curd. Toss it gently with the mushrooms. Put in the oyster sauce mixture. Cover, turn the heat to low and simmer very gently for 8 minutes. Then add the peas. Simmer, covered, for another 2 minutes. Remove the lid and take the wok off the heat. Stir the cornstarch mixture and pour it in. Put the wok back on the heat and add the sesame oil. Stir gently and cook on a low heat until the sauce has thickened.

BEAN SPROUTS WITH A SPICY COCONUT DRESSING

Malaysia

From Aminahbi at Restoran Minah in Penang

KERABU TAWGEH

Here is a very simple, refreshing vegetable dish-cum-salad. It has an unusual dressing of lime juice, tomatoes and roasted coconut. If you cannot get fresh coconut, use unsweetened dried coconut and roast it *before* soaking it in hot water. *Serves 4–6*

3 tablespoons uncooked rice

1 cup fresh coconut, grated (see page 282)
   or ⅔ cup unsweetened dried coconut

½ large red bell pepper

2 teaspoons shrimp or anchovy paste
   (optional)

3 tablespoons lime or lemon juice

2 canned peeled plum tomatoes, lightly
   drained

¼ teaspoon ground red (cayenne) pepper
   or to taste

1½ teaspoons salt

1½ teaspoons sugar

¾-inch cube fresh ginger

1 small onion

1 lb fresh bean sprouts

6 oz cabbage (about 2 packed cups when
   cut)

FOR THE GARNISHES (ALL OPTIONAL)

6 cherry tomatoes

2 scallions

Few tablespoons celery leaves

5–6 fresh hot green chilies

Set a small cast-iron frying pan over a medium heat. When it is hot, put in the rice. Stir the rice around until it is golden and roasted. Empty the rice onto a plate. Put the coconut into the same frying pan. Stir and fry it until it is golden brown in parts. Empty it onto a separate plate; or, if you are using dried coconut, empty it into a small bowl with ½ cup hot water and leave it to soak for 30 minutes. It will absorb most of the liquid. Put the rice into the container of a food processor and grind until it is powdery.

Seed the red bell pepper and dice it coarsely. Combine the red pepper, shrimp paste (if you are using it), lime juice, canned tomatoes, ground red pepper, salt and sugar in a blender. Blend until smooth.

Peel the ginger and grate it finely. Peel and finely slice the onion. Break off the threadlike tails at the end of each bean sprout, if you feel up to it. Cut the cabbage into fine long shreds.

Set a large pan of water over a high heat. When it comes to a rolling boil, drop in the bean sprouts and cabbage. Let the water return to a boil. Boil for about 1 minute or until the cabbage is barely limp. Drain and rinse under cold running water. Drain thoroughly again.

Prepare the garnishes, if you are including them. Cut the cherry tomatoes in half. Cut the scallions crosswise into fine rings. Finely chop the celery leaves. Just before serving, put the bean sprout-cabbage mixture into a bowl. Add the ground rice, roasted coconut, grated ginger and sliced onions. Mix well. Add the sauce from the blender and stir it in. Put the mixture into a serving dish. Sprinkle the scallions and celery leaves over the top. Garnish the edges with the tomato halves and whole green chilies.

Hong Kong

From Andy's Kitchen Restaurant in Causeway Bay

BRAISED LIMA BEANS

SHENGBIAN CANDOU

Y ou can make this Shanghai-style dish with fresh or frozen large lima beans. The hard outer skin around each individual bean may be popped open by the diner, just before it is devoured.   *Serves 3–4*

1 scallion
1½ cups fresh or frozen lima beans
   (shelled weight)
3 tablespoons vegetable oil
½ teaspoon salt
⅔ cup Chicken Stock, homemade
   (see page 77) or canned
½ teaspoon sugar
1 tablespoon sesame oil

Cut the scallion crosswise into very thin rounds.

Wash the lima beans and, if they are frozen, defrost them completely in a bowl of lukewarm water. Drain thoroughly.

Put the oil in a wok or large frying pan and set it over a high heat. When the oil is hot, put in the lima beans. Stir briskly for about 30 seconds and then add the salt, stock and sugar. Cover and cook on a high heat for 6–7 minutes or until the beans are just tender. Remove the lid and boil away all the liquid. Add the scallions and sesame oil. Toss and serve.

Green Beans and Carrots with Ginger and Chilies

Indonesia

From the Household of Usman and Rosalina Beka, Jakarta

TUMIS BUNCHIS

When little girls start learning how to cook in Indonesia, this is frequently one of the dishes they start with. A *tumis* is a stir-fried dish with just a little liquid in it. The beans (in Indonesia long beans are used) are often combined with bean curd or bean sprouts. If you wish to use either of these, you will need about 1½ cakes (4 oz) of pressed bean curd or about ½ lb fresh bean sprouts. Add them to the dish at the same time as the beans. The bean curd should be cut into pieces about the same size as the beans. I have used carrots instead, only because they are more easily available and because the West has so few imaginative carrot dishes. If you cannot get fresh galangal, just do without it.   *Serves 4*

1 lb green beans

2 medium carrots

3–4 fresh hot green chilies

1-inch cube fresh ginger

1-inch cube fresh galangal (optional)

4–6 garlic cloves

5 shallots (or 1 small onion)

3 tablespoons vegetable oil

8–10 fresh or dried curry leaves or 2 bay leaves

¾ teaspoon salt

Trim the beans and cut them into 1-inch pieces. Peel the carrots and cut them crosswise into 2-inch lengths. Cut each piece lengthwise into quarters and then halve these.

Finely chop the green chilies. Peel the ginger and cut it into paper-thin slices. Stack a few slices together at a time and cut them into minute dice. If you have fresh galangal, peel and dice it just as you have the ginger. Peel the garlic and shallots and chop them finely.

Set a wok over a high heat. When it is hot, swirl in the oil. When the oil is hot, put in the chilies, ginger, galangal, garlic, shallots and curry (or bay) leaves. Stir and fry briefly. As soon as the spices start to brown, put in the green beans, carrots and salt. Stir and fry for a minute. Put in ¾ cup water and cover. Turn the heat to medium and cook for about 5 minutes or until the vegetables are just tender.

Thailand

STIR-FRIED GREEN BEANS WITH PORK AND CHILIES

MOO PAD PRIK SAI TUA FAK YAO

Versions of this dish are to be found in many parts of Southeast Asia. I met an official in Hanoi who often lunches on this in his office. In the Sichuan province of China, beans are cooked with similar seasonings, but soy sauce is used instead of fish sauce. This particular recipe comes from a long-toothed lady with a food stall ensconced right in the middle of the Weekend Market in Bangkok. She served it to me for lunch along with a plate of plain rice. It was a simple but quite memorable meal.

You may make these beans as hot as you like by increasing the number of chilies. In Thailand fresh hot red chilies are used and they not only contrast stunningly in flavor with the green beans and brown pork, but add bright flecks of color as well. I tend to use green chilies as they are easier to find at my grocer's. If you like, you can throw in a small amount of finely diced red bell pepper in the last five minutes of cooking, just for the color. In Thailand long beans are preferred. If you cannot obtain them, use ordinary string beans.   *Serves 4*

1¼ lb green beans
12–16 garlic cloves
6–9 fresh hot green or red chilies
5 tablespoons vegetable oil
10 oz lean pork, ground
½ teaspoon paprika
1 teaspoon dark brown sugar *flakes*
3 tablespoons fish sauce or salt to taste

added soy & sesame oil at end
also chopped scallions

Wash and trim the beans. Cut them crosswise into ¼–⅓-inch rounds. Peel the garlic and chop it finely. Cut the chilies crosswise into very thin slices.

Put the oil in a wok and set it over a medium-high heat. When the oil is hot, put in the garlic and green chilies. Stir and fry until the garlic turns golden, then add the pork. Stir and fry, breaking up any lumps, until the pork has lost its raw look. Put in the beans, paprika, sugar, fish sauce and 1¼ cups water. Stir and cook on a medium-high heat for about 8–10 minutes or until the beans are tender and most of the water has been absorbed.

Stir-Fried Green Beans with Pork and Chilies (this page)

GREEN BEANS WITH SESAME DRESSING

SANDO MAME NO GOMA AYE

Y ou may choose from a variety of green beans to make this dish. French *haricots verts* should be trimmed and cut into 1½-inch lengths; all other green beans, the rounded and flat varieties, may be either sliced diagonally or first cut into 2-inch lengths and then into thin slivers.

This dish may be served as an appetizer or as an accompanying vegetable with any meat or fish. It may be made ahead of time and refrigerated. Take it out of the refrigerator at least 20 minutes before serving.   *Serves 4*

¾ lb green beans

1 tablespoon salt

1¼ cups Japanese Soup Stock (see page 78) or Chicken Stock, homemade (see page 77) or canned, at room temperature, lightly salted to taste

2½ tablespoons sesame seeds

About 1½ tablespoons Japanese soy sauce (shoyu)

1 tablespoon rice wine (mirin) or 1½ teaspoons sugar dissolved in 1½ teaspoons of the above stock

Trim the beans and cut as suggested above. Bring a large pan of water to a rolling boil. Add about 1 tablespoon salt to it and put in the beans. Boil rapidly for 2–5 minutes or until the beans are just tender but still crisp. Drain and quickly plunge them into cold water to set the color. Drain again and put the beans into a bowl. Pour the stock over them and set aside for 30 minutes or longer.

Now prepare the dressing. Put the sesame seeds in a small cast-iron frying pan set over a medium-high heat. Stir the seeds about for a few minutes until they are roasted and give out a nutty aroma. Reserve about ½ tablespoon of the seeds for garnishing the dish. Grind the rest in a clean coffee grinder or food processor, then empty them into a bowl. Add the soy sauce, *mirin* and 1 tablespoon stock taken from the soaking beans. (If you are using sugar and stock instead of *mirin*, just take another 1½ teaspoons of stock from the beans.) Mix well.

Drain the beans thoroughly. (Save the stock for soup or another dish.) Put them into a bowl, add the dressing and mix. To serve, Japanese-style, pile the beans in a little hillock in the center of each of 4 small bowls or plates. Sprinkle the reserved roasted sesame seeds over the top of each serving.

CABBAGE STIR-FRIED WITH RED PEPPER PASTE

SALA LOBAK

I discovered this absolutely delicious dish in the remote hills of Western Sumatra. Even though there was an array of fine foods laid out on the floor-cloth—curries of beef, chicken and fish—all hands went first to the cabbage and it was, indeed, the dish that was finished first.

There are two points of interest here. First, only the dark outer leaves of cabbage were cooked. I can think of no better way to use up a portion of a vegetable that is normally thrown away. If you are slightly short of the required weight of dark leaves, as I often am, use some of the inner cabbage as well. The mixture is exceedingly pleasant. Second, a small flat piece of dried fish was fried and added to the seasoning. I use a small amount of shrimp or anchovy paste instead.

You may serve this dish with any Eastern meal. It also goes particularly well with roast pork, roast lamb and various chops and cutlets.   *Serves 4*

---

1 lb dark outer cabbage leaves mixed with some of the inside leaves

1 small red bell pepper

5 medium shallots (or ½ large onion)

2 large garlic cloves

½ teaspoon shrimp or anchovy paste (optional)

¼ teaspoon ground red (cayenne) pepper

6 tablespoons vegetable oil

½ teaspoon salt

Wash the cabbage leaves. Stacking several of them together, cut them crosswise into long, fine, ⅛-inch-wide shreds. Seed the red bell pepper and chop it coarsely. Peel the shallots and garlic and chop them coarsely. Combine the pepper, shallots, garlic, shrimp paste, ground red pepper and 3 tablespoons water in an electric blender. Blend until a coarse paste results—it should not be too smooth.

Set a wok over a high heat. When it is hot, put in the oil. Once the oil has heated, put in the spice paste. Stir and fry for about 5 minutes or until the oil separates and the mixture has a dark red appearance. Add the cabbage and salt and stir for 30 seconds. Cover tightly, turn the heat to medium-low and cook for 8–10 minutes or until the cabbage is just done. (No water should be needed, but check after 5–6 minutes.)

Hong Kong
**From Bernadette
Au-Yeung**

SALAD OF CARROTS, CELERY, CUCUMBER AND HAM

LIANG BAN YANGCAI

This Shanghai-style salad is normally made with the addition of vermicellilike strands of vegetable gelatin known as agar-agar. Most health food shops stock agar-agar, but unfortunately they sell only a powdered version. Since the supply of the stranded version is limited to Chinese and Asian groceries, I have excluded it here. If you can find it, cut about ⅓ oz into 2-inch lengths with a pair of scissors and then soak it for 30 minutes in 2 cups water. Drain, pat it dry and add it to the salad ingredients. The dressing should, in any case, be mixed in only at the last minute.   *Serves 4*

2 small carrots
1 celery stalk
2 small Kirby cucumbers or 1 regular
    6-inch cucumber
1 oz lean ham
1 tablespoon Chinese light soy sauce
1 tablespoon distilled white vinegar
1 tablespoon sesame oil
¼ teaspoon sugar

Peel the carrots and cut them into fine, 2-inch-long julienne strips. Cut the celery crosswise into 2-inch lengths and then cut the segments lengthwise into fine julienne strips. Fill a medium-sized pan with water and bring it to a rolling boil. Drop in the carrots and celery and leave them for 30–40 seconds. (The water may not even come to the boil again during this time.) Drain the vegetables and immediately run cold water over them. Drain them again and put them into a bowl.

Peel the cucumber, cut it into fine, 2-inch-long julienne strips and add it to the bowl of vegetables. Cut the ham into fine, 2-inch-long julienne strips as well. Wrap it in plastic wrap and refrigerate if necessary.

Mix the soy sauce, vinegar, sesame oil and sugar in a small bowl and set aside. Just before serving, combine the vegetables and ham. Stir the dressing, pour it over the salad and toss to mix.

CAULIFLOWER AND CARROTS WITH A COCONUT DRESSING

GADANGAN

*T*his Javanese dish, eaten with slight variations throughout much of Indonesia, consists of nothing more than blanched mixed vegetables (they could be greens of various sorts or long beans or bean sprouts) that are tossed with an exquisite dressing that includes lime juice, coconut and red bell pepper. It is an inspired mixture. You may serve it hot, at room temperature or cold, though I feel that it is best to mix the dressing in while the vegetables are still hot.

If you cannot get fresh coconut, use ½ cup unsweetened dried coconut soaked in 4 tablespoons hot water for 30 minutes. The water will be absorbed by the coconut.   *Serves 4*

*1 small whole cauliflower (untrimmed) or
    15 oz cauliflower flowerets*

1½ medium carrots

½ small red bell pepper

1 garlic clove

4 teaspoons lime or lemon juice

1 teaspoon dark brown sugar

¼ teaspoon ground red (cayenne) pepper

4¼ teaspoons salt

*½ cup fresh coconut, very finely grated
    (see page 282) or dried coconut
    (see above)*

Trim the cauliflower and cut it into slim delicate flowerets—no piece should be wider than 1 inch or thicker than ½ inch, and no stem longer than 2 inches. Trim and peel the carrots. Cut them crosswise into 2-inch lengths. Quarter the thick end of each carrot lengthwise and cut the thinner portions in half lengthwise.

Coarsely chop the red bell pepper, discarding the seeds. Peel and chop the garlic. In an electric blender combine the red bell pepper, garlic, lime juice, sugar, ground red pepper and ¼ teaspoon salt. Blend until smooth. Taste the dressing; you may wish to add a little more salt.

Just before you are ready to eat, bring 5 quarts water to a rolling boil in a large pan. Throw in 4 teaspoons salt and stir it in. Put in the cauliflower and carrots and boil rapidly for several minutes or until the vegetables are just tender but still retain a hint of crispness. Drain them quickly and put them into a serving bowl. Toss the vegetables first with the dressing and then with the coconut. Serve immediately.

SMOKY EGGPLANTS IN A LIME SAUCE

CÀ TÍM NỬỐNG

This is a superb dish, inspired in every way. Eggplants, all smoky from being charred over a flame, are smothered with stir-fried pork and then submerged in a delicious lime sauce. You may roast the eggplants outdoors over charcoal in the summer, indoors in your fireplace during the winter or under your oven broiler at any time of year. I find that the most convenient way for me is directly on top of a gas burner. When buying the eggplants, make sure that they have their green sepals and a short length of stalk still attached. This makes the cooking easier and the presentation prettier. *Serves 4*

2 small eggplants

4 tablespoons Fish Sauce Seasoned with Lime Juice (see page 239)

1 small onion

1 garlic clove

1 scallion

1 tablespoon vegetable oil

¼ lb lean pork, ground

¼ teaspoon salt

Freshly ground black pepper

Do not trim the eggplants. Prick them lightly with a fork to prevent them from bursting during cooking. Line a burner on a gas stove with aluminum foil, leaving an opening for the gas. (Line two burners if you wish to cook both eggplants simultaneously.) Hold one eggplant by its stem end and stand it upright, directly on top of a medium-low flame. Let the bottom char. Now lay the eggplant down on top of the flame and let one side char. Keep turning the eggplant until all of it is charred and roasted and the entire vegetable has gone limp. You may need to hold it with a pair of tongs toward the end. Cook the other eggplant in the same way.

Peel the charred skin off the eggplants, picking them up carefully by the stem now and then and holding them under cold running water to wash away small bits of skin. The eggplants should stay intact though they will be somewhat flattened. If small portions do get loose, the eggplants can easily be reassembled. Put the eggplants side by side in a serving dish that has a slight depth to it as there will be a little sauce later. Pat them dry with paper toweling. (You can prepare the dish up to this point a day in advance. Cover and re-

Top: *Snow Peas Stir-Fried with Shrimps (page 203);* bottom: *Smoky Eggplants in a Lime Sauce (this page)* frigerate the eggplants. The following day, bring them to room temperature before proceeding with the next step.)

Make the Fish Sauce Seasoned with Lime Juice. Peel the onion and garlic and chop them finely. Cut the scallion crosswise into very fine rings.

Put the oil in a frying pan and set it over a medium-high heat. When the oil is hot, put in the onion and garlic.

Stir once or twice and add the pork, salt and lots of black pepper. Stir and fry for about 5 minutes or until the meat is cooked through, breaking up any lumps as you do so. Put in the scallion and stir for 10 seconds. Spread the pork over the eggplants. Pour the Fish Sauce Seasoned with Lime Juice over the top and serve.

Malaysia

*From Mrs.
Zaidah Ahmed in
Kuala Lumpur*

EGGPLANT IN A THICK, HOT, SWEET AND SOUR CHILI SAUCE

PACHERI TERONG

Another dish of Indian-Malay ancestry, this hot, sweet and sour *pacheri* may be made with fresh pineapple cubes as well.   *Serves 4*

2 large onions

1-inch cube fresh ginger

2 teaspoons whole cumin seeds

2 teaspoons ground coriander seeds

3–5 whole dried hot red chilies

4 whole cloves

2-inch cinnamon stick

1 medium eggplant

6 tablespoons vegetable oil

1 tablespoon paprika

3–4 tablespoons tamarind paste (see page 303) or 3 tablespoons lime juice mixed with 2 tablespoons dark brown sugar

1–2 tablespoons dark brown sugar

1½–2 teaspoons salt

Peel and finely slice the onions. Peel the ginger and cut it into fine shreds.

Put the cumin, ground coriander, dried chilies, cloves and cinnamon into a clean coffee grinder or the bowl of a food processor fitted with the metal blade. Grind as finely as possible.

Cut the eggplant into 1-inch cubes, leaving the skin on.

Put the oil in a large, preferably nonstick frying pan or large wok and set it over a medium-high heat. When the oil is hot, put in the sliced onions and the ginger. Stir and fry for about 4 minutes or until the seasonings have a dryish look but have not browned.

Add the spices from the spice grinder. Stir for 1 minute. Quickly put in 1¼ cups water and turn the heat down a little. Add the paprika, tamarind (or lime juice and sugar), sugar and salt. Stir to mix. Put in the cubed eggplant and bring to a simmer. Cover and cook gently for 20–30 minutes, stirring now and then, until the eggplant cubes are tender. Remove the lid, turn up the heat and cook most of the remaining liquid away. You should have just a thick sauce clinging to the eggplant pieces.

Thailand

GREENS WITH GARLIC AND OYSTER SAUCE OR "FLYING" GREENS

PAK BUNG LOY FA

*I*t all started, apparently, in the northern town of Phitsanulok with a simple stir-fried dish of swamp morning glory. These greens, also known as swamp cabbage and water spinach *(pak bung* and *kangkung)*, grow in or near water, are cheap, nourishing and utterly delicious, and are routinely eaten throughout Southeast Asia.

One day, or so this recent legend goes, a young chef in an open-air restaurant, having stir-fried the dish in a wok, tossed the dish into the air a few times before transferring it to a serving plate. He noticed that he had an audience. He threw it higher the next time, then higher and higher until he made an act out of it. Soon he was not content with throwing the greens 20 feet into the air and catching them. He decided to throw them across the street where an acrobatic second chef ran to catch them on a serving plate. Of course, a few strands did end up on telephone wires and in trees, but the dining audience was hooked! Nowadays members of the same family do their "act" in Chiang Mai and Pattaya as well, to great acclaim.

The greens taste good even if they are not airborne before being eaten. Most of us cannot get swamp morning glory, but luckily any greens will do—young collard greens, spinach, Swiss chard, the Chinese *choi sam* and *gai lan.*

In Chiang Mai, where I saw these greens being prepared, the ingredients were combined on a plate and then emptied into a very hot wok encircled by billowing flames. Because most of us cannot expect to get this sort of intense heat in our kitchens at home, I put the ingredients in my own slower order.   *Serves 2–4*

continued

¾ lb young collard greens or spinach
(trimmed weight)

3 garlic cloves

2 tablespoons any meat, poultry or
vegetable stock, homemade or canned or
water

1 tablespoon oyster sauce

2 teaspoons crushed yellow bean sauce or
soy sauce

3 tablespoons vegetable oil

Separate the leaves of the greens and trim them. Bring a large pan of water to a rolling boil. Drop in the greens and boil them at a high temperature for a few minutes or until they are just tender. Drain immediately and plunge them into cold water to fix the color. Drain thoroughly.

Peel the garlic and chop it finely. Combine the stock, oyster sauce and yellow bean sauce.

Set a wok over a high heat. When it is hot, put in the oil and let it heat. Then put in the garlic. Stir quickly once or twice or until the garlic is light brown, then add the greens. Stir them briskly for a brief minute. Add the stock mixture and stir and cook, still on a high heat, for another minute or so. Pour out the liquid, if there is any, into a serving dish. Give the greens another stir and then lift them out, laying them over the liquid in the dish.

Vietnam

*From Lửu Thanh
Nhàn in Hanoi*

KOHLRABI OR BROCCOLI STEM SALAD

NỘM SU HÀO

This very popular and delicious salad is served at most weddings in north Vietnam. It calls for kohlrabi, a vegetable that is probably still unfamiliar to many Westerners. When I was a child growing up in India, we four girls insisted that our father grow it in our vegetable garden. We loved it with a passion and devoured it raw while it was still young and tender. I did not care for it in its cooked version then, though I have since completely changed my mind and now love it in all its forms.

Kohlrabi belongs to the cabbage family. You have probably seen it in Chinese, Korean and Southeast Asian groceries. It consists of a pale green or purple turnip-shaped ball from which grow long edible leaves. Only the ball itself is required for this recipe (some shops sell only the ball). If you cannot obtain it, use the larger stems from heads of broccoli. Peel them before cutting them into julienne strips. You will need ½ lb peeled stems. The taste of the two is almost identical. When cutting kohlrabi, you will notice that almost a quarter of the bottom end is fibrous and very hard. This may be cut away entirely and discarded.   *Serves 4*

Peel the garlic and crush it or put it through a press. Add it to the lime juice. Chop the chilies very finely. Combine the garlic-lime juice mixture, chilies, shrimp paste, coconut, ground red pepper and salt in a large bowl and mix well.

Preheat the oven to 350° F. Wipe the mushrooms with a damp cloth and cut them into ¼-inch-thick slices. Put the mushrooms into the bowl with the spices. Toss well. Prepare a large piece of aluminum foil about 18 inches long. Empty the tossed mushrooms and all the spices right in the center of it. Fold the foil over the mushrooms from the top and the bottom and then from the sides to make a neat packet. Place the packet in the oven and bake for 30 minutes. Open carefully and empty the mushrooms into a serving bowl.

SPICY YELLOW SPLIT PEAS

Malaysia

*From Puan
Rashidah in
Kuala Lumpur*

PARPU

*T*his was originally a South Indian dish, as its Tamil name attests. It has changed, very slightly, as it moved through Malaysia. Here, though the traditional Indian *toovar dal* (Indian yellow split peas) is preferred, it is harder to find and more expensive. Hence yellow split peas are commonly used instead. This dish may be served with rice or with a bread such as *pita* or *chappati*.

Serves 4–6

1½ cups yellow split peas

2 2-inch cinnamon sticks

4–8 whole dried hot red chilies

½ teaspoon ground turmeric

2 smallish potatoes

1 large garlic clove

½-inch cube fresh ginger

1½ teaspoons salt

¾ cup coconut milk (see page 282)

1 small onion

1 teaspoon whole mustard seeds
   (black or yellow)

½ teaspoon whole fennel seeds

6–8 fresh or dried curry leaves (optional)

4 tablespoons vegetable oil or ghee
   (clarified butter)

Wash the peas, drain them and put them in a heavy-bottomed pan. Add the cinnamon, half the red chilies, the turmeric and 3¾ cups water. Bring to a simmer. Cover loosely, leaving the lid slightly ajar, and simmer gently for about 45 minutes or until the peas are almost tender.

continued

Meanwhile, peel the potatoes and cut them into pieces about ½ inch thick and about ¾ inch long. Peel the garlic and ginger and cut them into very fine strips. When the peas have cooked for 45 minutes, add the potatoes, garlic, ginger, salt and ½ cup water. Bring to a gentle simmer and cook, covered, for about 20 minutes, stirring now and then to prevent sticking. Stir the coconut milk and pour it in. Stir to mix and bring to a simmer. Cover and turn off the heat. Keep in a warm place.

Peel and finely slice the onion. Combine the mustard seeds, fennel seeds, remaining chilies and curry leaves in a small bowl. Heat the oil or *ghee* in a small frying pan. When it is hot, put in the onion. Stir and fry until the onion turns a medium brown color. Add the whole seasonings which you have mixed in the small bowl. Stir quickly once or twice. Lift the lid of the pan containing the peas and pour in the entire contents of the frying pan. Cover quickly to hold in the aromas.

Thailand

SPINACH WITH GARLIC AND FISH SAUCE

PAD PAK BUNG

*H*ere is a simple and delicious way to cook spinach in the Thai style.
Serves 4–6

1¾ lb fresh spinach
3 garlic cloves
5 tablespoons vegetable oil (preferably peanut)
4–5 teaspoons fish sauce or salt to taste

Pull the spinach leaves apart and wash them well. Drain. Bring a large pan of water to a rolling boil. Drop in the spinach. Bring the water to a boil again, and boil rapidly for 2 minutes or until the spinach is just done. Drain and rinse under cold running water to fix the bright green color. Drain again, squeezing out most of the water.

Peel the garlic and chop it finely.

Put the oil in a wok or large frying pan and set it over a medium-high heat. When the oil is hot, put in the garlic. Stir a few times or until the garlic turns golden. Add the spinach. Stir and fry for 3 minutes. Add the fish sauce or salt, a little at a time, stirring and tasting as you go. Cook for another minute, stirring frequently.

Snow Peas Stir-Fried with Shrimps

Philippines
From Tito Rey's Restaurant in Manila

SITSARO GUISADO

Many vegetables in the Philippines are cooked with just a few chopped shrimps or cockles or bits of pork in order to flavor them gently. This exquisite dish fits just as successfully into Western meals as it does into Eastern ones.

Serves 4

¾ lb snow peas

3 garlic cloves

½ small onion

About 4 medium shrimps

3 tablespoons olive oil

½ teaspoon salt

4 tablespoons stock (pork, chicken [see page 77] or duck)

Freshly ground black pepper

Snap the stem off each snow pea and then drag it along the "backbone" of the pod in order to string it. Peel the garlic and chop it finely. Peel the onion and chop it finely too. Peel and devein the shrimps. Wash them and pat them dry. Cut them crosswise into ¼-inch pieces.

Put the oil in a large wok or frying pan and set it over a medium-high heat. When the oil is hot, put in the garlic and onion. Stir for about 30 seconds or until the garlic and onion turn golden. Add the shrimps. Stir for 30 seconds and then put in the snow peas. Stir for another 30 seconds. Add the salt and stir to mix. Put in the stock and cover immediately. Cook on a medium-high heat for about 1½ minutes or until the vegetables are just done. Sprinkle the black pepper over the top, mix and serve.

SEASONED SPINACH

SIGUMCHI NAMUL

*E*ven though this recipe comes from Korea, a very similar dish is eaten in Japan as well. Both are offered at room temperature in relatively small quantities and served as appetizers. The Koreans tend to put the entire amount onto a single plate while the Japanese divide it up into individual portions and serve it mounded up into tiny hillocks.   *Serves 4*

10 oz fresh spinach
Salt
1½ tablespoons sesame seeds
1½ tablespoons Japanese soy sauce
    (shoyu)
1 teaspoon sugar
1 tablespoon sesame oil

Trim the spinach, separate the leaves, and wash them well. Bring a large pan of lightly salted water to a rolling boil and drop in the spinach. Boil it rapidly until the leaves have wilted. Drain well and immediately plunge the spinach into cold water to set the color. Drain and squeeze out as much water as possible. Cut the spinach into 2-inch lengths.

Now make the dressing. Put the sesame seeds into a small cast-iron frying pan set over a medium-high heat. Stir the seeds about for a few minutes until they are roasted and give out a nutty aroma. Empty the seeds into a clean coffee grinder, food processor or mortar and grind them coarsely. Put the ground seeds into a bowl. Add the soy sauce, sugar and sesame oil and mix together. Pour the dressing over the spinach and mix well. Taste to check whether the seasoning is as you like it. Add more soy sauce if you think you need it and mix again.

ZUCCHINI WITH PORK AND SHRIMPS

BẦU XÀO

When I asked a government official in Hanoi what he had had for his lunch that day, he said that he had brought it from home and that it consisted of green beans stir-fried with a little pork and some rice. Vegetables are nearly always cooked with pork or seafood, or both, in Vietnam. The amount of flesh is not necessarily large, but just enough to flavor the vegetables. For this recipe, I buy one large thin-cut pork chop and then take the meat off the bone.   *Serves 4*

3 small zucchini
½ teaspoon salt
¼ lb medium shrimps
¼ lb lean pork
1 small onion
1 garlic clove
7–8 tablespoons fresh coriander leaves
1 scallion
2 tablespoons vegetable oil
Freshly ground black pepper
2 tablespoons fish sauce or salt to taste

Trim the zucchini and cut them into quarters lengthwise. Cut away and discard most of the seeded area. Now cut the zucchini shells into fingers that are roughly 2½ inches long, ½ inch thick and ¼ inch wide. Put these into a bowl. Add the salt and toss. Set aside for 30 minutes. Then wash the zucchini under cold running water and pat them as dry as possible.

Peel and devein the shrimps and split them in half lengthwise. Hit each half with the flat side of a large knife to discourage its tendency to curl up. Cut the pork into ⅛-inch-thick slices that are about 2½ inches long and about ¼–½ inch wide. Peel the onion and garlic and chop them finely. Chop the fresh coriander leaves coarsely. Cut the scallion into fine rings along its entire length, including the green section.

Put the oil in a large frying pan or wok and set it over a high heat. When the oil is hot, put in the garlic and onion. Stir and fry for a minute. Add the pork and shrimps. Stir and cook for 2 minutes. Then put in the zucchini, black pepper and fish sauce. Stir and fry for about 3 minutes. Add the coriander leaves and scallion. Stir and cook for 30 seconds. Serve hot.

STIR-FRIED ZUCCHINI WITH SESAME SEEDS

HOBAK NAMUL

This superb, gently flavored dish may be served with almost any Asian meal as well as with roasted and grilled meats. It is good even with sausages and hamburgers. *Serves 6*

4 medium zucchini
2 teaspoons salt
4 garlic cloves
1 scallion
3 tablespoons vegetable oil
1 tablespoon sesame oil
2½ tablespoons roasted sesame seeds
  (see page 299)

Trim the zucchini and cut them in half lengthwise. Then cut the halves crosswise into ¼-inch-thick slices and put the slices into a large bowl. Sprinkle 1½ teaspoons of the salt over them, mix well and set aside for 30–40 min-utes. Drain thoroughly and pat dry. Meanwhile, peel the garlic and chop it finely. Cut the scallion into very fine rounds along its entire length.

Set a wok over a high heat. When it is hot, put in the vegetable oil. When the oil has heated, put in the garlic. Stir once or twice or until the garlic begins to color. Add the zucchini. Stir and fry for 4–5 minutes or until the zucchini are just done. Put in the re-maining ½ teaspoon salt, the scallion and sesame oil. Stir once or twice. Add the roasted sesame seeds. Stir once and serve. This dish may also be served cold as a salad.

SALAD OF ASSORTED VEGETABLES WITH A DELICIOUS PEANUT DRESSING

GADO-GADO

My family's idea of a perfect lunch is *gado-gado*. It is light and meatless, which suits us in the middle of the day. It also happens to be mouth-wateringly good and totally satisfying in a way many so-called light salads are not.

This Indonesian favorite may be described as a composed salad: vegetables of various humble sorts (cabbage, cauliflower, green beans, bean sprouts, carrots, potatoes, cucumbers), as well as hard-boiled eggs, are all neatly laid out on individual plates. Then a kind of cooked vinaigrette, rich with crushed peanuts, is poured over the top. The result is as magical as it is nutritious.

Even though I have suggested what vegetables to include in this recipe, you may change them or their quantities according to what you have available. It is the perfect way to use up the odd few carrots or the remaining quarter of a cabbage!

All the parts of this salad may be prepared several hours ahead of time. It can also be assembled in advance and covered with plastic wrap until you are ready to eat. The dressing should, however, be poured on at the last minute. In Indonesia Shrimp Wafers (*krupuk udang*, page 76) are always served on the side. You may do without them if you wish.   *Serves 4 as a main course or 8 as a first course or salad*

2 medium potatoes (preferably new)

3 eggs

¼ lb green beans

1 large carrot

5 oz cauliflower

¼ small cabbage

¼ lb bean sprouts

1 small cucumber

2 teaspoons salt

FOR THE PEANUT DRESSING

1¼ cups Roasted Peanuts (see page 247)

2 garlic cloves

3 medium shallots (or ½ small onion)

2 tablespoons vegetable oil

½ teaspoon ground red (cayenne) pepper

½ teaspoon salt

2 teaspoons dark brown sugar

Freshly ground black pepper

4–5 teaspoons lime or lemon juice

continued

Set the potatoes to boil. When they are done, cool but do not refrigerate them. Peel them and cut them into ¼-inch-thick slices. Hard-boil the eggs. Shell them and cut them lengthwise into quarters.

Keep all the raw vegetables separate as you prepare them. Trim the green beans and cut them into 2-inch lengths. Trim and peel the carrots. Cut them crosswise into 2-inch sections and then halve or quarter the sections lengthwise so that the carrots match the beans in size. Cut the cauliflower into small delicate flowerets. Cut the cabbage into fine long shreds. Break off the threadlike tails of the bean sprouts and rinse them well in a bowl of water. Drain. Peel the cucumber and cut it crosswise into round slices.

Set a bowl near the stove with a sieve balanced on it. Also set out several plates to hold the different vegetables as they are cooked.

Bring 2 quarts water to a rolling boil in a medium-sized pan. Add 2 teaspoons salt to it and stir. Put the green beans and the carrots together into the boiling water. Let the water come to a rolling boil again and boil rapidly for about 3 minutes or until the vegetables are just cooked through. Empty the contents of the pan, vegetables and water, into the sieve. Lift up the sieve and drain the vegetables. Rinse the vegetables under cold running water and put them on a plate. Pour the water in the bowl back into the pan and bring it to a rolling boil again. Put the cauliflower into the pan. Let the water return to the boil. Boil the cauliflower rapidly for about 1½ minutes or

until it is just tender but retains a hint of crispness. Empty the contents of the pan into the sieve, lift up the sieve and drain the cauliflower. Rinse the cauliflower under cold running water and put it on a plate. Cook the cabbage and bean sprouts in the same way, boiling the cabbage for about 1 minute and the bean sprouts for 30 seconds. Drain each and refresh under cold running water. Squeeze any excess moisture from the cabbage and bean sprouts and then separate the strands before putting them on separate plates.

Now make the dressing. Put the peanuts into a food processor and grind them as finely as possible. Peel the garlic and shallots and chop them finely. Put the oil in a small pan over a medium heat. When it is hot, put in the garlic and shallots. Stir and fry for about 1 minute or until the garlic and shallots have turned a medium brown. Put in 2 cups water, the ground red pepper, salt, sugar and ground peanuts. Stir and bring to a boil. Turn the heat to medium-low and simmer for 15–20 minutes or until the sauce has thickened. It should be no thicker than a creamy salad dressing. Stir now and then to break up any lumps.

Remove the cooked dressing from the heat and let it cool a little. Add the black pepper, beat in the lime juice and taste to check whether the seasoning is as you like it. Arrange the potatoes, eggs, green beans and carrots, cauliflower, cabbage, bean sprouts and cucumber side by side on 4 individual plates. Just before serving, pour about a quarter of the dressing evenly over each serving.

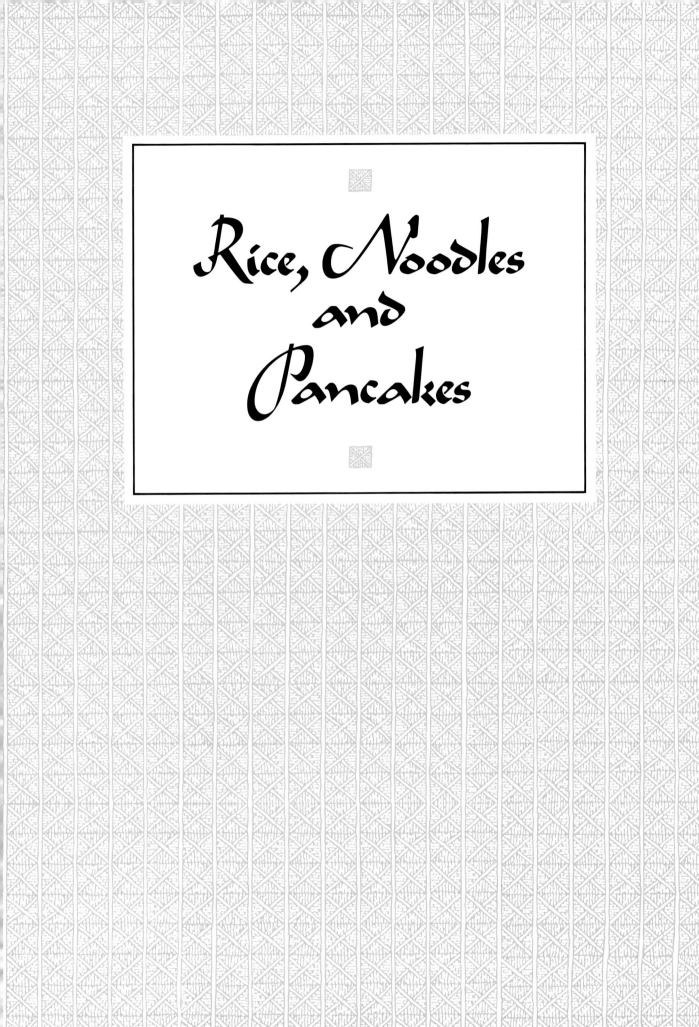

Rice, Noodles and Pancakes

PLAIN LONG-GRAIN RICE

2 cups long-grain rice

Put the rice in a bowl and fill the bowl with water. Rub the rice gently with your hands. When the water turns milky, pour it off. Do this several times in quick succession until the water runs clear. Now fill the bowl with fresh water and let the rice soak for 30 minutes. Drain.

Put the drained rice into a heavy medium-sized pan. Add 2⅔ cups water and bring to a boil. Cover with a tight-fitting lid. (If your lid is not the tight-fitting kind, cover the pan first with aluminum foil, crimping the edges, and then cover with the lid.) Turn the heat to very low and cook for 25 minutes. If left covered in a warm place, this rice will retain its heat for a good hour. *Serves 4–6*

PLAIN JAPANESE AND KOREAN RICE

GOHAN, PAB

The rice in Japan and Korea is a fat short-grain variety that develops a most pleasing stickiness when it is cooked. The grains not only adhere to each other, thus making them easy to pick up with chopsticks in small lumps, but they can also be easily rolled into ovals and rounds, all the better to be devoured with neat slivers of raw fish or roasted sesame seeds. Japanese food just does not taste the same to me without Japanese-style rice.

The brand to look for in Asian grocers' shops is *Kokuho Rose*. If you cannot find it, use long-grain rice and cook it according to the recipe for Plain Long-Grain Rice on page 210. Aromatic rices, such as *basmati,* are quite unsuitable for Japanese and Korean meals.

If you wish to cook more or less rice than suggested in the recipe below, remember that the proportion of rice to water, in volume, is 1:1¼. The cooking time remains exactly the same.   *Serves 4–6*

2 cups Japanese or Korean rice

Put the rice in a bowl and add water to cover it generously. Swish the rice around gently with your hand, kneading it lightly as you do so. Pour off the water when it has turned milky. Do this several times in quick succession, until the water remains almost clear. Drain the rice through a sieve. Leave the rice in the sieve for 30 minutes–1 hour to allow it to absorb the moisture that clings to it.

Put the rice into a heavy-bottomed pan. Add 2½ cups water and bring to a boil. Cover, turn the heat to very low and cook for 20 minutes. Turn the heat to high for 30 seconds and then turn it off. Let the pan sit, covered and undisturbed, for another 10–15 minutes.

GLUTINOUS RICE

Glutinous rice is also known as sticky rice and sweet rice. The grains are short and white and, when cooked, they turn translucent and slightly glutinous. They are *not* sweet, however. Throughout much of the Far East this rice is used for both sweets and stuffings. In the region around northern Thailand, however, it is the staple grain. At each meal it is served from a large basket. Each diner forms the rice into a little ball, combines that ball with a bit of meat and a bit of vegetable and then pops the morsel into his or her mouth. The two easiest ways to cook this rice are by steaming and by using a double boiler. Here is the double boiler method. *Serves 4–6*

2 cups glutinous rice

Wash the rice in several changes of water and drain it. Put it in a bowl, cover with plenty of water and leave it to soak for 6 hours. Drain, wash again, and drain thoroughly.

Heat some water in the bottom of a double boiler. When it starts to boil, fit in the top of the double boiler and into it put the rice and enough water to bring the level to ½ inch above the rice. When the water with the rice begins to boil, cover the pan and cook on a medium heat for 25 minutes.

MIXED RICE

Japan

Adapted from a recipe of the École Technique Hôtelière Tsuji in Osaka

KAYAKU GOHAN

This delightful mixture of rice, chicken and vegetables may be served all by itself with accompanying salads (and beer!) or, if you leave the chicken out, it may be served with all manner of simply grilled meats and fish. You may substitute any cubed white fish fillets for the chicken, in which case do not bother with the blanching. The rice will probably develop a slightly brown crustiness at the bottom: this is as it should be. *Seves 4–6*

2 cups Japanese rice

2 chicken thighs or 1 whole leg

1 small carrot

4 green beans

1 large or 2 small mushrooms

2½ cups Japanese Soup Stock (see page 78) or Chicken Stock, homemade (see page 77) or canned

3 tablespoons Japanese soy sauce (shoyu)

2 tablespoons rice wine (mirin) or 1 tablespoon sugar well dissolved in 1 tablespoon sake or water

About 15 snow peas

Salt

2 tablespoons sake (optional)

Put the rice in a bowl and add water to cover it generously. Swish the rice around gently with your hand. Pour off the water when it turns milky. Do this several times in quick succession, until the water remains almost clear. Drain the rice through a sieve and leave it in the sieve for 30 minutes–1 hour to allow it to absorb the moisture that clings to it.

Meanwhile, bone the chicken (follow the instructions on page 55). Skin the meat and cut it into ¼-inch dice. Drop the meat into a pan of boiling water for 10–15 seconds. Drain it quickly, rinse it briefly under cold running water, and then drain well.

Peel the carrot and cut it into 1-inch lengths. Cut these lengths into fine julienne strips. Trim the green beans and cut them into 1-inch lengths. Cut these lengths into fine julienne strips. Wipe the mushroom with a damp cloth and cut it into thin slices. Cut the slices into fine strips.

Combine the rice, chicken, carrot, green beans, mushroom, stock, soy sauce and *mirin* in a heavy-bottomed pan. Bring to a boil. Cover tightly, turn the heat very low and cook for 20 minutes.

Meanwhile, string the snow peas, cut into 1-inch lengths, then cut the lengths into fine strips. Throw the snow peas into lightly salted boiling water. Boil for 15–20 seconds. Drain, rinse under cold running water and drain again.

After the rice has cooked for 20 minutes, quickly put in the snow peas and *sake*. Cover the pan immediately with a clean dish towel and then with the lid. Take the pan off the heat and set aside for 10–15 minutes before serving, so that any excess moisture in the rice can be absorbed by the dish towel.

SPECIAL FRIED RICE WITH BEEF AND SHRIMPS

NASI GORENG ISTIMEWA

This fried rice, served with Shrimp Wafers (page 76) and Red Pepper Sauce (page 242) or Red Pepper Sauce with Shrimp Paste (page 243), can be a meal in itself. In Indonesia hot chilies and cucumbers, cut prettily to resemble tropical flora, decorate the rice plate like bunting, as do Egg Strips (page 251) and Crisply Fried Shallot Flakes (page 250). You may, if you like, choose a simpler garnish of chopped hard-boiled eggs and finely sliced scallions sprinkled over the rice and halved cherry tomatoes and cucumber slices arranged around the edges. Cooked shrimps may be used in this dish if uncooked ones are unavailable; if they are small, increase the quantity recommended.

It is a good idea to cook the rice itself well ahead of time so that it has time to cool off completely before you stir-fry it. For the best flavor, the rice should be stir-fried with all the other ingredients just before eating. *Serves 4*

1¼ cups long-grain rice
1 small red bell pepper
3 small shallots (or ½ small onion)
1 teaspoon shrimp or anchovy paste
1 teaspoon salt
¼ teaspoon ground red (cayenne) pepper
¼ lb lean beef steak
4 medium shrimps
2 cabbage leaves
4 tablespoons vegetable oil

Wash the rice in several changes of water, then drain it. Cover it generously with water and leave it to soak for 30 minutes. Drain again. Put the rice into a heavy-bottomed pan. Add 1⅔ cups water and bring it to a boil. Cover tightly, turn the heat to very low and cook for 25 minutes. Switch off the heat. Keep the pan covered and let the rice come to room temperature.

Coarsely chop the red bell pepper, removing all the seeds. Peel and coarsely chop the shallots. Combine the red bell pepper, shallots, shrimp paste, salt and ground red pepper in an electric blender. Blend until a smooth paste results.

Cut the steak across the grain into very thin slices. Cut the slices crosswise into ¼-inch-wide strips. Peel and devein the shrimps. Cut them crosswise into ¼-inch-wide segments. Cover both and set aside, refrigerating if necessary. Cut the cabbage leaves into very fine long shreds.

Just before you are ready to serve, set a wok over a medium-high heat. When it is hot, put in the oil. When the oil has heated, pour in the spice paste. Stir and fry for 3–4 minutes or until the spice paste turns dark red and the oil separates. Add the beef and shrimps. Stir and fry for 1 minute. Add the cabbage. Stir and fry for another minute. Now put in all the rice, breaking up any lumps with the back of a slotted spoon. Stir and fry for 4–6 minutes or until the rice has heated through. Garnish as suggested above, and serve.

PERFUMED RICE WITH VEGETABLES NONYA-STYLE

Malaysia

From the Hyatt Saujana Hotel in Kuala Lumpur

NASI ULAM

*T*his unusual rice dish is first perfumed with fresh herbs, then flavored with a little fish and finally topped with crunchy raw vegetables. It is exquisite, both in taste and appearance. Rather like fried rice, to which it is a very superior cousin, it may be eaten with other foods or all by itself. Use any tender green beans; in Malaysia long green beans would be used.

If you have a Southeast Asian grocer near you, try to obtain fresh lemongrass and fresh kaffir lime leaves as the dry ones just cannot be used in this dish. However, if you cannot get the fresh herbs, all is not lost. Western herbs, such as basil, chervil, tarragon and summer savory, may be substituted. The aromas are different but they do make the rice very interesting.

In Malaysia, where the climate is generally balmy, this rice is served at room temperature. I prefer to serve it hot or warm.   *Serves 4–6*

4–5 fresh kaffir lime leaves or 1½
    tablespoons grated lemon rind
1 stick fresh lemongrass or 15 fresh basil
    leaves, torn into small pieces
About ¼ of a regular cucumber
2½ oz tender green or long beans
3 medium shallots or ½ small onion
5 medium shrimps
4 tablespoons vegetable oil
Salt
2 cups long-grain rice

Cut the center vein out of the kaffir lime leaves and then cut the leaves crosswise into the thinnest hairlike strips. Trim the lemongrass, discarding its very hard bottom tip and its strawlike top. Cut the rest (which should be about 6 inches long) crosswise into very, very thin rounds. Combine with the lime leaves and cover. Peel the cucumber and cut it into ⅛-inch dice. If the cucumber has large seeds, discard them and use only the outer seedless section. Trim the ends of the beans and then cut them crosswise into ⅛-inch pieces. Combine the beans with the cucumber and cover. Peel the shallots and cut them into paper-thin slices. Peel and devein the shrimps and then cut them crosswise into ¼-inch segments.

Line a plate with paper toweling. Put the oil in a frying pan and set it over a medium heat. When the oil is hot, put in the shallots. Stir and fry until they turn medium brown and crisp. Remove them with a slotted spoon and spread them out over the paper toweling to drain. Put the cut shrimps into the same oil. Stir and fry for about 1 minute or until the prawns are cooked through. Remove them with a slotted spoon and put them into a bowl. Sprinkle the shrimps very lightly with salt, toss them and then cover. Save the oil in the pan.

Wash the rice in several changes of water. Drain. Cover well with water, soak for 30 minutes, and then drain again. About 30 minutes—1 hour before you intend to eat, combine the rice, 2⅔ cups water and 1 teaspoon salt in a medium-sized, heavy-bottomed pan. Bring the water to a boil, cover, turn the heat to *very* low and cook for 25 minutes. If you are not eating at once, keep the rice covered and keep it warm.

Just before serving, empty all the rice into a serving bowl, breaking up any lumps with the back of a slotted spoon. Put in the shrimps, the reserved oil in which they were cooked, the kaffir lime leaves and the lemongrass. If you are using basil leaves and lemon rind, add these now. Toss to mix. Scatter the cucumber and beans over the top, followed by the fried shallots, and serve.

RICE WITH SEAFOOD, CHICKEN AND SAUSAGES

Philippines
With help from
Ruby Roa

PAELLA

One of the glories of Spain, this dish now also decks the tables at fiestas and banquets all over the Philippines. While the main ingredients, rice and a touch of saffron, remain the same (the less affluent use coloring from caper-shaped Mexican *achiote* seeds instead), all other ingredients are left to the whim, and pocket, of the cook. In the poorer *barrios,* chicken, green peas and tomatoes suffice, while in the mansions of the rich, *paellas* come with shrimps, squid, clams and mussels peeping invitingly out of the rice.

Traditionally a *paella* was cooked on a *paellera,* and in some homes it still is. A *paellera* is a very large, round tray. Rice is cooked in it rather in the manner of an Italian *risotto* with frequent additions of hot stock and much stirring. Raw, partially cooked and fully cooked meats and seafood are embedded in the rice at frequent intervals and in a sequence that only practiced chefs have mastered. All ingredients must be ready at the same time.

Since most of us do not have *paelleras,* here is a delicious *paella* that is cooked in a saucepan. You do need a large, wide, heavy pan with a tight-fitting lid. If you are unsure of the fit of the lid, cover the pan first with aluminum foil.   *Serves 6*

2 sweet or hot Italian or Spanish sausages
    (such as chorizo), *weighing in total*
    about 6 oz
2 *whole chicken legs, each cut into*
    3–4 pieces
Salt
Freshly ground black pepper
6 *tablespoons olive oil*
8 *fresh clams*
8 *fresh mussels*

Generous pinch saffron threads
About 2 cups Chicken Stock, homemade
    (see page 77) or canned
12 *medium shrimps*
½ *large red bell pepper*
½ *large green bell pepper*
1 *large onion*
3 *garlic cloves*
1½ *cups fresh or frozen peas*
3 *cups long-grain rice*

continued

Prick the sausages with a fork and put them into a frying pan with ¾ cup water. Bring to a boil. Cover, turn the heat to medium and cook for 5 minutes. Uncover and continue to cook until the water boils away. Brown the sausages in the fat they have exuded. Let them cool, then cut them into ¼-inch slices.

Dust the chicken lightly with salt and pepper. Put the olive oil in a clean frying pan and set it over a medium heat. When the oil is hot, put in the chicken pieces and fry them for about 10 minutes or until they are brown on both sides. Remove them with a slotted spoon. Save the oil.

Clean the clams and mussels with a stiff brush under cold running water, pulling off any beards that may still be attached to the mussels. Put the clams and mussels into a pan with 3 cups water and bring to a boil. Cover the pan and simmer vigorously over a medium heat for about 5 minutes or until the mollusks open. Remove them as they open and wash them quickly under cold running water if they seem to be gritty. Cool, cover and set aside. Save the cooking liquid. Strain the liquid through a clean cloth and put it in a large measuring cup or bowl. Add the saffron and enough chicken stock to make up 1 quart.

Peel and devein the shrimps. Wash them and pat them dry. Seed the red and green bell peppers and cut them lengthwise into ¼-inch wide strips. Peel and thinly slice the onion. Peel and finely chop the garlic.

If the peas are fresh, boil them in 2½ cups water until they are just tender. Drain and refresh them under cold running water. Drain again and set them aside. If the peas are frozen, cook them for just 1 minute. Drain them, refresh under cold running water and drain them again.

In a large, wide, heavy pan put 5 tablespoons of the oil used for frying the chicken and set it over a medium-high heat. When the oil is hot, put in the onions and garlic. Fry for about 2½ minutes or until they are soft. Add the peppers. Stir and cook for another 2½ minutes. Now add the rice. Stir and fry for 2 minutes, turning the heat down a little if the rice seems to stick. Add the saffron-flavored clam-mussel liquor, the sausages, the chicken and 1 teaspoon salt. Bring to the boil. Cover, turn the heat to very low and cook for 20 minutes. Lift the lid and quickly bury the shrimps in the rice and scatter the peas over the top. Cover the pan again and cook for another 5 minutes. Lift the lid and quickly put in the clams and mussels. Cover and cook for another 2 minutes.

Rice with Seafood, Chicken and Sausages (page 217)

MADHUR JAFFREY'S FAR EASTERN COOKERY

TOMATO RICE

NASI TOMAT

Like many Malaysians, Aminahbi is of mixed Malay and Indian ancestry. Her exquisite food acknowledges her dual heritage with pride, as this recipe shows.

When rice is cooked in thick liquid, there is a tendency for the grains on top to remain slightly underdone. The solution is to turn the rice over halfway through the cooking. This has to be done rather fast as the minimum amount of steam should be allowed to escape.   *Serves 4–6*

2 cups long-grain rice
4 canned peeled plum tomatoes, lightly drained
4 tablespoons plain yogurt
5 medium shallots (or ½ small onion)
1-inch cube fresh ginger
8–10 fresh mint leaves
3 tablespoons vegetable oil
½ teaspoon whole cumin seeds
5 whole cloves
5–6 whole cardamom pods
2-inch cinnamon stick
1 whole star anise
1½ teaspoons salt

Wash the rice in several changes of water. Drain and put it in a bowl. Cover it generously with water and leave it to soak for 30 minutes. Drain. Meanwhile, mash the tomatoes to a pulp. Put the yogurt in a large measuring cup and beat it with a fork until it is smooth and creamy. Add the tomatoes and enough water to make up 2⅔ cups. Mix. Peel the shallots and cut them into fine slices. Peel the ginger and cut it into very thin slices and then into minute dice. Chop the mint leaves coarsely.

Put the oil in a medium-sized heavy pan and set it over a medium heat. When the oil is hot, put in the cumin, cloves, cardamom, cinnamon and star anise. Stir once or twice and add the shallots. Stir and fry until the shallots are reddish brown. Put in the ginger and stir once. Add the rice and stir for 2 minutes, turning the heat down a little if the rice starts to stick to the bottom of the pan. Put in the tomato-yogurt mixture, the salt and the mint. Bring to a boil. Cover well, first with aluminum foil and then with a lid. Turn the heat down to very low and cook for 15 minutes. Lift the lid, gently toss the rice with a slotted spoon so that the top layer is well buried at the bottom, cover again and continue cooking for another 15 minutes or until the rice is done.

POTATO PANCAKES

GANJA BUCHIN

Koreans eat these scrumptious, slightly glutinous pancakes as a snack with a spicy dipping sauce. They can also be served as part of a meal. I often serve them at brunch or at breakfast along with scrambled eggs. Once the potatoes have been grated and the batter mixed, you need to proceed apace and cook all the pancakes, for the batter tends to darken if not used straightaway. Use 2 frying pans at once if necessary. If you wish to make more than 8 pancakes, make another batch of fresh batter.   *Makes 8 small pancakes and serves 2–4*

Korean Dipping Sauce (see page 241)
2 medium (½ lb) potatoes
½ small onion
1 egg
1½ tablespoons cornstarch
¼ teaspoon salt
3–4 tablespoons vegetable oil

Make the Korean Dipping Sauce.

Peel the potatoes and put them into a bowl of water. Peel the onion and chop it very finely. Beat the egg and set it aside. Measure out the cornstarch and mix it with the salt. Just before eating, grate the potatoes finely so that they turn into pulp. Add the onion, egg and the cornstarch-salt mixture to them. Mix well.

Put just enough oil into 2 large frying pans to coat the bottom and set each over a medium heat. When the oil is hot, drop 1 rounded tablespoon batter into a corner of a frying pan, spreading it out with the back of a spoon until the pancake is about 3 inches in diameter. You should be able to fit 4 pancakes into 1 large frying pan. Cook each pancake for 2–3 minutes on the first side, or until it turns reddish brown. Turn the pancakes over and cook on the second side for another 2–3 minutes, or until that side develops reddish spots. Serve hot with the Korean Dipping Sauce.

CELLOPHANE NOODLES WITH BEEF AND VEGETABLES

CHAPCHAE

Also called transparent bean thread noodles, pea starch noodles and bean sticks, cellophane noodles are made from mung beans. They can be put into soups and combined with almost any meat and vegetable. Here is a Korean way of preparing them. *Serves 4*

2 oz cellophane noodles

4 scallions

4 garlic cloves

5 oz tender beef steak

4 teaspoons plus 1 tablespoon soy sauce
  (preferably Japanese—shoyu)

4 teaspoons sugar

Freshly ground black pepper

1 tablespoon plus 1 teaspoon sesame oil

5 dried Chinese mushrooms

1 medium carrot

1 small zucchini

½ (10 oz) package fresh spinach

5 tablespoons vegetable oil

Salt

1 tablespoon roasted sesame seeds
  (see page 299)

Put the cellophane noodles in a bowl. Pour warm water over them and let them soak for 30 minutes–1 hour or until they are soft. Drain them and cut them into 3-inch lengths. Cut the scallions into 3-inch lengths. Cut each piece lengthwise into 2–3 strips. Peel the garlic and chop it finely.

Cut the beef against the grain into very thin slices. Cut these slices, also against the grain, into thin julienne strips, each around 3 inches long. In a small bowl combine the beef with 4 teaspoons of the soy sauce, 2 teaspoons of the sugar, 1 tablespoon of the scallions, 1 teaspoon of the garlic, some black pepper and 1 tablespoon of the sesame oil. Toss to mix.

Soak the dried mushrooms in enough hot water to cover for 30 minutes or until they are soft. Lift them out of the water and cut off their hard stems. Slice the caps into ⅛-inch-thick strips. Peel the carrot and cut it into 3-inch lengths. Cut each section lengthwise into thin slices and then into fine julienne strips.

Trim the zucchini and cut it lengthwise into quarters. Cut away the seeded sections and then cut the lengths into 3-inch segments. Cut each segment into long julienne strips. Wash the spinach throroughly and discard any tough stems. Drop the spinach into a pan of boiling water. Boil for 1 minute or until the spinach has wilted. Drain and rinse under cold running water. Squeeze out as much water as possible and then separate the leaves. Combine the carrot, zucchini, spinach and remaining scallions in a bowl.

Put 3 tablespoons of the vegetable oil in a wok or very large frying pan over a high heat. When the oil is hot, put in the remaining garlic. Stir and fry for 30 seconds. Empty the bowl of vegetables into the wok. Stir and fry for 3–4 minutes or until they are tender-crisp. Salt and pepper lightly. Toss. Take the vegetables out of the wok and put them back into the bowl. Put the remaining 2 tablespoons vegetable oil into the wok. When the oil is hot, put in the meat and sliced mushrooms.

Stir and fry for 1–2 minutes or until the meat is just cooked through. Remove the meat and mushrooms with a slotted spoon, leaving the juices, if any, behind.

Turn the heat to low, add ¼ cup water to the wok along with the remaining 1 tablespoon soy sauce and 2 teaspoons sugar. Mix, then turn the heat to medium. Put in the cellophane noodles. Cook for about 2 minutes or until the noodles are heated through and tender. Empty the noodles and liquid into a serving bowl. Add the meat and mushrooms, the vegetables, the remaining 1 teaspoon sesame oil and the roasted sesame seeds. Toss and serve.

COLD SESAME NOODLES WITH CHICKEN AND VEGETABLES

BON BON JIHAN BANMIAN

The noodles in this dish can be cooked in advance, rinsed in cold water and then tossed with a little sesame oil. All the other parts of the dish can be prepared ahead of time as well. All you need to do at the last minute is mix everything together in a large bowl. It is, as a result, a perfect party dish. I have served it both as a first course and as a main dish.   *Serves 3 as a main course or 6 as a first course*

½ lb fresh or dried egg noodles (preferably fresh Chinese lo-mein noodles)

1 tablespoon sesame oil

¼ lb chicken breast, skinned and boned

Salt

1 small carrot

1 medium celery stalk

2 scallions

1 large Kirby or ½ regular cucumber

FOR THE SAUCE

4 tablespoons sesame paste (tahini)

2 tablespoons sesame oil

2 teaspoons Chili Oil (see page 237)

2 tablespoons Chinese light soy sauce

1 tablespoon distilled white vinegar

1 teaspoon sugar

⅛–¼ teaspoon ground red (cayenne) pepper (optional)

5 tablespoons Chicken Stock (see page 77)

Bring a large pan of water to a rolling boil. Drop in the noodles and cook for 3–5 minutes or until they are just done. Drain. Rinse with cold water and drain again. Put them into a bowl, add the 1 tablespoon sesame oil and toss. Cover well with plastic wrap and set aside, refrigerating if necessary.

Cut the piece of chicken breast lengthwise into ¾-inch-wide strips. Put the chicken strips in a medium-sized pan along with ¼ teaspoon salt and enough water just to cover the meat. Slowly bring to a simmer. Continue to simmer gently for 2–4 minutes or until the meat turns white all the way through. Drain the meat and allow it to cool. (Save the stock for use in this recipe or another dish.) Using both your hands, pull the cooked chicken into fine long shreds. Put the shredded chicken into a bowl.

Peel the carrot and cut it into 2-inch-long, very fine julienne strips. Cut the celery and scallions crosswise into 2-inch-long sections and then cut the sections lengthwise into very fine strips. Bring a medium-sized pan of water to a rolling boil. Drop in the carrot and celery. Bring to a boil again and cook rapidly for 40 seconds. Drop in the scallions and boil for another 10 seconds. Drain the vegetables and rinse them under cold running water. Drain again and pat dry. Put the vegetables in the bowl with the chicken, keeping aside just a few pieces for garnishing the finished dish. Peel the cucumber and cut it crosswise into 2-inch chunks. Cut these chunks lengthwise into fine julienne strips. Put most of these strips into the bowl with the chicken, saving a few for garnishing. Cover the chicken bowl with plastic wrap and refrigerate, if necessary. Wrap the vegetables reserved for garnishing in a piece of plastic wrap and set aside.

Now make the sauce. Put the sesame paste in a bowl and stir it well. Slowly add all the other sauce ingredients, mixing as you go. (You could do this in a blender if you wish.) Set aside. Just before you are ready to serve, put the noodles in a bowl. Add the chicken and vegetables. Stir the sauce and pour it over the top. Toss well and taste to check whether the seasoning is as you like it. Transfer to a serving dish or individual plates. Top with the vegetables reserved for garnishing.

RICE NOODLES IN SOUP WITH BEEF

PHỞ

In Vietnam *phở*, a soupy dish that derives its name from the fresh rice noodles that are in it, is a meal in itself. Millions of Vietnamese eat it for breakfast at the crack of dawn as they sit hunched in small restaurants, their chopsticks digging in with gusto. It is quite a sight. In Hanoi I saw huge cauldrons of all-purpose stock boiling away in the fronts of restaurants. A peep inside revealed beef and pork bones, chicken carcasses, chunks of fresh root ginger and onions. As orders came in—and at dawn they come fast—slithery white noodles were dipped in hot water to be heated and then divided into several bowls at the same time. They were topped with slices of cooked chicken or, for those who could afford it, beef, which is preferred rare. A veritable salad of fresh green herbs and seasonings, rich in vitamins, went in next: mints, fresh coriander, scallions and hot green chilies. Finally, a healthy ladle of the stock wilted the greens and released their varying aromas.

That was not all. At the table were more seasonings in the form of sauces—fish sauce, a sauce of hot red chilies and a third one of vinegar and chilies. There were lime wedges, too, for those who wanted them.

I am told by Vietnamese who have left Vietnam that true *phở* is made only with beef and beef stock and that the use of chicken is a change brought about by harder times. Here I give the more traditional recipe. Incidentally, even though *phở* is a much loved breakfast food, it is also eaten for lunch and dinner and as a snack.

The *phở* (pronounced "far") noodle is hard to find in the West except in cities with large Far Eastern or Chinese populations. Use any fresh flat rice noodle, if you can find it. Just heat it briefly in boiling water. Dried *phở* noodles, usually sold as *banh phở*, are available at many Chinese and Thai grocers' shops. They need to be soaked in water for 2 hours and then cooked very briefly in boiling water. If you cannot find any rice noodles, use flat egg noodles as a last resort, cooking them just before you intend to eat. *Serves 4–6*

10 oz dried flat rice noodles (preferably banh phở²) or flat egg noodles

½ lb tender beef steak, about 1 inch thick

2–3 fresh hot red or green chilies

1 scallion

6 tablespoons fresh coriander leaves

6 tablespoons small fresh mint leaves

1 lime

Red Pepper Sauce (see page 242)

1 small bowl fish sauce

Seasoned Vinegar (see page 247)

1½ quarts Beef Stock (see page 80) plus about ⅓ of the beef brisket used in making it, wrapped tightly and refrigerated

If you are using dried rice noodles, soak them in water for 2 hours or more. Drain them before cooking.

Cut the raw beef steak into paper-thin slices 1 inch wide and 2 inches long. (It helps if the meat is partially frozen.) Cut the chilies crosswise into very thin slices and arrange them at one end of a large plate. Cut the scallion into very fine rounds along its entire length, including the green section. Heap it up on the plate beside the chili slices. Wash and dry the fresh coriander leaves, snipping off their coarse stalks. Put the coriander near the scallion. Do the same with the mint and put it near the coriander. Cover the plate with plastic wrap. Cut the lime into wedges. Put the Red Pepper Sauce, fish sauce and the Seasoned Vinegar in separate bowls and set these on the dining table. Put the lime wedges in another small bowl and put it on the table. Cut the cold brisket against the grain into very thin slices 1 inch wide and 2 inches long.

Heat a large pan of water and drop the drained noodles into it. They will cook very fast—perhaps even in 1 minute—so keep testing them. When they are done, drain the noodles again and rinse them under cold running water. Leave the noodles in a bowl of cold water until they are needed.

Just before serving, heat the stock and keep it simmering. To heat the noodles, drain them and then either plunge them into hot water for a few seconds or put them into a microwave oven for 1 minute. (Fresh rice noodles need only to be dropped into boiling water for just a few seconds and then drained. If you are using egg noodles, cook them according to the instructions on the packet.) Divide the noodles among 4–6 individual serving bowls. Arrange a layer of cooked brisket slices over the noodles. On top of the brisket arrange a layer of the raw beef slices. Sprinkle some chili and scallion slices, coriander and mint over the sliced steak. Ladle some of the simmering stock over all this and serve. The diners season the dish themselves with sauces and freshly squeezed lime juice.

RICE NOODLES IN A COCONUT CURRY SOUP

CURRY MEE

Hig tea in England was never quite like this one served in Malaysia! At the Ming Court Hotel in Kuala Lumpur, early evening finds tables in the lobby groaning with cakes and pastries, mango sweetmeats, stir-fried noodles and curried soups. The ritual of tea drinking has been reclaimed by the former colony. With the beverage (and even without it) can be had not just the delicacies of the former rulers but also an array of Eastern snacks that no Malay would dream of doing without.

Rice Noodles in a Coconut Curry Soup is one of them. I think it is the finest curry soup I have ever eaten. Filled with slithery rice noodles, this coconut-enriched soup is permeated with the very Malay aromas of lemongrass and galangal. Even though there are many parts to this dish, it is easy to make.

Serves 4 as a light meal or snack, or 6 as a soup course

10 oz dried flat rice noodles (preferably banh phở) or flat egg noodles

1 stick fresh or 3 tablespoons dried sliced lemongrass

1-inch cube fresh or 8 large slices dried galangal

1 large onion

4 garlic cloves

1-inch cube fresh ginger

1 large red bell pepper

1 tablespoon paprika

1½ tablespoons shrimp or anchovy paste

½ teaspoon ground turmeric

¼–½ teaspoon ground red (cayenne) pepper

8 tablespoons vegetable oil

5 cups Chicken Stock, homemade (see page 77) or canned

1¼ cups thick coconut milk (see page 282)

Salt

Freshly ground black pepper

4½ oz chicken breast, skinned and boned

1 cup fresh bean sprouts

1 celery stalk (preferably from the middle of the bunch)

4 tablespoons Crisply Fried Shallot Flakes (see page 250; optional)

Lime wedges to serve

If you are using dried rice noodles, soak them in water for 2 hours or more.

If you are using fresh lemongrass, slice it crosswise into very thin rounds, starting at the bulbous bottom end and going up about 6 inches. Discard the strawlike top. If you are using dried sliced lemongrass, soak it in ¾ cup hot water for 30 minutes. If you are using fresh galangal, peel it and chop it coarsely. If you are using dried sliced galangal, put it into hot water (with the dried lemongrass, if applicable) and soak it for 30 minutes.

Peel the onion and chop it coarsely. Peel the garlic. Peel the ginger and chop it coarsely. Remove the seeds from the red bell pepper and chop it coarsely. In an electric blender combine the lemongrass (fresh or dried), the galangal (fresh or dried), any soaking liquid, the onion, garlic, ginger, red pepper, paprika, shrimp paste, turmeric and ground red pepper. Blend until smooth, adding a few tablespoons of water if needed to achieve a pastelike consistency.

Put the oil in a wide heavy pan and set it over a medium-high heat. When the oil is hot put in the paste from the blender. Stir and fry for about 15 minutes or until the paste is dark red and reduced, and the oil separates from it. Add the stock, stir and bring to the boil. Turn the heat to low and simmer for 15 minutes. Strain this soup, pushing out as much liquid as you can. If using canned coconut milk, stir well and add to the liquid. If you have made coconut milk from fresh coconut, use only the thick milk which rises to the top. Stir and bring to a simmer. Add salt and black pepper to taste. The soup is now ready; set it aside until later.

Put the chicken breast in a frying pan with water just to cover. Add a generous pinch of salt and bring it slowly to the boil. Turn the heat to low and simmer for 3–5 minutes, turning the breast around a few times until the meat is white all the way through. Lift the chicken out of the liquid and shred the meat. Cover and set aside.

Pluck off the threadlike ends of the bean sprouts and put them in a bowl of cold water. Chop the celery into minute dice. Cover and set aside.

Just before you are ready to serve, set the soup on a low heat. Bring a large pan of water to a rolling boil. If you are using dried rice noodles drain them and drop them into the boiling water and cook them until they are just done. This may take only 1 minute, so watch them carefully. If you are using egg noodles instead of rice noodles, cook them according to the instructions on the packet. Drain the noodles and divide them among the individual serving bowls. Ladle the hot soup over the noodles. Top with some chicken, bean sprouts, diced celery and Crisply Fried Shallot Flakes. Offer lime wedges on the side.

Noodles in Broth with Poached Egg and Vegetables

SANSAI UDON

Noodles are to Japan what hamburgers are to the United States. They are available everywhere and can be simple or elegant, cheap or expensive, just as you please. Whole restuarants are devoted to them. The Japanese love their noodles and are just as content to have them quite plain and icy cold in the summer with a light dipping sauce as they are to have them topped with an elaborate assortment of vegetables, meats, fish and eggs.

Japan, like all Far Eastern countries, has many types of noodles. *Udon* are thick wheat noodles that are obtainable flat or rounded. What follows is my effort to reproduce a dish served to me on a spring day by Keiko Okamoto, the wife of a prestigious potter living in the tea-growing Uji district just outside Kyoto. Most of the vegetables she used grew wild in the hills around her. Each had been cooked separately and then arranged over the noodles at the last minute. My vegetables, I am afraid are rather more prosaic, but the dish remains delightful—and very healthy, to boot.

Noodle dishes of this type are entire meals in themselves (this, with the addition of tea to drink, was our lunch), hence they are served in rather large, deep, individual bowls. Needless to say, our bowls had been handcrafted by the master potter himself and were objects of great beauty. The only "cutlery" we had was chopsticks. You are supposed to pick up the noodles with chopsticks and then suck them in with a deep intake of breath which cools them off. Loud noises made in the process are considered normal and are indicative of pleasure. All solids are picked up with the chopsticks. To drink the broth, chopsticks are left on chopstick rests and the bowl is picked up with both hands and brought directly to the mouth.

As far as poaching the eggs is concerned, I have never seen it done more casually or more successfully than it was by Keiko. She just put some water in a frying pan and it had barely come to a simmer when she cracked 4 eggs into it. Then, before the eggs were fully set, she loosely covered the pan and turned off the heat, leaving them to stand until they were done. The eggs were perfect—as mine are now that I do them this way.

Try to find Japanese *udon* noodles if you can, as there is no real substitute for them. (Many health food shops carry a whole-wheat version.) If you cannot get them, use either Italian *linguine* or flat egg noodles, cooking them according to the instructions on the packet only just before you are ready to serve. After you have drained your *linguine* or egg noodles, toss them with about 1 cup stock just to prevent them from sticking to each other as you arrange the vegetables over them.

If you are using ready-prepared *dashi-no-moto* instead of Japanese Soup Stock, omit the salt in this recipe entirely or add only a very small amount, tasting as you go. *Serves 4*

continued

Bottom: *Noodles in Broth with Poached Egg and Vegetables (this page);* **top:** *Rice Noodles in a Coconut Curry Soup (page 228)*

Carrots as Both Food and Garnish
(see page 255)

Green Beans as Both Food and Garnish
(see page 256)

Mushrooms as Both Food and Garnish
(see page 252)

Bamboo Shoot Tips as Both Food and
Garnish (see page 253)

Asparagus as Both Food and Garnish
(see page 254; optional)

2 quarts Japanese Soup Stock (see page 78)
or light unsalted Chicken Stock,
homemade (see page 77) or canned

3 tablespoons sugar

4 tablespoons sake

6 tablespoons Japanese soy sauce (shoyu)

1½–2 teaspoons salt

14 oz Japanese udon noodles or linguine
or flat egg noodles

4 eggs

Japanese seven-spice seasoning (shichimi)
or Sesame Seed Seasoning
(see page 299)

Cook the carrots, green beans, mushrooms, bamboo shoot tips and asparagus (if you are using it) according to their individual recipes. Each cooks very fast and you may make them even a day in advance and then cover and refrigerate them in their own liquid. Let them come to room temperature before you arrange them over the noodles so that they do not cool off the stock too much.

Prepare the Japanese Soup Stock. Add the sugar, sake, soy sauce and salt to it. Put it into a pan and simmer it very gently for 5 minutes. This too can be made a day ahead, covered and refrigerated. Heat it just before you are ready to eat.

Now cook the noodles. If you are using dried Japanese udon noodles, bring a very large pan of water to a rolling boil. Do not salt it. Now drop in the noodles. When the water comes to the boil again, put in an extra 1 cup cold water. Repeat this 3–4 times, each time waiting for the water to come to the boil again. Keep testing the noodles. When they are just done (there should be no hard core left in the center), drain them and rinse them under cold running water, rubbing them with your hands to remove all the starch. Leave them in a colander until you are ready to eat, at which time you will need to put them into a large pan of boiling water for a few seconds to heat them. Drain them quickly.

Poach the eggs just before you are ready to eat and when everything else is heated and ready. Put about ¾ inch water in a medium-sized frying pan. Bring it to a very low simmer. Break the 4 eggs into it so that they sit side by side. Let the water simmer very gently until the egg whites are almost set. Now turn off the heat and place a loose cover over the pan. As soon as the whites of the eggs have set, remove the cover. (This does not take very long.)

Assemble the dish quickly now. Divide the noodles between 4 large individual bowls. Lift the vegetables out of their liquid and arrange them over the noodles, laying them prettily side by side. Pour the hot stock over the top, dividing it among the 4 bowls. Place a poached egg in the center of each bowl. Serve at once. The seven-spice mixture (or Sesame Seed Seasoning) is generally sprinkled over the top. Each diner breaks the egg yolk with chopsticks, allowing it to mix with the broth.

NOODLES WITH PORK IN HOT AND SOUR SOUP

Hong Kong

*From the Wing
Lai Yuen
Restaurant in
Hong Kong*

SUANLA ZHA JIANGMIAN

*T*his spicy Szechuan specialty, which I enjoyed in a very humble restaurant on Hong Kong's Diamond Hill, is not quite a soup, though you may certainly serve it as one. It is really a meal in itself, especially when served with a Chinese-style vegetable on the side. All the different parts of the soup may be prepared in advance. You should assemble the soup just before you are to eat it.

Serves 2 as a meal or 4 as a soup

FOR THE NOODLES

½ lb fresh or dried egg noodles (preferably fresh Chinese lo-mein noodles)

1 tablespoon sesame oil

FOR THE PORK

3 scallions

2 garlic cloves

1 tablespoon vegetable oil

½ lb lean pork, ground

1½ tablespoons hoisin sauce

1 teaspoon chili bean sauce or ¼–½ teaspoon ground red (cayenne) pepper

1 teaspoon Chili Oil (see page 237)

1 teaspoon sugar

1 tablespoon Chinese dark soy sauce

⅔ cup Chicken Stock (see page 77) or chicken and pork stock or water

FOR THE SOUP

2 cups Chicken Stock (see page 77) or chicken and pork stock

3 tablespoons sesame paste (tahini)

1–2 teaspoons Chili Oil (see page 237)

1 tablespoon distilled white vinegar

4 teaspoons Chinese light soy sauce

FOR THE GARNISH

1 scallion

First prepare the noodles. Bring a large pan of water to a rolling boil. Drop in the noodles and cook for 3–5 minutes or until they are just done. Drain them and put them in a bowl. Add the sesame oil and toss. Let the noodles cool slightly and then cover with plastic wrap. Set aside and refrigerate.

Now prepare the pork. Cut the scallions crosswise into very fine slices along their entire length, including the green sections. Peel the garlic and chop it finely. Put the oil in a wok or frying pan and set it over a high heat. When the oil is hot, put in the garlic and scallions and stir for 1 minute. Put in the pork and stir and fry, breaking up the lumps, until the meat has lost all signs of pinkness. Add the hoisin sauce, chili bean sauce, Chili Oil, sugar and dark soy sauce. Stir and fry for 30 seconds. Add the stock, cover and simmer for 10 minutes.

Next prepare the soup. Combine all the ingredients for the soup in a pan.

continued

(Stir the sesame paste well before adding it.) Mix well, taste and adjust the seasoning if necessary.

Finally, prepare the garnish. Cut the scallion crosswise into very fine slices along its entire length, including the green section.

To serve, set a large pan of water to boil and place a colander in the sink. Heat the pork and the soup in separate pans. When the soup is boiling, divide it among individual soup bowls. Plunge the noodles into the boiling water for 10–20 seconds to heat them through. Drain them in the colander and then divide them among the soup bowls, piling them up in the center of the soup so that their "peaks" are well above it. Top the noodles with the pork, again dividing it among the bowls. Sprinkle the scallions over the very top and serve.

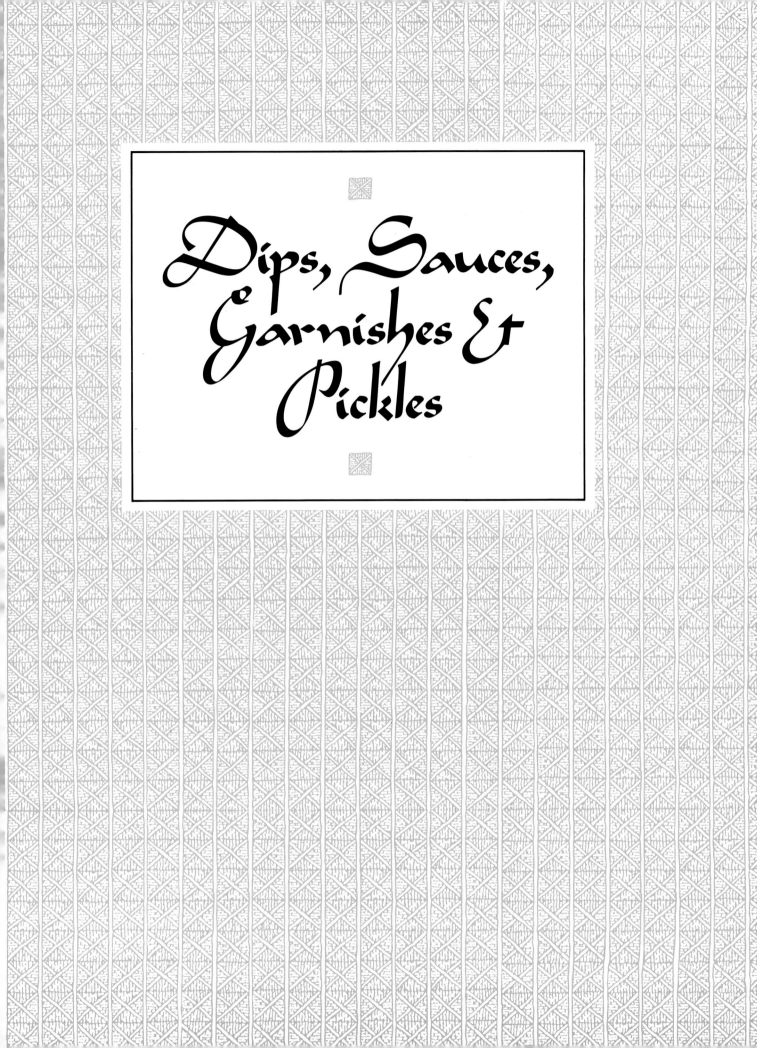

Dips, Sauces, Garnishes & Pickles

EAST-WEST SAUCE

TONKATSU SOSU

This sauce is a mixture of Eastern and Western ingredients. It contains, among other things, tomato ketchup and Worcestershire sauce. We must remember, though, that ketchup is an Asian word for an Asian suace and that tomato ketchup may well have been an attempt to replicate the kind of sweet and sour sauces found all over the Far East. Also, Worcestershire sauce, which is used in this recipe, has ingredients like tamarind in it. Tamarind is very much an Eastern ingredient. This may well be a case of an idea for a sauce traveling from the East to the West and then back to the East in a new incarnation.

East-West Sauce is served with Breaded Pork Cutlets (see page 118). You can, however, use it with any meat, fried chicken or fried fish. Since this sauce is prepared commercially in Japan, where it is known as *tonkatsu sosu*, I never could get an exact recipe for it. However, by tasting it again and again I have come up with a good approximation, which I give below.   *Serves 4–6*

½ teaspoon dry mustard
4 tablespoons tomato ketchup
4 teaspoons sake
4 teaspoons Japanese soy sauce (shoyu)
4 teaspoons Worcestershire sauce
4 teaspoons sugar
4 teaspoons distilled white vinegar
¼ teaspoon ground allspice
Dash ground cloves

Put the dry mustard in a small bowl. Add 4 teaspoons hot water and mix thoroughly. Add all the remaining ingredients and mix.

CHILI OIL

LAJIAO YOU

*O*range-colored chili oil is offered as a seasoning on the tables of most restaurants in Hong Kong. A few drops, or more liberal doses, are dribbled onto any foods that need extra "heat." It is also a common seasoning in Chinese kitchens serving Szechuan-style food. You can buy it ready-made at Chinese groceries, but it is easy enough to make at home. I find that it needs to be strained a couple of times if I want it to be really clear.   *Makes about ⅔ cup*

¾ *cup vegetable oil (preferably peanut)*

1 *tablespoon ground red (cayenne) pepper or pure chili powder made just with ground red chilies*

Put the oil in a small pan and set it over a medium-high heat. When the oil is hot, remove it from the heat and put in the ground red pepper. Mix and leave to cool, then strain the oil through a clean cloth. It is now ready to be used. You may, however, let it sit for a few hours and strain it a second time. If you have an empty bottle or jar in your cruet set, you could use it for your chili oil.

FISH SAUCE SEASONED WITH LIME JUICE AND CHILI

NAM PLA PRIK

You may put this sauce on the table when you are serving any Thai meal.
Serves 4

1 *fresh hot green or red chili*
4 *tablespoons fish sauce*
2 *tablespoons lime or lemon juice*

Cut the chili crosswise into very fine rounds. Put it in a small bowl. Add the fish sauce and the lime or lemon juice. Stir to mix.

FISH SAUCE WITH VINEGAR AND LIME JUICE

NƯỚC CHẤM THÔNG DỤNG

This is a wonderful dipping sauce to use with spring rolls and grilled or boiled meats. *Serves 4*

5 *tablespoons fish sauce*
3 *tablespoons distilled white vinegar*
1½–2 *tablespoons lime or lemon juice*
2 *tablespoons sugar*
1–2 *fresh hot green or red chilies*

Combine the fish sauce with 3 tablespoons water, the vinegar, lime or lemon juice and sugar in a jug. Mix well. Slice the chilies crosswise as thinly as possible and add them too. Divide the sauce equally among 4 small bowls and serve.

FISH SAUCE SEASONED WITH LIME JUICE

Vietnam

*From Biche
Lombatière*

NƯỚC MẮM TỎI ỚT

I am told that the popularity of a Vietnamese restaurant often rests with the quality of this ever-present sauce.   *Serves 4*

1 garlic clove
4 tablespoons fish sauce
4 tablespoons lime or lemon juice
3 tablespoons sugar or less to taste
3–4 fresh hot red or green chilies

Peel and crush the garlic. Combine it with the fish sauce, lime or lemon juice, sugar and 4 tablespoons water. Mix well and pour into 4 individual bowls. Cut the chilies crosswise into very thin rounds and divide them among the bowls.

Vietnam

FISH SAUCE SEASONED WITH VINEGAR

NƯỚC CHẤM

When serving this sauce, give each diner an individual bowlful. This recipe is enough for 4 small bowls.

8 tablespoons fish sauce
6 tablespoons distilled white vinegar
1 tablespoon sugar
3–4 fresh hot green or red chilies

Combine the fish sauce, vinegar and sugar. Mix thoroughly. Cut the chilies into fine rounds and put them into the sauce.

HOT FERMENTED BEAN PASTE

KOCHU CHANG

*E*very household in Korea has a tall earthenware jar of Hot Fermented Bean Paste (*kochu chang*) sitting serenely in a courtyard, on a balcony or in some other convenient nook. It is an essential seasoning and is one of the several bean pastes used with great frequency throughout Korea. It serves as a cross between a relish and a spice.

Its method of preparation is elaborate and long, calling for barley or glutinous rice powder to be mixed with malt, cooked slowly into a thick paste and then mixed with fermented soybean powder, ground red chilies and salt. The resulting paste is red in color (because of the chilies) and very thick. It is added to dipping sauces, to meats that are just about to be stir-fried, and to stews. Dollops of it are also served as a kind of salty sweet-and-hot chutney.

Kochu chang is available only in Korean shops. It can, however, be approximated at home with ingredients available to most of us. It is best to buy brown or reddish *miso* for this recipe. This, when mixed with ground red pepper, paprika and a little sugar, tastes and looks very much like real *kochu chang*.   *Makes approximately ¼ cup*

4 tablespoons brown or red miso
1½ tablespoons paprika
1 teaspoon ground red (cayenne) pepper
1 tablespoon sugar

Combine all the ingredients and mix well.

KOREAN DIPPING SAUCE

YANK NYUM JANG

This all-purpose sauce may be served with plain heated bean curd, with chicken patties and with potato pancakes.   *Serves 4*

1 small garlic clove

1 scallion

4 tablespoons soy sauce (preferably Japanese—shoyu)

2 tablespoons distilled white vinegar

1 tablespoon sesame oil

1 teaspoon sugar

1 teaspoon roasted sesame seeds (see page 299)

¼ teaspoon ground red (cayenne) pepper (optional)

Peel the garlic and crush it to a pulp. Cut the scallion crosswise into very thin rounds (you only need 1 tablespoon of this). Combine the garlic, 1 tablespoon sliced scallion, the soy sauce, vinegar, sesame oil, sugar, sesame seeds and ground red pepper in a small serving bowl and mix well.

CARAMEL WATER

NỬỚC HÀNG

This is used in Vietnam to add color and extra flavor to food.
Makes about 1¼ cups

3 tablespoons sugar

Put the sugar in a small cast-iron frying pan and let it warm up, without stirring, over a low heat. The sugar will begin to caramelize. Tilt the pan slowly back and forth to move the sugar, but do not stir it. When all the sugar has turned brownish, slowly pour in ¾ cup warm water. It will bubble vigorously, so be careful. Stir and mix. Pour the sauce into a bowl. Add another ⅔ cup boiling water and mix. Allow to cool and then store in a covered jar in the refrigerator.

RED PEPPER SAUCE

In Vietnam this sauce is made by pounding red chilies and salt in a mortar, cooking the mixture and then passing it through a sieve. Some countries do not bother with the cooking and straining. Others add a little sugar and vinegar. My method is very simple: I let a blender do all the work.   *Serves 4*

2–3 whole dried hot red chilies
1 small red bell pepper
¼ teaspoon sugar
½ teaspoon distilled white vinegar
¼ teaspoon salt or to taste

Put 3 tablespoons water in a small cup and crumble the dried red chilies into it. Soak for 30 minutes. Coarsely chop the pepper, discarding all the seeds. Combine the soaking chilies and their liquid with all the other ingredients in a blender. Blend until smooth.

RED PEPPER SAUCE WITH SHRIMP PASTE

SAMBAL TERASI

*T*his spicy relish (or *sambal*) may be served with all Indonesian meals. It will keep for at least a week in the refrigerator. Store it in a tightly lidded jar. Ideally, it should be made with good quality *terasi,* a semidry shrimp paste only sold in Southeast Asian groceries. Anchovy paste is the nearest substitute.

Makes about 1 cup

2 small red bell peppers
2 teaspoons shrimp or anchovy paste
½ teaspoon salt
½ teaspoon ground red (cayenne) pepper
4 tablespoons vegetable oil
1 teaspoon dark brown sugar
2½ tablespoons lime or lemon juice

Dice the red bell pepper coarsely, discarding all the seeds. Put the red bell pepper, shrimp paste, salt and ground red pepper in an electric blender. Blend until smooth.

Set a wok over a medium-high heat. When it is hot, put in the oil. When the oil has heated, put in the paste from the blender. Stir and fry for about 5 minutes, turning down the heat a little if necessary, until the paste turns dark red and the oil separates. Add the sugar and stir to mix. Take the paste off the heat and put it into a bowl. Beat in the lime or lemon juice. Taste and adjust the seasoning if necessary.

RED CURRY PASTE

NAM PRIK KAENG DANG

*T*his curry paste recipe makes approximately ½ cup, enough for 2 dishes, each serving 4 people. You can freeze any of the paste that you do not use immediately. *Makes about 8 tablespoons*

7 large or 10 medium whole dried hot red chilies

2-inch cube fresh or 4–6 slices dried galangal or 2-inch cube fresh ginger

2–3 pieces dried or 3 ½-inch pieces fresh kaffir lime rind (optional)

1 stick fresh or 2 tablespoons dried sliced lemongrass

3 garlic cloves

About 4–5 roots from fresh coriander, if available

6 shallots or ½ medium onion

1½ teaspoons shrimp or anchovy paste

2 teaspoons paprika

½ teaspoon ground coriander seeds

½ teaspoon ground cumin seeds

¼ teaspoon ground turmeric

1/16 teaspoon ground cinnamon

1/16 teaspoon ground cardamom

½ teaspoon salt

Remove and discard the seeds from the red chilies. Combine the chilies and the dried galangal, dried kaffir lime rind and dried lemongrass (if you are using them) in a small bowl. Cover with about ¾ cup water and set aside for 40 minutes–1 hour.

If you are using fresh galangal (or ginger), peel and coarsely chop it. If you are using fresh lemongrass, cut it crosswise into very fine slices, going up about 6 inches from the root end. Discard the strawlike top. Peel the garlic. Wash the coriander roots well and pat them dry.

Combine the soaked seasonings and their soaking liquid—or their fresh counterparts, where applicable—with all the remaining ingredients in an electric blender. Blend well.

GINGER SHREDS IN SWEET VINEGAR

HARI SHOGA

*E*ven though this is a Japanese relish, I keep it on hand to serve with Western-style roast lamb and grilled chicken.   *Serves 4*

2-inch cube fresh ginger
4 tablespoons distilled white vinegar
4 tablespoons sugar
¼ teaspoon salt

Peel the ginger and cut it crosswise into very thin slices. Stacking a few slices at a time together, cut them into very fine julienne strips. Combine the vinegar, sugar and salt in a bowl and mix well until the sugar is dissolved. Put in the ginger and stir. Set aside for at least 10–15 minutes. Lift the ginger shreds out of the liquid before serving.

QUICK SPICY RELISH

NAM PRIK NUM

*T*his relish is so good that you will want to eat it with everything—including potato chips. It is found only in northern Thailand. In fact, Thai visitors from the south buy kilos of it to take back home. It *is* hot, so small portions are recommended.   *Serves 4–6*

6 shallots
3 garlic cloves
6 fresh hot green chilies
½–1 teaspoon shrimp or anchovy paste

6 cherry tomatoes
1 tablespoon fish sauce or salt to taste
1 tablespoon lime or lemon juice

continued

Preheat the oven broiler. Peel the shallots and garlic. On a broiler rack lined with aluminum foil, spread out the shallots, garlic and green chilies in a single layer. Make a patty of the shrimp paste, if you are using it, and place it on the rack as well. (If you are using anchovy paste, set it aside for the time being.) Put the rack under the broiler and brown lightly. (This will happen quite quickly.) Turn everything over and brown the other side. Now either chop up everything you have broiled or put it all into an electric blender and blend briefly until you have a coarse paste. Empty the paste into a bowl. Chop the tomatoes into small pieces and add them (as well as the anchovy paste, if you are using it), the fish sauce (or salt) and the lime or lemon juice to the bowl. Mix. Taste the seasoning and adjust if necessary.

SWEET GLAZING SAUCE

TERIYAKI NO TARE

This Sweet Glazing (or *teriyaki*) Sauce, sweet and salty at the same time, is generally made with equal parts of Japanese rice wine (*sake*), soy sauce, *mirin* (a sweetened syrupy *sake*) and a little sugar. I have substituted sugar for the hard-to-find *mirin*. If you do manage to obtain it, add ⅔ cup of it to the soy-*sake* mixture and reduce the sugar to 2 teaspoons.

Generally speaking, *teriyaki* sauce is brushed onto grilled foods such as fish, chicken and beef when they are slightly more than half-cooked. It gives them a glorious glaze, as well as the sweet and salty *teriyaki* flavor. You may, if you like, add a little juice from grated fresh ginger to the sauce as well.   *Serves 4*

⅔ cup Japanese soy sauce (shoyu)
⅔ cup sake
6 tablespoons sugar

Combine the soy sauce, *sake* and sugar in a small pan and bring to a boil. Lower the heat to medium and simmer for about 5 minutes or until the sauce turns very slightly syrupy. (If the sauce is to be used as a marinade as well, it should be allowed to cool off first.)

SEASONED VINEGAR

*T*his seasoning is found in all the Asian countries where the Chinese have lived or settled—Hong Kong, Vietnam, the Philippines, Malaysia, Thailand and Indonesia. Of course, the actual vinegar varies not only from country to country but often from village to village. Diners usually add just a few drops of the hot vinegar to their food. If they want to, they can also take a few chili slices from the vinegar.   *Serves 4*

2 fresh hot green or red chilies
4 tablespoons distilled white vinegar

Cut the chilies crosswise into very thin rounds. Put the vinegar into a very small bowl. Add the chilies and let them steep for 30 minutes.

ROASTED PEANUTS

*C*rushed roasted peanuts are a common seasoning throughout most of Southeast Asia. They add a nutty taste, a crunchy texture and protein to a dish.

Raw peanuts are sold in every market in this region, usually still covered with their red inner skins. To roast them at home, put them into an ungreased, well-heated cast-iron wok or frying pan over a medium heat. Stir the peanuts around until they are roasted, reducing the heat if necessary. The red skins will turn crisp and papery. When the peanuts have cooled rub them with both hands and blow the skins away. To crush them, lightly or finely as required, either whir them for a few seconds in a clean coffee grinder or food processor or, if only a few tablespoons are needed, chop them up with a large knife.

CABBAGE PICKLE

KIMCHEE

*I*t is not surprising that *kimchee* is used in Korean rituals and rites. After all, there is not a single meal, from breakfast until dinner, when it is not served. According to the Kimchee Museum in Seoul, there are at least 160 varieties of this pickle. It can be made from radish, cucumber and even from fresh ginseng, but the most common *kimchee* remains the one made from cabbage.

Koreans use a fat, elongated cabbage that many call Chinese cabbage or Napa cabbage. A single head can weigh as much as 4½ lb. An extended family of 10 people eats about 200 heads of this pickled cabbage in 3–4 months.

Around late November, when the cabbage and red chili crops are ready, whole villages fall to the task of making their supply of winter *kimchee*. On the first day, cartloads of cabbages are trimmed, washed and left overnight in salted water to wilt and soften. The next day they are washed again while another group of workers prepares the stuffing. Large white radishes are julienned, scallions and Chinese celery are cut, ginger is chopped and red chilies crushed. This mixture, along with shucked oysters, salt and tiny salted shrimps, is slapped between each leaf of the cabbages. The cabbage heads are then packed into large, Ali Baba–sized vats, where they seethe, bubble and ferment until they turn deliciously sour. In the villages the vats are buried up to their necks in the earth to prevent the pickle from freezing. In city homes all vats stand like sentinels, lined up on balconies.

Makes enough to fill a 2-quart jar

1 lb or about ½ head Chinese cabbage
   (halve it lengthwise)
Salt
1 lb long white Oriental radish
3-inch cube fresh ginger
8–10 large garlic cloves
8 scallions
2 teaspoons ground red (cayenne) pepper
1 teaspoon sugar
10 shucked oysters, or 10 canned anchovy
   fillets
1 tablespoon unbleached, all-purpose flour

Trim away the very bottom of the cabbage but keep the leaves attached. If the half-head is very thick, cut it in half again lengthwise. Wash the cabbage well, carefully removing the dirt between each leaf.

In a large bowl, combine 1½ quarts water with 3 tablespoons salt. Put the cabbage into the solution. Weight it down with a clean heavy plate so that it does not float. Cover loosely and leave for 8 hours.

Prepare the "stuffing." Peel the radish and cut it crosswise into 2-inch chunks. Now cut each chunk lengthwise into ⅛-inch-thick slabs. Cut each slab into ⅛-inch-thick julienne strips.

Peel the ginger and garlic and chop them coarsely. Put them into an electric blender with 3 tablespoons water. Blend until smooth. Cut the scallions into fine rounds along their entire length, including the green section.

In a large bowl combine the radish, ginger-garlic paste, scallions, ground red (cayenne) pepper, sugar and oysters. If you are using anchovy fillets, wipe off the oil and chop them finely before adding them. Mix. Add 1 tablespoon salt and mix again. Put the flour in a small pan and slowly add 1½ cups water, mixing as you go. Bring this water to a simmer. Simmer gently until slightly thickened.

Remove the cabbage from the salt water and rinse thoroughly several times. Keep the leaves attached. Drain. Starting with the outside leaves, put some stuffing in between each cabbage leaf. Tuck the largest leaf under so that it will hold the "package" together. If you have a second cabbage section, stuff it in the same way. Fit the cabbage packages tightly inside a clean, wide-mouthed, 2-quart crock or jar. Pour the flour water over the top. Make sure that there is some room on top of the jar for the fermenting pickle to expand. Cover and set aside for 3–7 days, depending upon the weather; the hotter it is, the quicker the cabbage will pickle. Taste the pickle now and then to see if it has turned sufficiently sour. Once the pickle is ready, it should be refrigerated.

To serve, remove just as much of the cabbage from the liquid as you need and put it in a small bowl. In Korea the liquid is used to flavor stews and soups.

CRISPLY FRIED SHALLOT (OR ONION) FLAKES

A young lady in Padang, Indonesia, told me with great authority that shallot flakes turn much crisper if they are soaked in lightly salted water before being fried. Theories abound: this one makes sense, however, as salt draws out some of the moisture. I think that starting the frying at a medium-hot rather than a very hot temperature also helps.

In much of Southeast Asia shallots are cheap and used rather as onions are used in the West. Crisply Fried Shallot Flakes serve both as a garnish and as a seasoning. Often they are fried in bulk and kept in tightly lidded jars to be used as needed. If you cannot obtain shallots, use onions. Cut them in half lengthwise and tien crosswise into very fine half-rings. Fry them just as you would the shallots. (Small amounts of shallots, intended for use the same day, may be fried without first being soaked in salted water.)   *Makes enough to fill a 12-oz jar*

16 medium shallots (or 2 medium onions)
Salt
Vegetable oil for deep-frying

Peel the shallots and cut them lengthwise into fine slivers. Put them in a bowl. Add ½ teaspoon salt and toss lightly. Cover with 2 cups water and leave for 30 minutes. Drain them well and pat them dry.

Put about 2 inches oil in a wok set over a medium heat. When the oil is hot, put in the shallots. Stir and fry for 1 minute. Turn the heat down to medium-low and keep stirring and frying until the shallots are reddish brown and crisp. Remove them with a slotted spoon and spread them out on paper toweling to drain. When they are cool and crisp, store them in a tightly lidded jar until needed.

EGG STRIPS

*T*hese strips are a popular garnish for rice and noodles in many parts of Southeast Asia. They are also used in salads and soups.   *Makes about 1½ cups*

3 eggs
1 teaspoon sugar
⅛ teaspoon salt
About 2 teaspoons vegetable oil

Break the eggs into a bowl and add 1 tablespoon water. Beat, but not to a froth. Add the sugar and salt and beat lightly to mix.

Brush a 7–8-inch nonstick frying pan with about ½ teaspoon of the oil and set it on a medium heat. When it is hot, pour in a quarter of the egg mixture. Tilt the pan around so that the egg flows evenly to the edges. Let the mixture set, which it will do quite quickly. Turn the pancake over carefully and cook the second side until it is just firm (a matter of seconds). Remove the pancake to a plate and cover it with wax paper. Make 3 more pancakes in this way, putting them on top of each other with a layer of wax paper in between. Allow them to cool, then roll them up one at a time and cut them crosswise at ⅛-inch intervals. Put the resulting strips into a covered container and store in the refrigerator if you are not going to use them immediately.

MUSHROOMS AS BOTH FOOD AND GARNISH

KINOKO

*I*f you are using prepared *dashi-no-moto* instead of Japanese Soup Stock, omit the salt.   *Serves 4*

8 medium mushrooms
⅔ cup Japanese Soup Stock (see page 78)
    or light unsalted Chicken Stock,
    homemade (see page 77) or canned
1 tablespoon sake
2 teaspoons Japanese soy sauce (shoyu)
2 teaspoons sugar
¼ teaspoon salt

Wipe the mushrooms with a damp cloth and cut them in half lengthwise. Combine the stock, *sake*, soy sauce, sugar and salt in a small pan and bring it to a simmer. Put in the mushrooms and cook them for about 2½ minutes over a medium-low heat, stirring now and then. Turn off the heat and let the mushrooms cool in their liquid. Drain and serve.

BAMBOO SHOOT TIPS AS BOTH FOOD AND GARNISH

TAKENOKO

Since the bamboo shoots in this recipe need to look as good as they taste, only the tips are used. These are sometimes available in cans (the cans are labeled "winter bamboo shoots") and come in conical shapes of various sizes. They need to be washed and then cut vertically into wedges that are about ⅛ inch thick on the outside, while their inside looks like the teeth of a comb. Tender bamboo shoot chunks can be used as a substitute. They can be cut into triangular slices about 2 inches long and ⅛ inch thick. Do not make this dish if you can get only sliced bamboo shoots. If you are using prepared *dashi-no-moto* instead of Japanese Soup Stock, omit the salt.   *Serves 4*

3 oz canned bamboo shoot tips or chunks

⅔ cup Japanese Soup Stock (see page 78) or light unsalted Chicken Stock, homemade (see page 77) or canned

1 tablespoon sake

2 teaspoons Japanese soy sauce (shoyu)

1 tablespoon sugar

¼ teaspoon salt

Slice the bamboo shoot tips as suggested above and wash them well in water. Combine the stock, *sake,* soy sauce, sugar and salt in a small pan and bring to a boil. Drop in the bamboo shoots and simmer on a medium-low heat for 5 minutes, turning the shoots around now and then. Leave them to cool in the liquid, again turning the pieces around several times so that they pick up the color evenly.

ASPARAGUS AS BOTH FOOD AND GARNISH

ASUPARA

*T*he asparagus here may be used as a garnish for meats, fish or chicken, or placed over a dish of noodles in broth. If you are using prepared *dashi-no-moto* instead of the Japanese Soup Stock, omit the salt that is added to the stock.
  Serves 4

12 *medium-thick asparagus spears (prepared weight about ¼ lb)*

Salt

⅔ cup ice-cold Japanese Soup Stock (see page 78) or light unsalted Chicken Stock, homemade (see page 77) or canned

Trim away the woody section of each asparagus spear and then peel the lower half. Cut each spear into 2–2½-inch sections.

Bring about ½ inch water to a boil in a medium-sized frying pan. Add ¼ teaspoon salt to it and put in the asparagus. Cover, lower the heat and cook for about 3 minutes or until the asparagus pieces are just tender. Drain and immediately plunge the asparagus pieces into the cold stock. Add ¼ teaspoon salt and mix in gently. Let the asparagus sit in the stock for at least 15 minutes.

CARROTS AS BOTH FOOD AND GARNISH

NINJIN

Small quantities of carrots provide a colorful accent, and a third dimension, to plates of chicken or fish in Japan. These carrots can also be arranged, along with other vegetables, over a bowl of noodles. You could easily double or triple the quantities given below if you wish to serve the carrots, Western-style, as an accompanying vegetable at a meal. The cooking time will remain the same. If you use prepared *dashi-no-moto* instead of Japanese Soup Stock, omit the salt.   *Serves 4*

2 small carrots

4 tablespoons Japanese Soup Stock (see page 78) or light unsalted Chicken Stock, homemade (see page 77) or canned

2 teaspoons sugar

¼ teaspoon salt

Peel the carrots. Cut them crosswise into 2½-inch segments and then cut each segment lengthwise into ⅛-inch-thick slices. You may leave the slices like this or cut them, again lengthwise, into ⅛-inch-wide julienne strips.

Combine the carrots, stock, sugar and salt in a small pan and bring to a boil. Boil for about 1 minute. The carrots should retain some crispness. Immerse the pan in a bowl of cold water to cool off the carrots quickly. When serving, lift the carrots out of their liquid and arrange as required.

GREEN BEANS AS BOTH FOOD AND GARNISH

INGEN

When Japanese food is presented, sometimes just a few vegetables are used as a kind of garnish or arranged over noodles along with several other similarly prepared vegetables, fungi and roots. You could always increase the quantity if you wish to serve the beans at a Western-style meal. If you are using prepared *dashi-no-moto* instead of Japanese Soup Stock, omit the salt that is put into the ice-cold stock. *Serves 4*

¼ lb green beans

1¾ teaspoons salt

½ cup ice-cold Japanese Soup Stock (see page 78 or light unsalted Chicken Stock, homemade (see page 77) or canned

Trim the green beans and cut them into 2½-inch lengths. Combine 2½ cups water and 1½ teaspoons of the salt in a pan and bring to a boil. Put in the beans and boil rapidly for about 4 minutes (this depends on the size of bean) or until they are crisp but tender. Drain them and immediately drop them into the ice-cold stock. Add the remaining ¼ teaspoon salt to the stock and stir it in. Leave the beans in the liquid for at least 15 minutes or until you are ready to use them. When serving, lift the beans out of the liquid and arrange as required.

Desserts and Drinks

PLATE OF FRESH FRUIT

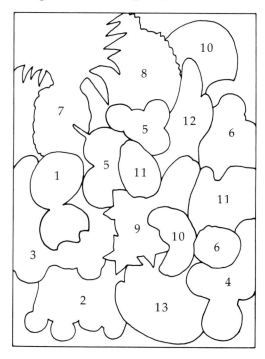

In much of Asia meals end not with puddings and desserts, but with fruit. Sometimes it is just one glorious seasonal fruit, such as perfumed summer mangoes chilled in ice water, or it could be a collection of several fruits, all pared and cut into neat mouthfuls. In Korea these neat mouthfuls sit on a common platter set in the center of the table. Each piece of fruit is pierced with a small 2-pronged fork so that it can be picked up with ease and nibbled at will. In Thailand, where a whole school is devoted to the art, fruit comes carved in the most elaborate floral and geometric designs; you cannot even get a simple papaya in your hotel room without some slight hint of delicate fingers at work. In Japan I was stunned by a plate that held just a whole orange and a bunch of black grapes. The orange had been peeled in one neat spiral and sectioned, then reassembled so that the fruit looked whole. Each grape, too, had been seeded and loosened inside from its coarse skin (how did they do this?). All I had to do was hold a grape to my lips and just suck in the smooth insides.

While I do not suggest that you spend all day carving fruit, here are helpful hints on fruits that you may be unfamiliar with, which are sold in many Western shops and supermarkets.

Key to photo opposite (see pages 259–62 for identification of fruit)

MANGO[1]*

Sweet, juicy and, at its best, smooth-textured, a mango to me is the king of fruit. There are hundreds of varieties, each with its own taste, texture and color. Most varieties in the northern hemisphere ripen in the summer, from late April to early July, so that would be the best time to buy them. Mangoes sold by most shops in the West tend to be hard and underripe. Smell the mango at its stem end, and if it seems to have the potential of being sweet, buy it. You will be taking a bit of a chance, but if it works out once, look for the same variety again. When you get home, wrap the hard mango in newspaper and put it in a basket or an open cardboard box. Do not refrigerate it. You can ripen several mangoes together in this way, wrapping each one separately in newspaper first. In Thai villages, bas-

* Superscript numbers refer to photo key.

kets of mangoes are left to ripen under the bed. When the perfume becomes overwhelming, the household knows that the mangoes are ready to be eaten! Examine your mangoes every day. They should eventually yield very slightly to the touch, but should *not* have black spots on them. You may now chill the mangoes in the refrigerator, or put them to cool in a bucket of water to which you have added plenty of ice.

While there are people who believe that mangoes are best eaten with the hands, and in a bathtub, there is a neater approach for those who would like to use an implement—and stay at the table. The mango usually has two flatter sides. Cut a thick slice lengthwise off each of these sides as close to the stone as you can. (Peel the remaining mango and devour it in the kitchen by yourself. This is your reward for the work you are putting in.) Put these two slices on a plate. This is one serving. The mango pulp may now be scooped decorously out of the skin with a spoon. You could also cut a cross-hatch pattern in the flesh, making rows at about ½-inch intervals with a sharp knife. Cut all the way down to the skin, but not through it. Now put the fingers of both your hands under the skin and push upwards. The flesh of the mango will rise up in an arc and open in a most interesting pattern. Eat it with a spoon. You could, if you like, peel the mango, slice it and cut it into dice. Serve the stone only to those who do not mind using their fingers.

a Slice the mango down beside the stone, lengthwise. Cup the mango section you have just sliced off in your hand and make a grid pattern in the flesh with a knife, taking care not to pierce the skin.

b Turn the mango section inside out.

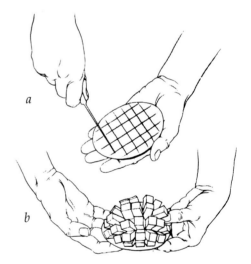

LITCHIS[2]

These, to my mind, must always be eaten in quantity. Eating one or two is like eating one or two peanuts. Litchis have a red or reddish brown, somewhat tough, crisp skin. As you peel the egg-sized fruit, a sweet, clear juice begins to drip from it. The inside is white, translucent and glistening, not unlike the skin of a peeled squid. Pop the litchi into your mouth, but remember that there is a long stone in the center.

Chill the litchis before serving. You may put a whole bunch of litchis in a bowl in the center of your table and let people break off their own, peel them and eat them. Or you can peel the litchis yourself and arrange them on a plate with other cut fruit. Do not remove the stone; that is the least people can do for themselves.

RAMBUTAN[3]

This is a large red litchi with red hairlike spikes on the outside. It tastes a little like a litchi, but is much less juicy. The Thais often leave half-peeled rambutans on a fruit plate to show off their interesting skins. Rambutans also have seeds in them.

MANGOSTEEN[4]

The fruit that has won the most kudos among Western travelers is perhaps the mangosteen. One ancient traveler compared it to nectar and ambrosia, saying that it "surpassed the golden apples of the Hesperides and was, of all the fruit of the Indies, the most delicious." I remember sitting on a park bench in Malacca and greedily devouring about a dozen of them, sticky juice dripping all over me.

In spite of its name, the mangosteen is in no way related to the mango. It is purplish or reddish brown on the outside, the size of a tangerine and quite hard. There is a knack to cracking it open with a good twist, which I have now finally mastered, but I will suggest an easier method. Take a sharp knife and make an equatorial cut all around the fruit. Do not cut all the way through; you do not want two equal halves. Now pull the top off like a cap. Sitting propped up inside a natural cup, like a scoop of ice cream, will be 5–8 white, juicy, translucent segments. You may eat them with a spoon. They will be sweet with just a hint of sourness, and very good. I long for one as I write this.

PASSION FRUIT[5]

From the outside, this looks like a dented egg of purplish (or sometimes yellow) color. Split it open and you will find crunchy seeds covered with a clear, gelatinous flesh nestling in the hollow. At its best, passion fruit has a sweet and sour taste that seems to combine the flavor of limes and berries. If it is too sour, a little sugar should be sprinkled over the pulp before it is eaten. The pulp may also be strained and then served over ice cream or used to flavor sorbets and soufflés.

CUSTARD APPLE[6]

This is a heart-shaped fruit that seems to be covered with a green alligator skin. It must be fully ripe when it is bought, which means that it should yield easily to the touch when pressed. Serve each person a whole chilled custard apple. You can easily split it open lengthwise, using nothing but your hands. The inside is filled with white, creamy, sugar-sweet buds that often harbor smooth, black seeds. Ease your spoon into the custardlike pulp. The art of eating this fruit lies in knowing how to dislodge the seeds from the pulp while the buds are still in your mouth and then how to delicately spit out the seeds while retaining your dignity.

PINEAPPLE[7]

By now, I am sure, you know how to serve a pineapple. When buying one, smell it; it should smell sweet. Look at its color—the yellower the tip, the riper it will be. Feel its very top, near the leaves—it should have a little give. To prepare a pineapple, peel it, remove its "eyes," core and then serve it cut in wedges as they do in Southeast Asia, or in round slices. It is best when it is chilled. If it is not too sweet, sugar may be added, but remember that sugar will make it syrupy, so it will not be suitable for a fruit plate.

DURIAN[8]

Dare I mention it? This is the fruit that is banned from hotels and airplanes because of its lingering odor. Southeast Asians are always surprised when a Westerner can allow himself or herself to go near it, let alone eat it. I love it passionately and recommend it without hesitation.

It looks unprepossessing—large, green and full of murderous spikes, a football made by a dinosaur for a dinosaur. It needs to be cracked open with a hatchet wielded by a practiced hand. Lying inside its five compartments are pale, off-white segments of the creamiest, smoothest texture imaginable. These segments are sweet, in flavor and texture the most heavenly blend of cream, bananas and flowing ripe brie.

In Indonesia the durian is considered to be an aphrodisiac and, the saying goes, "When the durian comes in, the sarongs go up." Might that induce you to try it?

STAR FRUIT[9]

When this yellowish-colored fruit is cut crosswise into slices, each slice looks like a star—hence its name. Its flavor can be sour, sweet and sour, or just sweet, depending upon the type. It is exceedingly juicy. Once, when we were grilling fish outdoors in Sumatra on a particularly hot day, I remember my hostess breaking off a star fruit from a bunch that hung above us and offering it to me. "It will quench your thirst and cool you down," she said. As I bit into it, juice went flying in every direction. It was just as good as drinking an icy lemonade.

Slices of star fruit can be added to a plate of fruit served at the end of a meal. They can also be left on the table, along with herbs and lettuce leaves, to be nibbled upon at will during the course of a Vietnamese, Thai or Malaysian meal.

POMELO[10]

This is best described as an extra-crisp, crunchy, flaky grapefruit. Once it has been peeled, its wedgelike sections can be separated and the papery skin on each wedge pulled off with ease. This makes it ideal for fruit plates and salads. Each peeled wedge can be flaked by separating all the individual "buds" in it. In Thailand the "flaked" version is used in everyday salads.

PAPAYA[11]

This should be very ripe and sweet. It should yield slightly to the touch and have a nice yellowish color on the outside. Chill it first, then cut it in half lengthwise. Scoop out all the seeds. You may now cut it into long slices, or you may serve a whole half with a wedge of lime, or you may peel the papaya halves and cut them into cubes.

BANANAS[12] AND WATERMELON[13]

Sliced bananas and watermelon chunks may be added to any plate of tropical fruit that you wish to serve.

SWEET WALNUT SOUP

WAIYOU HETAO TANG

*T*here is a neat clean restaurant in Hong Kong, freshly done up in peach and shining white formica, that specializes in desserts. Policemen, politicians and bankers in Rolls-Royces all haunt its pristine quarters and can be found there during the after-dinner hours.

One of the specialties is hot sweet soup. Machines in the back whir busily, grinding sesame seeds to a fine paste for sweet sesame seed soup. One may order sweet red bean soup, or almond cream soup, or a sweet walnut soup.

This soup may be served chilled in the summer.   *Serves 4*

2 teaspoons cornstarch
1 cup shelled walnut halves
½ cup peanut oil
3½ tablespoons sugar
½ cup heavy cream

Mix the cornstarch with 2 tablespoons water and set aside. Drop the walnuts into 1¼ quarts boiling water and boil for 10 seconds. Drain the walnuts and leave them in a sieve.

Put the oil in a wok or small pan over a medium heat. Do not let the oil get very hot: the temperature should be around 325°F. Put in the walnuts and immediately take the wok or pan off the heat. Stir the walnuts for 5 seconds and then remove them with a slotted spoon.

Put the walnuts in a blender, add 1 cup water and blend until smooth. Pour the walnut mixture into a clean pan. Some of the mixture will cling to the blender, so pour in another 1 cup water and blend again for a few seconds. Pour this liquid into the pan as well. Add the sugar, mix and bring to a simmer. Give the cornstarch mixture a stir and add that to the pan as well. Stir and cook for 30 seconds or until the soup has thickened slightly. Add the cream and heat through. Pour into Chinese soup bowls or any other bowls of your choice and serve hot.

CARAMEL CUSTARD FILIPINO-STYLE

LECHE FLAN

I have such a weakness for soothing, slithery milk desserts—especially for caramel custard. It is made particularly well in the Philippines where, as in Spain, it could be considered the national dessert. What do the Filipinos do differently? They never seem to use fresh milk, for one thing. Their love affair with canned American products continues unabated and, I must say, in this case works to great advantage. The dessert is rich, creamy and, as one of my daughters pronounced, the best ever.

All households in the Philippines seem to agree on the use of canned evaporated milk but seem to disagree on the number of eggs and whether they should be used whole or in part. One is apt to hear comments like, "I make my *leche flan* with 3 eggs [and then a face is made as if to say that this custard is, well, tolerable] but you should really have my mother's. She uses 8 egg yolks. Hers is delicious." The recipe I give below calls for 3 whole eggs and 2 egg yolks, a very happy middle ground.

In the Philippines caramel custard is served on special occasions with a topping of slivered *macapuno*, a mutant glutinous coconut. *Macapuno* in syrup is available canned from some Southeast Asian grocers. If you find it, you might wish to give it a try. If you want to invert the custard onto a serving plate to bring it to the table, you should butter the mold lightly before pouring in the liquid custard.

Serves 4

FOR THE CUSTARD

3 large eggs

2 large egg yolks

A scant ½ cup sugar

Pinch of salt

3 cups canned evaporated milk

1½ teaspoons vanilla extract

Butter for greasing (optional)

FOR THE CARAMEL

A scant ½ cup sugar

Preheat the oven to 325°F.

Pour about 1 inch hot water into a roasting pan large enough to hold a custard mold of about 5 cups capacity or 4 individual molds. Place this pan in the oven.

Put the eggs and egg yolks into a bowl. Beat them lightly, but not to a froth. Add the sugar and salt and mix in. Heat the evaporated milk until it is very hot. Slowly pour the hot milk into the bowl with the eggs, whisking vigorously as you do so. Add the vanilla and mix in.

If you are intending to invert the

Bottom: *Candied Walnut Halves (page 266);* **top:** *Caramel Custard Filipino-Style (this page)* custard when serving, grease the custard mold or 4 individual molds with butter. Put the sugar for the caramel into a heavy frying pan or other wide heavy pan, spreading it over the bottom. Heat it over a medium heat. Do not stir. As the sugar melts and turns brown, tilt the pan around so that the sugar moves a little. When all the sugar has caramelized, pour it into the custard mold (or divide it among the 4 individual molds). Tilt the mold(s) around so that the sides are coated a little as well as the bottom. The sugar will harden: this is as it should be. Now strain in the hot liquid custard and place the mold(s) in the roasting pan with the water. Cook in the oven for 1 hour–1 hour and 10 minutes, or until a knife inserted into the center of the custard comes out clean and the custard seems set. Let the custard cool somewhat before inverting it, if that is what you want to do. You may serve it warm (I love it like this) or cold in the traditional way.

Korea

From Mrs. Choi Sang In

CANDIED WALNUT HALVES

HOTOO TWIKIM

*F*ried candied walnuts are often served as after-dinner treats or snacks in both China and Korea. Here is the Korean version. *Serves 4*

4 tablespoons sugar
1 heaping cup shelled walnut halves
1¼ cups peanut oil

Put the sugar in a wide bowl or saucer. Bring a large pan of water to a rolling boil. Drop in the walnuts. Boil rapidly for 20 seconds. Drain the walnuts thoroughly and toss with the sugar. The sugar should cling to the nuts. Spread the walnuts out on a clean plate and let them cool off and dry for 30 minutes.

Set a strainer over a bowl. Put the oil in a wok or small frying pan and set it on a medium-low heat; the oil should heat to about 250°F. Put in the walnuts. Stir and fry for 5–6 minutes or until the walnuts begin to glisten with a soft brown color. Do not let them darken or they will taste bitter. Immediately pour the oil and walnuts into the strainer. Spread the walnuts out on a plate or tray, separating each one. Allow them to cool. Spread them on two changes of paper toweling to absorb any remaining frying oil. Store the walnuts in a tightly lidded jar.

COCONUT MILK CUSTARD

SANKHAYA

Instead of making custard with milk, many countries of Southeast Asia use coconut milk. The results are superb. You may, if you like, garnish the top of each custard with dried coconut, sweetened or unsweetened, though I like it quite plain with nothing to mar its smoothness.

This custard is cooked in a steamer. If you do not have one, you can improvise. Use a wok with a steaming rack. You could also use a large pan and balance a flat trivet on an empty can inside it (cut out the top and bottom of the can). It is important that the water stays below the trivet or steaming tray and that it is kept at a bare simmer so that the custard is not filled with bubbles.

Canned coconut milk, well stirred, is of the correct consistency for this custard.

Serves 4

2 eggs
1 cup thick coconut milk (see page 282)
6 tablespoons light brown sugar

Beat the eggs lightly. Stir the coconut milk well and add it and the brown sugar to the eggs. Stir to mix. Strain this mixture into a heavy pan or a double boiler set over boiling water. Cook gently, stirring all the time with a whisk, until the mixture has thickened into a custard. Watch carefully and do not let the eggs curdle. (If very slight curdling does occur, it can be strained out.) Strain the custard into 4 small bowls. Cover lightly with upturned saucers or aluminum foil and steam *very* gently for 15–20 minutes or until the custard is just set. Cool.

APPLE OR GUAPPLE PIE

The El Ideal Bakery in the Negros township of Silay makes some of the best pies in the country. A crumbly guapple pie is only one of its superb offerings. What is a guapple? It is a big, round, hard guava. To prepare it, remove the seeds, coarsely chop it and then, to give it the tartness it lacks, toss it with lime juice, as well as with the more usual cinnamon and sugar. While the bottom of the pie has a regular short crust, the top is all crumb. If you can find very hard guavas, do use them for this recipe. I have used apples instead. You will need 1–2 limes to provide 1½ tablespoons finely chopped rind.   *Serves 6*

FOR THE BOTTOM CRUST

1 cup unbleached, all-purpose flour plus
    extra for dusting

3 tablespoons chilled margarine

2 tablespoons chilled lard

About 2 tablespoons ice-cold water

FOR THE FILLING

¾ cup sugar

¾ teaspoon ground cinnamon

1½ tablespoons finely chopped lime or
    lemon rind

2 lb hard sour apples (such as Granny
    Smith)

1½ tablespoons cornstarch

FOR THE CRUMB TOPPING

¾ cup plus 2 tablespoons unbleached,
    all-purpose flour

1 cup sugar

6 tablespoons chilled unsalted butter

First make the bottom crust. Sift the flour into a bowl. Cut the margarine and lard into small pieces and add them to the flour. Using 2 knives, or a pastry cutter, or your fingertips, cut or rub in the fat until the mixture resembles coarse breadcrumbs. Sprinkle in just enough ice-cold water—about 2 tablespoons—so that you can gather the dough into a ball. Knead lightly and quickly with the heel of your hand and then form a ball again. Spread a sheet of wax paper about 16 inches long on your work surface. Put the ball of dough on it and flatten it a little. Place another sheet of wax paper on top of the dough. Now roll the dough from the center outward, keeping it between these sheets of paper, until you have a round that is about 10 inches in diameter. Lift up and remove the top sheet of paper. Now lift up the dough with the help of the lower sheet of wax paper and overturn it on top of an 8-inch pie plate or tin. Fit the pastry in. Trim away the uneven edges and then press down on the rim with the prongs of a fork. Refrigerate the pie plate containing the bottom crust.

Prepare a shelf in the lower third of your oven. Preheat the oven to 425°F.

Next make the pie filling. Put the sugar and cinnamon into a large bowl. Add the finely chopped lime or lemon rind to the sugar mixture and toss. Peel, core and quarter the apples one at a time. As you cut each quarter, slice it crosswise into ¼-inch-thick pieces and let the pieces fall into the sugar mixture in the bowl. Toss them every now and then. When all the apples have been cut, add the cornstarch to the bowl and toss again.

Now make the crumb topping. Put the flour in a bowl. Add the sugar and mix. Cut the butter into very small pieces and rub it in with your fingers. The mixture should resemble coarse breadcrumbs.

You are now ready to assemble the pie. Take the bottom crust out of the refrigerator. Put into this crust all the apples and their juice. Sprinkle the crumb topping over the apples. Put the pie in the oven on the prepared shelf and bake for 10 minutes. Turn the oven temperature down to 350°F. Bake for another 45–50 minutes, or until the pie is nicely browned on the top. Serve lukewarm.

FLUFFY PANCAKES WITH SWEET SESAME-PEANUT FILLING

Malaysia Indonesia

With the help of Risnawati Agus in Padang and Lim Suan Har in Penang

BAN CHAN KUAY, MARTABAK

A thick sweet pancake with crumpetlike holes, this is a very popular street snack in both Malaysia and Indonesia. Its origins probably go back to the *appam* (or "hopper," as the British called it) of South India. I found it very interesting that a similar pancake, cooked today by Muslim fisherwomen of the southern Philippines, is still called an *appam*. In the former times the leavening for this dish was provided by fermented palm toddy. Today most people seem to use either packaged yeast or baking powder.

In the streets of Padang in Western Sumatra the filling often consists of butter, sugar, crushed peanuts and—would you believe it—chocolate sprinkles! In Penang in Malaysia the chocolate is left out and roasted sesame seeds are added to the peanuts. Both versions are very good.

To make these pancakes, you need a heavy cast-iron frying pan or an old-fashioned cast-iron crêpe pan. It should be about 6 inches in diameter, though a larger one would be acceptable. A lid is also required. (You can improvise with anything that fits.) These pancakes must be eaten hot. Since each pancake takes about 6 minutes to cook. I often have two pans going at the same time.

Makes 6 pancakes

continued

1¼ cup unbleached, all-purpose flour

2 teaspoons plus 2 tablespoons superfine
  sugar

2 teaspoons baking powder

¼ teaspoon salt

1 large egg

1⅓ cups milk

4 teaspoons vegetable oil

3–4 tablespoons Roasted Peanuts
  (see page 247)

3 tablespoons unsalted butter

3 tablespoons roasted sesame seeds
  (see page 299)

2 tablespoons confectioners' sugar
  (optional)

Sift the flour, the 2 teaspoons super-fine sugar, baking powder and salt into a bowl. Beat the egg lightly. Make a well in the center of the flour and drop in the egg, milk and oil. Mix until you have a smooth batter. (You could mix all the ingredients in a blender if you like.) Cover and set aside for 2 hours or longer.

Crush the peanuts to a coarse powder in a mortar, a clean coffee grinder or food processor. Let the butter soften slightly. Put the remaining superfine sugar and the roasted sesame seeds in separate bowls and keep them and the crushed peanuts near you when you start to cook.

Each pancake will require about 4 generous tablespoons of the batter. Pour that amount of water into a small cup or ladle just to get a rough idea of how much batter you will be scooping up each time. Discard this water and wipe your cup or ladle dry.

Set a cast-iron frying pan on a medium-low heat. When it is hot, put in ½ teaspoon of the butter. Stir the batter quickly. The pour in one measure of the batter, cover immediately and turn the heat to low. Cook for 3 minutes or until the top turns whitish and bubbles appear. Quickly spread 1 teaspoon of the butter over the pancake and top with 1 teaspoon super-fine sugar, followed by 1½ teaspoons sesame seeds, followed by 1 table-spoon peanuts. Cover again and cook for another 2½–3 minutes or until the pancake is done. Uncover and fold the pancake in half. Serve it as is or dusted with 1 teaspoon confectioner's sugar. Wipe out the frying pan thoroughly before making the next pancake. Make all the pancakes in this way, stirring the batter each time.

PEANUT CANDY

You need palm sugar for this candy, which is made throughout Southeast Asia. If you cannot get it easily, a good substitute is jaggery, sold by Indian groceries. It is sold in lump form and the best kind is crumbly and breakable, not hard as a rock.   *Serves 4*

1 cup raw shelled unskinned peanuts
2 teaspoons peanut oil
6 oz (roughly 4 egg-sized balls) palm
    sugar or jaggery

Set a medium-sized, preferably cast-iron frying pan to warm up on a medium heat. Put in the peanuts. Stir and roast them for about 3 minutes or until they just begin to show signs of browning. Turn the heat down to medium-low. Continue to stir and cook for another 6–7 minutes or until the peanuts are roasted. Empty the peanuts onto a piece of paper toweling and let them cool enough to handle. Now rub off the papery skins with the help of the paper toweling and either blow them away or pick out the peanuts and put them in a bowl. Wipe out the frying pan.

Brush a 7-inch pie tin with 1 teaspoon of the oil.

Break up the palm sugar into small lumps and put it, as well as the remaining 1 teaspoon oil and 2 tablespoons water, into the frying pan. Set it over a medium heat. When it is bubbling, turn the heat to low and let the palm sugar melt. Cook very gently for about 5 minutes for chewy candy, and about 8 minutes for hard, more brittle candy. The palm sugar will become thicker as it cooks. Take it off the heat. Put all the peanuts into the pan and immediately pour its contents into the oiled pie tin, letting the mixture spread evenly. Cool and then pull, tear or break the candy into pieces.

SERVING JAPANESE RICE WINE

SAKE

Japanese habits are changing. It is now considered chic to drink whisky with a meal, and it is quite common to have beer, but *sake*, the indigenous rice wine, remains the national drink. Famed as the mythical drink of the gods in ancient times and limited to exclusive consumption by nobles and priests through the Middle Ages, today *sake* is available to the masses even in cardboard cartons that are sold out of vending machines just like Coca-Cola.

Sake is colorless, like vodka, though much less potent. Its alcoholic content can range from 15 to 17 percent for the general market, and up to 20 percent for some very special domestic varieties. At weddings and banquets it may be served cool, straight out of specially ordered cedar casks, rather like beer out of barrels. These days, it may also be served chilled. Chilled *sake* is being promoted quite a bit now in Japan to lure back the infidels who have been seduced by the fashionable white wines of France.

The most common way to drink *sake,* however, is not cooled or chilled, but warmed. Warming releases its aromas and allows the alcohol to enter the bloodstream with a more pronounced sense of urgency. *Sake* that has been warmed once is not considered good for drinking any more as its aromas have been dispersed. (It is, however, good for cooking.) It is for this reason that only small quantities of *sake* are warmed at a time. Servings, too, are small as the entire amount—a few thimblefuls—is supposed to be drunk at one go, before it has a chance to cool off. It is considered polite to serve one's neighbors when their glasses are empty and to let them do the same for you. It is *not* quite the done thing to serve oneself when in company. *Sake* can be drunk through every course of a Japanese meal.

Once a bottle of *sake* has been opened, it behaves rather like wine and it is best to drink it all up. You may, if you have to, keep it for 2–3 weeks in a cool place or in a refrigerator, but its life is limited.

For heating and serving this drink, *sake* bottles and cups are sold by many oriental shops. If you do not wish to buy a set, it is very easy to improvise. For drinking, use the smallest liqueur glasses in your possession. The size will probably be just right. For heating and serving, use any pretty glass or ceramic bottle of roughly 1¼-cup capacity. Fill it with *sake*. Half-fill a medium-sized pan with water and stand the bottle of *sake* in it. Heat the water gently. The *sake* should be very warm but not very hot. The temperature you should aim for is around 130°F. Heat several batches, one after the other, as you need them. By the way, the word for "cheers" is *kampai!*

GINGER TEA

SALABAT

Ginger tea in some form or other is drunk nearly everywhere in the Far East. It is meant to be very good for coughs and colds and is also a digestive. In the Philippines it is often offered at breakfast and with midday snacks or *merienda*.

Serves 4

3 1-inch cubes fresh ginger

4–5 teaspoons honey or brown sugar to taste

Peel the ginger and chop it coarsely. Put it into a small pan along with 1 quart water and the honey or sugar. Bring to a boil. Turn the heat to low and simmer gently for 15–20 minutes. Strain and serve. You may also serve this tea cold.

GINGER COFFEE

KOPI JAHE

*I*ndonesians grow their own coffee and one of the ways they drink it is very sweet, with a strong ginger flavor. It is quite easy to make such coffee at home. Whether you drink the instant version or use a filter, all you have to do is prepare a ginger broth and make your coffee with that instead of water. (Perhaps it is *not* advisable to make this coffee in a drip coffee machine in case the chemicals in ginger affect its inner workings.)   *Serves 4*

1-inch cube fresh ginger

Coffee (instant or ground for filtering) enough for 4 cups

Brown or white sugar to taste

Peel the ginger and dice it coarsely. Put it into a pan with about 4¼ cups water. Bring the water to a boil, turn the heat to low and simmer gently for 15 minutes. Strain. If you are making instant coffee, put about 1 teaspoon coffee (or whatever amount you like) into each cup and pour the hot ginger broth over it. Stir it to mix. If you are using a filter, measure out just enough coffee for 4 people and put it into the filter. Pour the hot ginger broth over the coffee and let it filter through. Hand the sugar around separately when you serve the coffee.

INGREDIENTS

Far Eastern cuisines depend for their distinctive flavors on some special ingredients. It is worth making the effort to seek these out from specialist grocers. Some ethnic grocers operate a mail-order service (see page 311 for details). For the recipes in this book I have suggested substitutes for those ingredients which may be harder to find; in such cases the authentic ingredient is always given first, followed by the suggested substitute.

AGAR-AGAR This is a vegetarian gelatin made from a seaweed. It is available from Japanese, Korean and Chinese groceries as powder, flakes and sticks. The sticks, which look like uneven clear noodles, can be melted and used just like ordinary gelatin but this book only requires them to be used in salads. To do this, you should first soak them in cold water until they are soft but retain a nice crunch. Drain them and then cut them into any size you desire. They may now be added to any salad and dressed.

ANCHOVY PASTE This is the best substitute I can think of for the various types of shrimp paste used in Southeast Asia. Most of the better supermarkets, delicatessens and certainly all speciality food shops sell it. If you like, you could drain canned anchovies thoroughly and then pulverize them in a blender or food processor.

BAMBOO SHOOTS Unfortunately, we cannot usually get fresh bamboo shoots in the West and must make do with canned ones. Good canned bamboo shoots should be creamy white and crisp with a clean, refreshing taste. Among the better brands available here is Companion, whose win-ter bamboo shoots in water are generally of excellent quality. You can buy tinned bamboo shoots in rather large hunks which may then be cut up into cubes of the desired size, or you can sometimes buy the cone-shaped and very tender bamboo shoot tips which are usually cut into comblike wedges. Some tinned bamboo shoots come ready-sliced. Try to get the chunks instead if possible.

All bamboo shoots that come out of a can have a faint tinny taste. They should be washed in fresh water and drained before use. Any bamboo shoots that are unused may be covered with clean water and stored in a lidded jar in the refrigerator. In order to keep the bamboo shoots fresh, the water should be changed every day.

BASIL Many different types of fresh basil are used in Southeast Asia. Each country—sometimes each province within a country—has different names for the basils. There is sweet basil (*bai horapha* in Thailand); holy basil with thin purplish leaves (*bai ka-prow* in Thailand) and lemon basil (*bai manglak* in Thailand). Ordinary basil and fresh mint are the best Western substitutes for the very aromatic Southeast Asian basils.

ANCHOVY PASTE

EGGPLANT

AGAR-AGAR

BAMBOO SHOOTS

THAI BASILS

BEAN CURD

ENGLISH BASIL

CHINESE LONG BEANS

BEAN CURD   This is made from the "milk" of soaked, mashed and strained soybeans and takes the form of white, milky, custardlike squares. Bean curd is sold by all Chinese groceries and health food shops. It can be soft (silken tofu) or firm. For the recipes in this book, use firm bean curd. Bean curd squares are sold packed in water. If you do not intend to use them immediately after buying them, put them in a bowl, cover them with fresh water and refrigerate. Change the water every day.

BEANS, LONG   Also known as asparagus beans and yard-long beans, these can indeed be very long. In the Far East they come in two colors, pale and dark green, the dark being the crisper of the two. In the West we have to use what we can get, though good Chinese groceries here usually stock long beans. The beans are generally cut into smaller lengths and then used just like string beans. The best substitute is, indeed, string beans.

BEAN SAUCE, BLACK   Commercially prepared sauces made of fermented soybeans are used throughout Malaysia and other parts of Southeast Asia. They can be very thick, filled with crumbled beans, or smooth and somewhat thinner. Use any bottled or canned black bean sauce that is available, such as that sold under the brand name of Amoy. Once you have opened a bottle you should store it, tightly closed, in the refrigerator.

BEAN SAUCE, YELLOW   Like black bean sauce, this is commercially prepared from fermented soybeans, only it has a very pale brown, almost yellowish color. It can be smooth but I like to use the kind that has whole or halved beans in it, usually labeled as "crushed yellow bean sauce."

BEAN SPROUTS   These are crisp sprouts grown from the same mung beans sold in Indian stores as whole *moong*. They can now be bought fresh in supermarkets and health food stores as well as Chinese groceries. They are good when they are crisp and white. When you buy fresh sprouts, rinse them in cold running water and then put them into a bowl of fresh water. The bowl should be covered and refrigerated. If the beans are not used by the next day, you should change the water again.

It is considered proper to "top and tail" bean sprouts before using them. This means pinching off the remains of the whole bean at the top as well as the threadlike tail at the bottom. It requires a lot of patience. The sprouts do indeed look better after this treatment, but I have to admit that I very rarely bother with it. Bean sprouts are also sold in cans. I never use the canned variety as they do not have the necessary crunch.

BLACK BEANS, SALTED   These are salted, spiced and fermented soybeans. In their dry form they are sold in plastic bags. They need to be rinsed slightly to remove any excess salt and then chopped before use. They are also available in cans as "black beans in salted sauce." These are whole black beans usually floating in liquid. Lift them out of their liquid, chop them and use them as the recipe suggests.

BONITO STOCK *See Dashi*

BONITO, DRIED Known as *katsuo-bushi* in Japan, this fish of the mackerel family is filleted and dried until it becomes as hard as wood. It is then shaved rather like wood with a plane. These shavings are an essential ingredient in Japanese Soup Stock. The shaved flakes are sold in specialty and Japanese shops as *hana-katsuo*.

CANDLENUTS Called *kemiri* in Indonesia and *buah keras* in Malaysia, these nuts are used in curry paste to give it thickness and texture. As they are not easily available in the West, a reasonable substitute would be raw cashew nuts or macadamia nuts, both of which are sold in health food shops and many supermarkets.

CARDAMOM, WHOLE PODS These small green-colored pods have the most aromatic black seeds inside them. The pods are used to flavor curries, rice dishes and Indian-style desserts. In the West bleached whitish pods can be found in most supermarkets. They are less aromatic but may be used as a substitute for the green variety.

CASHEW NUTS These nuts traveled from the Americas via Africa and India all the way to China. For the recipes in this book they are used in their raw form as a substitute for candlenuts. (In fact all so-called raw cashews have been processed to remove the prussic acid they contain in their natural state.)

CASSIA BARK This is Chinese cinnamon, sometimes known as "false cinnamon." It is thicker, coarser and generally cheaper than true cinnamon but with a stronger flavor.

CHILI BEAN SAUCE This reddish brown, very hot and spicy sauce is made of soybeans, red chilies and other seasonings. It is used in the cooking of Western China and is sold in jars by Chinese groceries. The Yu Kwen Yick brand is the best.

CHILI OIL This is an orange-colored oil that gets its heat and its color from red chilies. Small amounts of it can be put into dishes as they are being cooked to add a bit of pep to them. Many Chinese restaurants have small bottles of chili oil on the table for those who wish to season their own foods further. Chili oil can be bought from any Oriental grocery. If you wish to make your own, see the recipe on page 237.

CHILI PASTE, THAI The Thai chili paste (*nam prik pow*) is made by frying shallots and chilies together and then combining them with sugar and tamarind until the seasonings have the consistency of a thick jam. *Nam prik pow* is sold by Thai grocers. Unfortunately, the bottles are not always labeled as such. It is best to ask for help and tell the shop attendant whether you want it hot, medium or mild, as it comes in all three strengths. If you cannot obtain it, you can add a certain amount of similar seasoning to your food by combining one part each of ground red (cayenne) pepper and sugar with two parts vegetable oil.

CHILIES, WHOLE DRIED HOT RED These can be small and thin or long and fat. The small variety is the most easily available. When used for making a spice paste they are usually soaked in water before being ground with other spices.

CHILIES, FRESH GREEN AND RED Chilies originated in the Americas and then traveled via Africa and India all the way to China and Korea. The East has adopted them with a passion almost unmatched in the countries of their origin. Red chilies are just ripe green chilies. However, their flavor is slightly different, though their intensity can be exactly the same. Red chilies are used in hundreds of Southeast Asian curry pastes not only for their heat but also for the beautiful color they provide to the sauce. I find that a combination of our more common red bell pepper with paprika and ground red (cayenne) pepper makes the best substitute when I cannot obtain fresh red chilies.

Chilies are a very rich source of iron and vitamins A and C. As they vary tremendously in size, shape and heat, it might take a little experimenting to find the chilies you like best. To store fresh red or green chilies, wrap them first in newspaper, then in plastic, and place in the refrigerator. They should last for several weeks. Any that begin to soften and rot should be removed as they tend to infect the whole batch. Chilies used in cooking (not garnishing) may also be washed, dried and then frozen whole in plastic containers. Hot chilies must be handled carefully. When you are cutting them, be careful not to touch your eyes or your lips with your fingers or they will burn. Wash your hands thoroughly afterward.

Chilies are not only used for their taste and heat in Southeast Asia, but also to provide a decorative element to a dish. Sometimes they are sliced into rings, at other times into slivers, and often they are cut to resemble flowers.

To make chili flowers Just cut off a tiny piece of the very tip, leaving the stem attached. Make four cuts lengthwise in the chili, starting from a little below the stem and going all the way down to the tip. You should now have four sections still attached at the stem. Remove all the seeds and soak the chilies in cold water until they open into flowers.

CHINESE CABBAGE There is great confusion about what Chinese cabbage is. To me, Chinese cabbage, sometimes called Napa cabbage, is the very chunky, pale green, long, wide-ribbed cabbage that is generally about 5–6 inches or more in diameter. Its leaves resemble those of the vegetable sold as Chinese celery cabbage. They are, however, much wider and have greater flavor. This is the vegetable that is used to make the Korean cabbage pickle called *kimchee*. If you cannot get it, use Chinese celery cabbage, which is widely available, as a substitute.

CHINESE CELERY This resembles Italian flat-leafed parsley. It is larger and coarser and its thin stalks have a distinct celery flavor. Celery stalks, finely diced, and celery leaves can be used as substitutes: follow the directions in individual recipes.

CHINESE CELERY CABBAGE This is an exceedingly slim version of Chinese cabbage. *See above.*

CHINESE CHIVES The leaves of Chinese chives are flat and have a pronounced garliclike flavor. During the season in which the plant is budding, buds, still attached to their stalks, are also sold. They add a wonderful touch to stir-

BLACK BEAN SAUCE

CRUSHED YELLOW BEAN SAUCE

BEAN SPROUTS

CANNED BLACK BEANS

DRIED SALTED BLACK BEANS

BONITO FLAKES

CANDLENUTS

CARDAMOM PODS

CASHEW NUTS

CASSIA BARK

CHILI BEAN SAUCE

DRIED CHILIES

CHILI OIL

CHILI PASTE

GROUND RED (CAYENNE) PEPPER

CHILIES

fried dishes. Ordinary chives can be used as a substitute (use their young buds as well).

COCONUT, FRESH When buying a coconut, look for one that shows no signs of mold and is free from cracks. Shake the coconut. If it has a lot of water in it, it has a better chance of being good. People generally weigh a coconut in each hand and pick the heavier.

To break open a coconut, use the unsharpened side of a cleaver or heavy knife and hit the coconut hard all around its circumference. You can hold the coconut in one hand over a large bowl while you hit it with the other, or you can rest the coconut on a firm solid surface while you hit it and then rush it to a bowl as soon as the first crack appears to catch the coconut water. Some people like to drink the water; I do. This coconut water is not used in cooking but it is a good indication of the sweetness and freshness of the coconut.

You should now have two halves. Before proceeding any further, cut off a small bit of the meat and taste it. It should have a sweet flavor. If it is lacking in sweetness, this can be endured, but if it is at all rancid or moldy you must discard the coconut. Now remove the tough outer shell by slipping a knife between it and the meat and then prizing the meat out. Sometimes it helps to crack the halves into smaller pieces to do this.

The coconut meat is covered on the outer side with a thin brown skin. If your recipe calls for grated fresh coconut, remove the skin with a vegetable peeler or knife, cut the meat into small cubes and put these into a food processor or blender. Instead of the paste you might expect, the result will resemble grated coconut. You can freeze what you do not use. Grated coconut freezes very well and it is a good idea to keep some on hand.

As a substitute for grated fresh coconut you can use unsweetened dried coconut which is sold in most health food stores. To get the equivalent of 8 tablespoons of grated fresh coconut, soak 5 tablespoons dried coconut in 4 tablespoons of hot water for 1 hour.

COCONUT MILK This may be made with fresh coconut or can be prepared from powdered coconut milk, unsweetened dried coconut, or block coconut in cream; or it can be bought canned. No coconut milk of any sort keeps well—this includes canned milk after it has been opened. Even if you refrigerate it, it generally does not last more than a few days.

Using fresh coconut First prize the flesh off the shell as described above. Whether you also peel off the brown skin depends on the dish you are making. If it needs to look pale and pristine, remove the skin; if not, leave it on. Grate the coconut meat in a food processor or blender as explained above.

To make about 1½ cups coconut milk, put 2 cups of grated coconut into a blender or food processor. Add 1¼ cups very hot water. Blend for a few seconds. Line a sieve with a piece of muslin or cheesecloth and place it over a bowl. Empty the contents of the blender into the sieve. Gather the ends of the cloth together and squeeze out all the liquid. For most of the recipes in this book, this is the coconut milk that is needed. If you leave this milk to stand for a while, cream will rise to the top. That is why I recommend stirring the coconut milk before using it. If just the cream or thick coconut milk is required, spoon it off the top.

Canned coconut milk is available from most Chinese and Indian groceries but the quality varies. A brand that I like very much and use frequently is Chaokoh from Thailand. It is white, creamy and quite delicious. Canned coconut milk is generally thicker than fresh milk and is very good for soups and sauces. The cream tends to rise to the top in a can, as it does in fresh coconut milk. Always stir it well before using it. Sometimes, because of the fat in it, canned coconut milk tends to become very grainy. To rectify this you can either whir the milk for a second in a blender or beat it well. I find that whereas you can cook, say, a fish in fresh coconut milk for a long time, canned coconut milk, which behaves differently, is best added toward the end of the cooking time.

Powdered coconut milk You can now buy packets of powdered coconut milk from Oriental grocers and supermarkets. Their quality varies from good to poor, the poor ones containing hard-to-dissolve globules of fat. I like the Emma brand, which comes from Malaysia. Directions for using the powder are given on the packet. To use the powder in any of the recipes in this book calling for coconut milk, mix an equal volume of powder and hot water and then stir well until the powder dissolves. If unwanted granules or globules remain, strain the milk before using it. I find that it is best to add coconut milk made of powder toward the end of the cooking period as it tends to separate easily.

Using unsweetened dried coconut Put 5 cups dried coconut into a pan. Add 2½ cups water and bring to a simmer. Now pour the contents into a blender or food processor and blend for 1 minute. Strain the resulting mixture through a double thickness of muslin or cheesecloth, pushing out as much liquid as you can. You should get about 2½ cups coconut milk.

Using creamed coconut This, available in block form at Indian and Southeast Asian groceries, can also be turned into coconut milk. I do not advise you to use it if you need large quantities of milk, but if you require just a few tablespoons, mix equal quantities of creamed coconut and hot water. The thick coconut milk that will result should be put into dishes only at the last moment.

CORIANDER, FRESH This is the parsley of the eastern half of Asia. Generally just the delicate, fragrant, green leaves are used. In Thai curries, however, the white root is ground in as well, and in China the stems are diced finely and put into sauces. The best way to keep fresh coriander is to stand it in a glass of water, cover it with a plastic bag and refrigerate the whole thing. Break off the leaves as you need them.

CORIANDER SEEDS These are the round, beige seeds of the coriander plant. They are sold either whole or ground. You can grind them yourself in a coffee grinder or food processor and then put them through a fine sieve.

CUMIN SEEDS Cumin was brought into Southeast Asia by Arab and Indian traders. Sometimes the seeds are used

CHINESE CELERY

CHINESE CHIVES

CHINESE CABBAGE

FRESH COCONUT

DRIED COCONUT

CANNED COCONUT MILK

CINNAMON STICKS

CHAOKOH
COCONUT MILK
NƯỚC CỐT DỪA
GATA

NET CON 14 FL.OZ. (400 ML)
ชาวเกาะ

COCONUT WATER

GRATED FRESH COCONUT

CREAMED COCONUT

POWDERED COCONUT MILK

FRESH CORIANDER

CORIANDER SEEDS

CUMIN SEEDS

GROUND CORIANDER

GROUND CUMIN

whole, though in this region they are generally ground with the spice paste for curries.

CURRY LEAVES These highly aromatic leaves are used in many areas of Southeast Asia. In Indonesia, where they are known as *daun salaam,* they are always used in their fresh form. They are not easily available fresh in the West, however. You could use the dried leaf, but I think a better substitute is the Indian curry leaf *(kari patta),* which is sometimes available both fresh and dried in Indian shops. Fresh curry leaves may be frozen flat in a plastic bag or box.

DASHI This is Japanese soup stock. The most common kind is made with a combination of shavings from dried bonito fillets and a dried kelp *(konbu).* See the recipe on page 78.

DASHI-NO-MOTO This is instant *dashi,* available in granules and generally salted. It is sold under many brand names. The kind I use requires 2 teaspoons of the granules to be mixed with 2 cups hot water to make a basic Japanese stock. To season this stock for soup, add 1 tablespoon sugar, 3 tablespoons Japanese soy sauce *(shoyu)* and 2 tablespoons *sake.* Simmer it gently for a few minutes until the sugar dissolves.

EVAPORATED MILK Available in cans, this is milk that has been condensed but not sweetened. It is popular in Malaysian and Filipino cooking.

FENNEL SEEDS These seeds look and taste like aniseed, but they are larger and plumper. To grind fennel seeds, put a few tablespoons into a clean cof-

fee grinder or food processor and grind as finely as possible. Store in an airtight container.

FISH SAUCE Known as *nam pla* in Thailand, *nước mắm* in Vietnam and *patis* in the Philippines, fish sauce is used in these countries much as soy sauce is used in China. A thin, salty brown liquid made from salted shrimp or fish, it has a very special flavor of its own. It is obtainable from Chinese and Far Eastern groceries. You can either use salt as a substitute or improvise a sauce by combining 1 tablespoon water with ½ teaspoon salt, ¼ teaspoon soy sauce and ¼ teaspoon sugar.

FIVE-SPICE POWDER A Chinese spice mixture, this contains star anise, fennel, cloves, cinnamon and Szechuan peppercorns. It is sold already ground by Chinese groceries and many supermarkets. To make it yourself, combine 2 whole star anise, 1 teaspoon whole fennel seeds, 1 teaspoon whole cloves, a 2-inch stick cinnamon or cassia bark and 1 tablespoon Szechuan peppercorns. Grind as finely as possible in a clean coffee grinder or food processor and store in a tightly lidded jar.

FRUIT, FRESH See pages 259–262.

FUNGUS, BLACK Also known as *moer* mushrooms and cloud ears, this tree fungus is a speciality of Szechuan province. It is sold in Chinese groceries in the form of little dried, curled-up black chips. Once these have been soaked, they enlarge considerably. At this stage you should feel with your fingers for the little hard "eyes" they have and snip them off. Rinse them well as they tend to be very gritty. They have no particular flavor of their own but add a very nice crunchy texture.

GAI LAN   This is the Chinese name for a wonderful member of the cabbage family. Deep green in color, it is close in taste to broccoli but has no head. It is basically all leaves with tasty stems and small flowers. It is usually available in Chinese groceries, where it may be labeled *kai lan*.

GALANGAL   Known as *Laos* and *lengkuas* in Indonesia, *langkuas* in Malaysia and *kha* in Thailand, this gingerlike rhizome has a very distinct earthy aroma of its own. Unfortunately, it is rarely available in its fresh form in the West. In the recipes that require it, I have suggested that you use dried sliced galangal. This has to be soaked in water before being ground with other spices to make curry paste. The dried slices are available from some Chinese and Far Eastern groceries. Ground dried galangal (frequently labeled "Laos powder") is also obtainable.

GARLIC   This is used in large quantities in Southeast Asia. Very often it is sliced, fried into crisp chips and either scattered over foods as a garnish or mixed in with them to give them an added delicious flavor.

GHEE   This is butter that has been clarified so thoroughly that you can even deep-fry in it. As it has no milk solids left in it, it does not need refrigeration. It has a nutty, buttery taste. All Indian grocers sell it and I find it more convenient to buy it ready-prepared. If, however, you need (or

want) to make your own, put 1 lb unsalted butter in a pan over a low heat and let it simmer very gently until the milky solids turn brownish and cling to the sides of the pan or fall to the bottom. The time this takes will depend on the amount of water in the butter. Watch carefully toward the end of the heating period and do not let the *ghee* burn. Strain the *ghee* through a triple layer of muslin or cheesecloth. Homemade *ghee* is best stored in a refrigerator.

GINGER, FRESH   You almost cannot cook without fresh ginger in the Far East. This rhizome has a sharp, pungent, cleansing taste and is a digestive to boot. Its brown skin is generally peeled, though in Chinese cookery it is often left on.

When a recipe calls for finely grated ginger, it should first be peeled and then grated on the finest part of a grater so that it turns into pulp. If a recipe requires a 1-inch piece of ginger to be grated, you will find that it is easier to grate that length while it is still attached to the large knob, so saving you from grating your fingers.

Ginger should be stored in a cool dry place. Many people like to bury it in dryish sandy soil. This way they can break off and retrieve small portions as they need them, while the rest of the knob generously keeps growing.

HOISIN SAUCE   This is a thick, slightly sweet, smooth Chinese bean sauce with a light garlic flavor. It may be used in cooking or as a dip. It is sold by Chinese groceries and many supermarkets. Store in a tightly lidded jar in the refrigerator.

CURRY LEAVES

DASHI-NO-MOTO

DASHI STOCK

DILL

EVAPORATED MILK

FENNEL SEEDS

GROUND FENNEL

FISH SAUCE

FIVE-SPICE POWDER

BLACK FUNGUS

GAI LAN

DRIED SLICED GALANGAL

GALANGAL OR LAOS POWDER

FRESH GALANGAL

HOLY BASIL *(bai kaprow)*   *See* Basil.

JAGGERY   A form of raw lump cane sugar. You should look for the kind that crumbles easily and is not rock-hard. It can be bought at Indian groceries. This is the best substitute for the palm sugar that is used in Southeast Asia.

JAPANESE SEVEN-SPICE SEASONING   *See Shichimi.*

KAFFIR LIME, LEAVES AND RIND   Kaffir lime is a dark green knobbly lime whose peel and leaves are used in Southeast Asian cookery. They are highly aromatic and there is no real substitute for their flavor. If you are lucky enough to obtain fresh leaves, you should tear them in half and pull off their coarse center veins before using them. Leftover leaves can be stored in a plastic bag in the freezer. Whole limes may be frozen as well. Both leaves and rind are sometimes available dried. You should use them in whatever form you can find. The leaves, dried rind and the lime itself are sold by Far Eastern and some Chinese groceries. You may have to ask for help in locating the rind, which may be labeled in Thai as *"piwma grood."*

KOCHU CHANG   A spicy paste made with fermented soybeans and red chilies, this is a very common seasoning in Korea. It is sold by Korean groceries that specialize in Korean foods. Korean groceries selling general foodstuffs always have some on hand for themselves. They will often sell you some or get you some if you beg nicely. You can improvise by using the recipe on page 240.

KOKUM   Various souring agents are used in Indonesian cookery. *Asem candis,* the dried skin of a mangosteen-like fruit, is very popular in Western Sumatra. As it is hard to find in the West, I use the Indian *kokum,* which is very similar.

KONBU   This green, calcium-rich dried kelp used for making stock *(dashi)* in Japan is sometimes sold as *dashi-konbu.* It resembles large long leaves and is available either folded up or cut into small pieces. *Konbu* (sometimes called *kombu*) should never be washed as its flavor resides near the surface. It should be wiped with a damp cloth just before use. *Konbu* may be allowed to simmer gently, but never boil vigorously. It is obtainable from Japanese and some Chinese groceries, where its price is generally a good indication of its quality.

KRUPUK   These Indonesian wafers, somewhat similar to Indian poppadums, can be served with most meals. They are available in different flavors. The base, however, is usually tapioca. When dried, they are hard and brittle. When fried, they expand and turn very crisp. They are obtainable from Far Eastern and some Chinese groceries. Once a packet has been started, any unused wafers should be transferred to a tightly lidded jar.

LEMONGRASS   Known as *sereh* in Indonesia, *serai* in Malaysia and *takrai* in Thailand, lemongrass is a tall, hard, grayish-green grass often used in Southeast Asian dishes for its aroma and flavor. It is available in Southeast Asian groceries. Usually only the bottom 6 inches are used and the straw-like top is discarded. The lemongrass may be used whole, its bottom first bruised with a hammer or other heavy object, or it can be sliced.

Lemongrass is fairly hard. To slice it, first cut off the hard knot at the very end and then slice crosswise into paper-thin slices. Even when lemongrass is to be ground to a pulp in a blender it needs to be sliced thinly first or it does not grind properly. Lemongrass is best stored with its bottom end in a little water. This prevents it from drying out. You can also freeze stalks of lemongrass.

In Southeast Asia lemongrass is always used fresh. Unfortunately, many of us in the West have to make do with the dried variety. I buy the dried sliced lemongrass and then soak it before I use it. As its name suggests, lemongrass has a citrus flavor and aroma. The best equivalent is lemon rind, though it is nowhere near as good as the real thing.

LIME AND LIME JUICE Limes of various sorts are plentiful in East Asia and are used with some abandon. The Philippines have the very small *kalamansi* lime, which is squeezed over many foods and makes excellent limeade. There is the kaffir lime of Indochina with its unmatched aroma, and then there is the lime that we know in the West, though here it is generally found in a smaller size. If you cannot get limes, use lemons as a substitute.

MINT Mints of various sorts fill the vegetable shops of Southeast Asia. They are used in cooking and also nibbled at on the side during meals or, as in Vietnam, added to morsels of food just as they are about to be eaten. Nothing but fresh mint can be used for this.

MIRIN This is sweetened *sake* that is used for cooking. Even though *mirin* is an essential ingredient in Japanese cookery, I have not used it too often in this book as it is exceedingly hard to find in the West. You can, however, make a reasonable substitute by combining equal parts of *sake* and sugar and then cooking them gently until the sugar dissolves and the liquid is reduced by half. I have tended to use this combination in my recipes instead of *mirin*. If you have access to a Japanese grocery, do try to get the real thing.

MISO A Japanese paste made from fermented soybeans, *miso* also contains other fermented grains. Among the *miso* easily available in the West is *aka-miso*, a reddish brown variety. *Miso* can usually be found in health food shops. Sometimes it is labeled according to its color—"red," "brown," "yellow," or "white." In Japan, where *miso* is used a great deal, it is available in almost every shade and texture. It can be used for soups and stews, it can be slathered onto vegetables such as eggplants before they are grilled, and it can also be used in the preparation of pickles and dressings. To make soup, *miso* needs to be dissolved in water and then strained. It should never be allowed to boil vigorously.

MUNG BEANS, WHOLE These yellow beans with green skins are sold in supermarkets, health food stores and Oriental groceries.

MUSHROOMS Hundreds of varieties of mushroom are sold in East Asia, from tiny pinheads to large meaty ones. In the West we can get only some of

GARLIC

GHEE

GINGER

HOISIN SAUCE

JAGGERY

KAFFIR LIME FRUIT

DRIED KAFFIR LIME RIND

DRIED AND FRESH KAFFIR LIME LEAVES

KOCHU CHANG

KOKUM

KOHLRABI

KONBU

KRUPUK

LEMONGRASS

LIME JUICE

DRIED SLICED LEMONGRASS

them and then only in their dried or canned forms. (*See also* Fungus, black.)

Dried Chinese mushrooms These are available in Chinese shops. Price is generally an indication of quality. The thicker the cap, the meatier the texture. The mushrooms need to be soaked in warm water before they are used. The texture of the stalks remains hard, even after soaking, so they need to be cut off. The water in which the mushrooms have soaked should be strained and saved; it can be added to stocks or used to cook vegetables.

Straw mushrooms Smooth and meaty, there is nothing quite as delicious as a fresh straw mushroom. I eagerly await the day when they will be as commonly available in the West as they are in the East. Meanwhile, we have to make do with the canned variety. Drain them first, rinse them and then use according to the instructions in the recipe.

MUSTARD SEEDS, BLACK AND YELLOW
Black mustard seeds are used in curry pastes in some parts of Southeast Asia. The seeds are tiny, round and of a blackish or reddish brown color. They can be bought from Indian groceries. Yellow mustard seeds may be substituted for the black ones.

NOODLES Noodles probably originated in the Far East. They are sold both dried and fresh, made of wheat or rice, and there are literally hundreds to choose from.

Fresh Chinese egg noodles These are usually sold in plastic bags in the refrigerated section of Chinese groceries. A 1-lb package usually serves 4–6 people. If you intend using smaller portions, divide the noodles as soon as possible after purchase, wrap well and freeze what you are not going to use that day; the rest can be refrigerated until you are ready to cook them.

The best way to cook fresh egg noodles is to put them into a large pan of boiling water. As soon as the water comes to the boil again, add a cup of fresh water. Repeat this about three times or until the noodles are just tender. The noodles can now be drained and used as the recipe suggests. Frozen egg noodles defrost quickly and easily when dropped into boiling water: just stir them about at first to ensure that they separate.

Dried Chinese egg noodles When fresh noodles are not available, use dried ones. Put them into a large pan of boiling water and cook them as you would fresh noodles.

Fresh rice noodles These are white, slithery and absolutely delicious. In Southeast Asia they are available in all sizes and shapes. Their freshness generally lasts for just a day. Many do not need to be cooked at all; others should be heated through very briefly. Unfortunately, these noodles are very hard to find in the West.

Dried rice noodles We usually have to make do with dried rice noodles in the West. For most of the recipes in this book, buy *banh phở* or any other flat rice noodles, soak them for about 2 hours or until they are soft, and then cook them very briefly in a large pan of boiling water. Drain them and rinse them in cold water before using them as the recipe suggests. *Banh phở* is the noodle to use for making the Vietnamese noodle soup called *phở*.

Cellophane noodles These noodles, also called bean thread or transparent noodles, are made from ground mung beans. Chinese groceries sell them dried. They are very fine and white in color, and should be soaked 10–15 minutes before use.

Udon These are white, slightly rounded or flat Japanese wheat noodles. They can be bought in the West mostly in their dried form. Cook them as you would Chinese fresh egg noodles, but then rinse them under cold running water.

OILS For most of the recipes in this book, I would recommend using peanut or corn oil. If the oil is used for deep-frying, it can be reused. Skim off all extraneous matter with a slotted spoon or a Chinese mesh skimmer and then drop a chunk of ginger or potato into it and let it fry: this will absorb most of the unwanted flavors. When it is cool enough to handle, strain the oil through a triple thickness of muslin or cheesecloth or a large clean handkerchief. Let it cool completely and then store it in a bottle. When reusing, mix half old oil with half fresh oil.

Olive oil This is used only in the Philippines because of its Spanish heritage.

Sesame oil See the separate entry Sesame oil.

OYSTER SAUCE A thick, brown, Cantonese-style sauce made with oysters, this is salty and slightly sweet at the same time. It is used to flavor all sorts of dishes from vegetables to noodles. Once opened, a bottle of oyster sauce should be stored in the refrigerator. It keeps indefinitely. It can be obtained at some supermarkets and delicatessens and at Chinese groceries. The Yu Kwen Yick brand is the best.

PALM SUGAR This is a delicious, raw, honey-colored sugar used in many parts of Southeast Asia. It comes in lump or fairly flowing forms. The best substitutes for it are either Indian jaggery or brown sugar.

PAPRIKA Not generally used in Southeast Asian food. I use it frequently in place of fresh red chilies in order to give dishes their traditional color.

PEANUTS Raw peanuts can be obtained at supermarkets, health food stores and ethnic groceries. For roasting and crushing peanuts, see page 247.

PEPPERS, RED AND GREEN BELL Cooked foods in Southeast Asia are often garnished with strips of fresh hot red and green chilies. Since this tends to make the dishes even hotter than they already are, I frequently substitute strips of sweet red and green bell peppers. The curry pastes of this region often require a pounded paste made from fresh red chilies, which are very hard to obtain in the West. The best substitute is a combination of sweet red bell pepper and paprika.

RADISH, WHITE Also known as *daikon* in Japanese groceries, this radish is large, long, thick and mild. It can be as large as 3 inches in diameter. It should be peeled before use.

MINT

MIRIN

MISO

MUNG BEANS

DRIED CHINESE MUSHROOMS

STRAW MUSHROOMS

YELLOW MUSTARD SEEDS

BLACK MUSTARD SEEDS

CELLOPHANE NOODLES

RICE VERMICELLI

DRIED RICE *PHỞ* NOODLES

FRESH RICE NOODLES

DRIED EGG NOODLES

FRESH EGG NOODLES

UDON NOODLES

PEANUT OIL

OLIVE OIL

RED PEPPER, GROUND (CAYENNE) This powder is made by grinding only dried hot red chilies. You can add as much or as little to a dish as you like, depending on how hot you like your food.

RICE This is the staple in most parts of the Far East. Each country, sometimes each province within each country, favors its own special rice. For the purposes of this book, two types of rice should suffice: long-grain for all the dishes from Indonesia, Malaysia, Vietnam, Thailand, the Philippines and Hong Kong; and Japanese short-grain for Japanese and Korean dishes. The rice is generally washed before use. Directions for cooking these two types of rice can be found on pages 210 and 211 respectively.

In some regions of Indochina, such as northern Thailand, glutinous rice is the staple. The grains are short and opaque. Directions for cooking glutinous rice are on page 212.

RICE PAPER, VIETNAMESE This is the thin translucent wrapper used to make Vietnamese spring rolls. It generally comes with the markings of the mats on which it was dried still imprinted on it. It needs to be dampened in order to become soft. Rice papers are available in various sizes from just a few select Asian groceries.

RICE WINE, CHINESE Several rice wines are used in Chinese cookery, the most common being Shao-Hsing. This is whisky-colored with a rich sweetish taste. A reasonable substitute is dry sherry. I find that La Ina comes the closest in flavor.

SAFFRON This is the whole stigma of the autumn crocus, which is available dried and has a threadlike appearance. Look for a reliable source for your saffron as it is very expensive and there can be a great deal of adulteration.

SAKE This is the Japanese rice wine used for both cooking and drinking. It is available from many good liquor stores and Japanese groceries. For more information see page 272.

SESAME OIL Oriental sesame oil is made from roasted sesame seeds. It therefore has a golden color and a deliciously nutty taste and aroma. It is not used for cooking as such. Small amounts are added to dressings and foods just to give them a sesame flavor and sometimes a sheen. Store sesame oil in a cool place away from the light but not in the refrigerator, as it turns cloudy there.

SESAME PASTE Chinese and Japanese sesame pastes are made from roasted sesame seeds and have a darker color than Middle Eastern sesame paste (tahini). If you cannot get the former, use the latter. All sesame paste has oil floating on the top. You need to mix the contents of the jar or can thoroughly before using it. It can be very hard initially but mixing softens it up. Store sesame paste in the refrigerator. Sesame paste is available from specialty grocers. *Tahini* is sold at most health food shops.

SESAME SEEDS You may use white sesame seeds or the beige ones for all the recipes in this book calling for these seeds.

To roast sesame seeds, set a small cast-iron frying pan over a medium-low heat. When it is hot, put in 1–3 tablespoons of sesame seeds. Stir them around until they turn a shade darker and give out a wonderful roasted aroma. Sesame seeds do tend to fly about as they are roasted. You could turn down the heat slightly when they do this, or cover the pan loosely. Remove the seeds from the pan as soon as they are done. You may roast sesame seeds in advance of when you need to use them. Cool them and store them in a tightly lidded jar. They will last several weeks in this way, though they are best when freshly roasted.

SHALLOTS For Westerners who tend to use shallots in small quantities, it is always rather startling to see Southeast Asians use them in massive amounts. The shallot is the onion of this region. It is ground into curry pastes, sliced into salads and fried into crisp flakes to be used both as a garnish and as a wonderful flavoring.

SHICHIMI This Japanese seven-spice seasoning is also sold as "seven-spice red pepper" *(shichimi togarashi).* Available only from Japanese groceries, it contains a coarsely crushed mixture of red bell pepper, a special Japanese pepper called *sansho,* roasted sesame seeds, roasted white poppy or hemp seeds, white pepper and tiny bits of orange peel and seaweed. Use my easy mixture called Sesame Seed Seasoning as a substitute.

To make Sesame Seed Seasoning, set a small cast-iron frying pan over a medium-low heat. When it is hot, put in 1 tablespoon sesame seeds, 1 tablespoon Szechuan peppercorns and 1 small dried hot red chili. Stir these around until the sesame seeds turn golden brown. Allow the mixture to cool, then grind it together with ¼ teaspoon salt in a clean coffee grinder, food processor or mortar until you have a fairly smooth powder.

SHRIMP PASTE This paste made of fermented shrimp is used as a seasoning throughout Southeast Asia. It comes in many forms ranging from a gray watery paste to crumbly brown blocks. Only Southeast Asian groceries sell an array of shrimp pastes.

To make your own substitute for the thin gray shrimp paste, buy a can of 12 anchovy fillets in oil, drain well and then blend them with about 1½ tablespoons water.

There is really no substitute for the blocks, which are known variously as *blachan* and *terasi.* I have used anchovy paste in desperation. When *blachan* or *terasi* are used in uncooked dishes, they need to be roasted first. To do this, break off the amount you need and either hold it over a low gas flame with a pair of tongs, turning it around until it is roasted, or spread it out on a piece of aluminum foil and grill it. You could, if you like, fry it in a tiny amount of oil instead.

SHRIMPS Only raw shrimps should be used for most of the dishes in this book. For instructions on peeling and deveining a shrimp, see page 57.

After you have prepared them, it is a good idea to wash shrimps with salt to remove any sliminess and refresh them. To do this, put the peeled shrimps in a bowl. Sprinkle a tablespoon or so of coarse salt over them and rub them lightly. Then wash them in cold water. Repeat once more, making sure that all the salt is washed away.

OYSTER SAUCE

PALM SUGAR

PAPRIKA

PEANUTS: RAW, ROASTED, AND ROASTED AND GROUND

FRESH SHRIMPS

BELL PEPPERS

JAPANESE RICE

LONG-GRAIN RICE

GLUTINOUS RICE

MOOLI

RICE PAPERS

CHINESE RICE WINE

SAFFRON

SOY SAUCE Many different soy sauces are used in East Asia. Not only do countries have their own brands of soy sauces but regions, towns and even individual villages within these countries sometimes proudly boast of producing their very own. All soy sauces are made from fermented and salted soybeans. They range from salty to sweet, from light to dark, from thick to thin, and have many different textures. Dark soy sauces tend to be thicker than the light ones and generally add a dark color to the dish to which they are added. Light soy sauce tends to be thinner and saltier. There are several thick, textured, slightly sweet sauces that are used in parts of Southeast Asia, many of which are unavailable in most Western markets. Very often black bean sauce is the best substitute. Since soy sauces vary so much in their saltiness, it is always advisable to use slightly less than the amount required in the recipe—you can always add more later.

Kecap manis is a thick, very sweet—indeed, syrupy—soy sauce used in Indonesia. If you cannot find it, you can make an approximation of it yourself by combining 1 cup dark soy sauce with 6 tablespoons molasses and 3 tablespoons brown sugar and simmering them gently until the sugar has dissolved.

Japanese and Chinese soy sauces have very different flavors. Hence, it is best to use Japanese soy sauces (sold in health food shops as *shoyu*) when called for and Chinese soy sauces as required. The best brand of Chinese soy sauce is Pearl River, which is sold by Chinese groceries. It is most confusingly labeled: "soy su-perior sauce" is dark and "superior soy" is light. The best-known Japanese soy sauce is Kikkoman.

STAR ANISE A flower-shaped pod of a brownish color, this spice has a decided aniseed flavor. It is used in Chinese-style braised dishes. Store it in a tightly lidded jar.

SZECHUAN PEPPERCORNS Reddish brown, highly aromatic pods, these are very slightly larger than ordinary peppercorns. They are available from Chinese groceries. Store them in a tightly lidded jar.

To roast Szechuan peppercorns, set a small cast-iron frying pan over a medium-low heat. When it is hot, put in the peppercorns. Stir and fry until they release their fragrance. They might smoke a little, but the smoke will be highly aromatic. To grind roasted Szechuan peppercorns, allow them to cool, then put them into a clean coffee grinder, food processor or mortar and grind until you have a powder.

TAMARIND This is a beanlike fruit of a tall tree. When ripe, the beans are peeled, seeded and packed in lumps or bricks. Tamarind is sold by Southeast Asian and Indian groceries.

To make your own tamarind paste, break off ½ lb from a pound brick of tamarind and tear it into small pieces. Put the tamarind into a small china, glass or stainless-steel bowl, cover with 2 cups very hot water and set aside for 3 hours or overnight. (You could achieve the same result by simmering the tamarind in a pan for 10 minutes.) Set a sieve over another china, glass or stainless-steel bowl and empty the tamarind and its soaking liquid into it. Push down on the tamarind with your fingers or the back of a wooden spoon to extract as much pulp as you can. Put whatever tamarind remains in the sieve back into the soaking bowl. Add ½ cup hot water to it and mash a little more. Return it to the sieve and extract as much more pulp as you can. Some of this pulp will be clinging to the underside of the sieve: do not fail to retrieve it.

This quantity will make about 1½ cups. Whatever paste is left over may either be put into the refrigerator, where it will keep for 2–3 weeks, or it can be frozen.

TURMERIC Many countries of Southeast Asia use fresh turmeric. Fresh turmeric is a rhizome not unlike ginger but smaller in size, more delicate in appearance and quite yellow inside. Many Indian stores sell it. Even though the ground turmeric available in most supermarkets is adequate, use fresh turmeric whenever possible. A 1-inch piece of fresh turmeric is equal to about ½ teaspoon ground turmeric. Like ginger, it needs to be peeled and ground. This grinding is best done

with the help of a little water in an electric blender.

VINEGAR There are probably as many vinegars in the East as there are soy sauces, with every district in every country producing its very own brand. China, for example, has red, black and white vinegars. The Philippines have a pale, slightly milky vinegar made from palm toddy, and Japan is proud of its very mild rice vinegars. To make matters easy for those of you who are going to use this book, I have specified distilled white vinegar almost all the way through. Occasionally, when Japanese rice vinegar is called for and you cannot obtain it, make your own version by combining 3 parts distilled white vinegar with 1 part water and ¼ part sugar.

WATER CHESTNUTS Dark-skinned and chestnut-sized, these grow in water. They are sold fresh only by some Chinese groceries. The inside flesh is deliciously crisp and white. Canned water chestnuts do not compare but may be used in cooked dishes.

YELLOW BEAN SAUCE *See* Bean sauce, yellow.

SAKE

SESAME OIL

SHALLOTS

CYPRESSA

LIGHT
TAHINI
PULPED
SESAME SEEDS
340 g

SESAME SEEDS

SESAME PASTE AND TAHINI

SHICHIMI

SHRIMP PASTE

SZECHUAN PEPPERCORNS, ROASTED AND GROUND

SZECHUAN PEPPERCORNS

CHINESE DARK SOY SAUCE

CHINESE LIGHT SOY SAUCE

JAPANESE SOY SAUCE

SWEET INDONESIAN SOY SAUCE

STAR ANISE

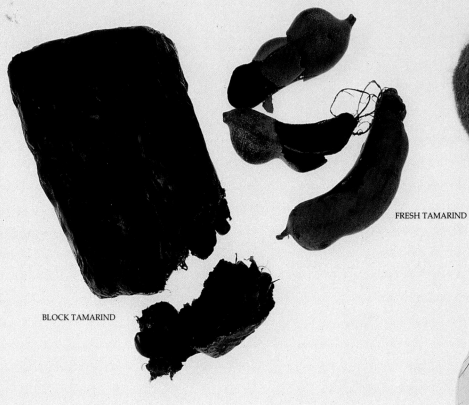

BLOCK TAMARIND

FRESH TAMARIND

TURMERIC

DISTILLED WHITE VINEGAR

JAPANESE RICE VINEGAR

WATER CHESTNUTS

MENUS

*T*here is no reason why you should feel compelled to put together meals with dishes from just one country. However, in case you want to, here are typical menus from each of the eight countries I visited. In each case the first menu is for a simple family meal, the second for a more elaborate dinner party. At the end of this list I also suggest a couple of mixed menus.

Malaysia

RICE NOODLES IN A COCONUT CURRY SOUP
BEAN SPROUTS WITH A SPICY COCONUT DRESSING

SQUID IN CHILI AND GARLIC SAUCE
SPICY SHRIMP AND CUCUMBER CURRY
PERFUMED RICE WITH VEGETABLES NONYA-STYLE
EGGPLANTS IN A THICK, HOT, SWEET AND SOUR CHILI SAUCE
FLUFFY PANCAKES WITH SWEET SESAME-PEANUT FILLING

Thailand

HOT AND SOUR SHRIMP SOUP
GROUND CHICKEN STIR-FRIED WITH BASIL
GREENS WITH GARLIC AND OYSTER SAUCE
PLAIN RICE

CHICKEN, SHRIMP AND FRUIT SALAD
FISH STEAMED WITH LEMONGRASS
EASY BEEF CURRY
PLAIN RICE
FRESH FRUIT OR COCONUT MILK CUSTARD

Indonesia

WHOLE BROILED FISH, SOUR AND SPICY
CAULIFLOWER AND CARROTS WITH A COCONUT DRESSING
PLAIN RICE
FRESH FRUIT

SPICY CHICKEN KEBABS WITH PEANUT SAUCE
BEEF CHUNKS COOKED IN COCONUT MILK
SPICED MUSHROOMS IN A PACKET
PLAIN RICE
SHRIMP WAFERS
FRESH FRUIT

Korea

STIR-FRIED PORK WITH RED BELL PEPPER
SEASONED SPINACH
PLAIN JAPANESE (OR KOREAN) RICE
CABBAGE PICKLE

SAVORY EGG CUSTARD WITH SHRIMPS AND MUSHROOMS
MARINATED AND BROILED BEEF STRIPS
STIR-FRIED ZUCCHINI WITH SESAME SEEDS
PLAIN JAPANESE (OR KOREAN) RICE
CABBAGE PICKLE
FRESH FRUIT

Philippines

PORK COOKED IN A PICKLING STYLE
PLAIN RICE
SNOW PEAS STIR-FRIED WITH SHRIMPS
CARAMEL CUSTARD FILIPINO-STYLE

MACKEREL "COOKED" IN LIME JUICE
GLORIOUS SEAFOOD SOUP
LAMB OR GOAT STEW WITH POTATOES, PEPPERS AND OLIVES
PLAIN RICE
SNOW PEAS STIR-FRIED WITH SHRIMPS
APPLE OR GUAPPLE PIE

Vietnam

PORK AND CRAB SOUP
EASY BEEF KEBABS
PLAIN RICE
GREEN SALAD WITH LETTUCE, MINT AND BASIL

SAVORY PORK AND CRAB TOASTS
AROMATIC AND SPICY BEEF STEW
SMOKY EGGPLANTS IN A LIME SAUCE
KOHLRABI OR BROCCOLI STEM SALAD
PLAIN RICE
FRESH FRUIT

Hong Kong

COLD SESAME NOODLES WITH CHICKEN AND VEGETABLES
LAMB WITH SCALLIONS
PLAIN RICE
BRAISED LIMA BEANS
FRESH MELON

COLD CHICKEN WITH SESAME AND CHILI SAUCE
GLAZED GINGERY SPARERIBS
FISH FILLETS WITH BLACK BEAN SAUCE
SALAD OF CARROTS, CELERY, CUCUMBER AND HAM
PLAIN RICE
SWEET WALNUT SOUP

Japan

FERMENTED BEAN PASTE SOUP WITH BEAN CURD
BREADED PORK CUTLETS
EAST-WEST SAUCE
PLAIN JAPANESE RICE
GREEN BEANS WITH SESAME DRESSING

GREEN BEANS WITH SESAME DRESSING
STUFFED MUSHROOMS
GRILLED MACKEREL WITH SWEET SOY SAUCE
ASPARAGUS AS BOTH FOOD AND GARNISH
PLAIN RICE
FRUIT

Mixed Menus

HOT AND SOUR SHRIMP SOUP
AROMATIC AND SPICY BEEF STEW
STIR-FRIED ZUCCHINI WITH SESAME SEEDS
PLAIN RICE
FRUIT

CHICKEN BITS ON A SKEWER
FISH, SHELLFISH AND BEAN CURD STEW
GREEN BEANS AND CARROTS WITH GINGER AND CHILIES
PLAIN RICE
GINGER TEA
CARAMEL CUSTARD FILIPINO-STYLE
CANDIED WALNUT HALVES

MAIL-ORDER LIST

There are now many ethnic groceries throughout the United States. It is best to start in your own area. Look in the yellow pages under Japanese, Korean, Southeast Asian, or Philippine groceries. They might be all lumped under "Oriental Groceries" or "Specialty Foods." Specialty stores, such as Balducci's and Dean & De Luca's in New York and the Oakville Grocery in San Francisco, do indeed carry many Far Eastern ingredients, both fresh and dried. The foods of many Asian nations overlap—Korean stores may have Japanese ingredients, and Thai stores may have Indonesian goods. Health-food stores carry many of the basics: sesame oil, sesame seeds, soy sauce, bean curd, mung beans, azuki beans, and bulgar wheat.

What you cannot get easily in your area, you can send for. Following is a list of stores that specialize in Far Eastern groceries. Those that definitely accept mail orders are marked with an asterisk (*) but many of the unmarked groceries will accept mail orders as well; just call or write first to inquire. Make sure that you request all ingredients be labeled in English.

The dry spices used in these recipes can be purchased through mail order from Madhur Jaffrey's Gourmet Foods, Ltd. Call or write:

Madhur Jaffrey's Gourmet Foods, Ltd.
45-15 Barnett Ave.
Long Island City, NY 11104
Tel. (718) 392-5640

KOREAN GROCERIES

East-West Food Center
3300 West 8 St.
Los Angeles, CA 90005

Kal's Mart
606 South Beaumont Ave.
Los Angeles, CA 90005

Pacific Food Market
2147 Clement St.
San Francisco, CA 94121

Oriental Market
4700 Geary Blvd.
San Francisco, CA 94118

East-West Grocery Store
3810 West Lawrence
Chicago, IL 60625

Tong Yang Market
5131 North Western Ave.
Chicago, IL 60625

Korea House
615 Orange St.
New Orleans, LA 70130

New Seoul
1555 Rockville Pike
Rockville, MD 20852

Sam Bok
3012-18 Edwin Ave.
Fort Lee, NJ 07024

Sammi Oriental Grocery
Store
444 Broad Ave.
Leonia, NJ 07605*

Sam Bok Grocery Store
127 West 43 St.
New York, NY 10036*

Daewoo Oriental Food
Market
42 West 36 St.
New York, NY 10018

Tong Dae Moon Grocery
Store
12 West 32 St.
New York, NY 10001

Korea Super Market
6427 Bissonet
Houston, TX 77074

VIETNAMESE GROCERIES

Viet Nam Thuc Phan
Menlo Park, CA 94025

A Dong Thuc Pham
6001 Eldercreek
Sacramento, CA 95824

Hillcrest Oriental Food Center
426 University Ave.
San Diego, CA 92103
Tel. (714) 298-0747

continued

Que Huong
9087 Bolsa Ave. (Bolsa Plaza)
Westminster, CA 92683

China Trading
271 Crown St.
New Haven, CT 06511

Vietnam House
242 Farmington Ave.
Hartford, CT 06105
Tel. (203) 524-0010

Asia Market
1241 East Colonial Drive
Orlando, FL 32803

Kim Thanh
3003 Florida Blvd.
Baton Rouge, LA 70803

Tien Nha Trang
1804 Baratario Blvd.
Marrero, LA 70072

Tan Duc (Sonico)
214–216 Grand St.
New York, NY 10013

Thuan Nguyen
82 Mulberry St.
New York, NY 10013

Viet Nam Market
2702 E. 15 St.
Tulsa, OK 74104

Vietnam
Christian St.
Philadelphia, PA 19147

Hoa Binh
2800 Pravis St.
Houston, TX 77006

Vietnam Plaza
2200 Jefferson St.
Houston, TX 77006

Xuan Thu
P.O. Box 720065
Houston, TX 77006

Tan Viet Market
10332 Ferguson Rd.
Dallas, TX 75228
Tel. (214) 324-5160

Viet Nam Food
610 South State Ave.
Salt Lake City, UT 84111

Mekong Center
3107 Wilson Blvd.
Arlington, VA 22201
Tel. (703) 527-2779

Vietnam Imports
922 West Broad St., Rte. 7
Falls Church, VA 22046

Viet-My Corporation
1007 St. Stephen Rd.
Alexandria, VA 22304
Tel. (703) 370-2234

THAI, INDONESIAN AND OTHER SOUTHEAST ASIAN GROCERIES

Bangkok Market
4804–6 Melrose Ave.
Los Angeles, CA 90029*

Thai Food Market
5902–4 Hollywood Blvd.
Hollywood, CA 90028

Thai and Oriental Market
25795 East Highland Ave.
San Bernardino, CA 92404

Thai Grocery
1090 South Raritan St.
Denver, CO 80223

Krung Thai Grocery
10141 Montview Blvd.
Aurora, CO 80010

Merapi Inc.
139 White St.
Danbury, CT 06810*

Thai Market
3323–5 South Dale Mabry
    Hwy.
Tampa, FL 33609

Thai Grocery
5014 North Broadway
Chicago, IL 60640*

Bangkok Grocery
412A Hunger Ford Dr.
Rockville, MD 20850

Asia Market
1101 East Charleston Blvd.
Las Vegas, NV 89104

Asian Food Market
5 Towne Center
Black Horse Pike
Turnerville, NJ 08012

Bangkok Market
106 Park St. (off Mott)
New York, NY 10013*

Siam Grocery
2754 Broadway
New York, NY 10025

Southeast Asia Trading Co.
68A Mott St.
New York, NY 10013

Thai Binh
8th St.
Philadelphia, PA 19147

Mrs. De Wildt
R.D. #3
Bangor, PA 18013*
(Mail order by catalog only)

Thai Asian Market
2537 University Blvd.
Houston, TX 77005

Thailand Market
2216 West Granwyler
Plymouth Park Shopping
Irving, TX 75061

Thai House Groceries
1733 Wilson Blvd.
Arlington, VA 22209

JAPANESE AND OTHER ORIENTAL GROCERIES

K. Sakai Co.
1656 Post St.
San Francisco, CA 94115

International Market
2019 Fillmore St.
San Francisco, CA 94115

Asia Food Market
2000 Judah Street
San Francisco, CA 94122*

JFC International, Inc.
Consumer Services Department
445 Kauffman Court
South San Francisco, CA 94808

Hillcrest Oriental Food Center
426 University Avenue
San Diego, CA 92103

Dobashi Co.
240 East Jackson St.
San Jose, CA 95112

Oriental Grocery
3433 El Camino Real
Santa Clara, CA 95051

Orient Grocery
337 8 St.
Oakland, CA 95051

Yaohan U.S.A. Corporation
2121 West 182nd St.
Torrence, CA 90504

Ai Hoa Market
860 North Hill St.
Los Angeles, CA 90012*

Hughes-El Rancho Market
320 West Colorado Blvd.
Pasadena, CA 91105

Ann's Oriental Grocery
315 West Colorado Blvd.
Pasadena, CA 91105

Pacific Mercantile Grocery
1925 Lawrence St.
Denver, CO 80202*

East-West Trading Co.
68 Howe St.
New Haven, CT 06511

Kim's Oriental Shop
202 Park Rd.
West Hartford, CT 06129

Oriental Grocery
1705 Concord Pike
Wilmington, DE 19803*

Oriental Food and Gift
1531 South Dale Mabry Hwy.
Tampa, FL 33609

Asian Supermarket
2581 Piedmont Rd.
Atlanta, GA 30324

Daido Foods
2390 Carroll Avenue
Chamblee, GA 30341

Oriental Food and Gift
3635 Buena Vista Rd.
Columbia, GA 31097

Far East Trading Co.
2837 North Western Ave.
Chicago, IL 60618*

Star Market
3349 North Clark St.
Chicago, IL 60657*

Jung's Oriental Food Store
913 East University Ave.
Des Moines, IA 50316*

Tokyo Foods
1005 Pierce St.
Sioux City, IA 51105*

Oriental Food
2111 Rogers Ave.
Fort Smith, KS 72901

Arirang House
7918 Georgia Avenue
Silver Spring, MD 20910

Yoshinoya
36 Prospect St.
Cambridge, MA 02111

Sun Sun Co.
34 Oxford St.
Boston, MA 02111

Oriental Food Store
18919 West Seven Mile Rd.
Detroit, MI 48219

International House
of Foods
75 West Island Ave.
Minneapolis, MN 55401*

Kim's Mart
6692 Enright Ave.
St. Louis, MO 63114*

Oriental Market
611 North 27 St.
Lincoln, NB 68503

Oriental Food
953 East Sahara, E-31
Las Vegas, NV 89104

Aki Oriental Food Co.
1635 Lemoine Ave.
Fort Lee, NJ 07024

Asian Food Market
217 Summit Ave.
Jersey City, NJ 07306*

Katagiri Company
224 East 59 St.
New York, NY 10022*

Tanaka and Company
326 Amsterdam Ave.
New York, NY 10023*

Whole Foods in Soho
117 Prince St.
New York, NY 10012*

Dayton Oriental Foods
812 Xenia Ave.
Dayton, OH 45410

Japan Imported Foods
808 N.W. 6 St.
Oklahoma City, OK 73106

Albertsons #505
5415 S.W.
   Beaverton-Hillsdale Hwy.
Portland, OR 97221

Asia Products Corp.
226 North 10 St.
Philadelphia, PA 19107

Persimmon Oriental Food
Market
University Heights Shopping
   Plaza
Providence, RI 02904

Daido Foods
1138 Westheimer St.
Houston, TX 77042

Eastern Foods
8626½ Long Point
Houston, TX 77055

Kobawoo Oriental Market
5732 Cedar Springs Rd.
Dallas, TX 75235

Oriental House
7816 Richmond Hwy.
Alexandria, VA 22306

Albertsons #429
11656 68 Ave.
Seattle, WA 98178

Uwajimay
P.O. Box 3003
Seattle, WA 98114*

Mikado
4709 Wisconsin Ave.
Washington, DC 20016

Mihamaya
392 Powell St.
Vancouver, Br. Columbia
Canada VGA 1G4*

Iwaki Japanese Food Store
2627 Yonge St.
Toronto, Ontario
Canada M4P 2J6

CHINESE GROCERIES

The Chinese Grocer
209 Post St.
San Francisco, CA 94108*

Shing Chong and Co.
800 Grant Ave.
San Francisco, CA 94108

Kwa On Lung Co.
686 North Spring St.
Los Angeles, CA 90015*

Wing Chong Lung Co.
   Grocery
922 South San Pedro St.
Los Angeles, CA 90015

China Trading
271 Crown St.
New Haven, CT 06511

South and Eastern Food
   Supply
6732 N.E. 4 Ave.
Miami, FL 33138*

Asia Trading Co.
2581 Piedmont NE
Atlanta, GA 30324

Kam Shing Co.
2246 South Wentworth St.
Chicago, IL 60616

A.B. Oriental Grocery
3707 Suit Shadeland Ave.
Indianapolis, IN 46226*

continued

Asia House Grocery
2433 Saint Paul St.
Baltimore, MD 21218*

Wing Wing Imported
  Groceries
79 Harrison Ave.
Boston, MA 02111

Sun Sun Co.
340 Oxford St.
Boston, MA 02111

Legal Sea Foods Market
237 Hampshire St.
Cambridge, MA 02139

Joyce Chen Unlimited Inc.
172–174 Massachusetts Ave.
Arlington, MA 02134

Kwong Tung Noodle
  Manufacturing Co.
326 Cedar Ave.
Minneapolis, MN 55404

King's Trading
3736 Broadway
Kansas City, MO 64111*

Lee's Oriental Gifts and
  Foods
3053 Main St.
Buffalo, NY 14214*

Cathay Food Products
115 Broadway
New York, NY 10004

Kam Man Food Products
200 Canal St.
New York, NY 10013*

Wing Woh Lung Co.
50 Mott St.
New York, NY 10013*

Wing Fat Co. Inc.
33–35 Mott St.
New York, NY 10013*

Delicacies Shop,
  Bloomingdale's
1000 Third Ave.
New York, NY 10022

Far East Co.
247 West McMillan St.
Cincinnati, OH 45219*

Sam Wah Rick Kee Co.
2146 Rockwell Ave.
Cleveland, OH 44114

International House
  of Foods
712 Washington Ave. SE
Columbus, OH 43206

Harmony Oriental
247 Atwood St.
Pittsburgh, PA 15213*

Wing On
1005 Race St.
Philadelphia, PA 19107

Oriental Import-Export Co.
2009 Polk St.
Houston, TX 77003

Adler's Fine Foods
2012–14 Broadway
San Antonio, TX 78209

Super Asian Market
2719 Wilson Blvd.
Arlington, VA 22201

Oriental House
4816 Richmond Hwy.
Alexandria, VA 22306

Mee Wah Lung Co.
608 H Street NW
Washington, DC 20001

Wang's Co.
800 7 St. NW
Washington, DC 20001

Chinamart Trading Co.
210 Spadina Ave.
Toronto, Ontario
Canada

INDEX